T0349022

AI Integration in Software Development and Operations

Transformation Through AI Infusion in DevOps, Testing, and SRE

Abhinav Krishna
Vamshidhar Meda

Foreword by Sorabh Singhal

Apress®

AI Integration in Software Development and Operations: Transformation Through AI Infusion in DevOps, Testing, and SRE

Abhinav Krishna
2nd Floor, Block 2
Bengaluru, Karnataka, India

Vamshidhar Meda
McKinney, TX, USA

ISBN-13 (pbk): 979-8-8688-1043-5
https://doi.org/10.1007/979-8-8688-1044-2

ISBN-13 (electronic): 979-8-8688-1044-2

Copyright © 2024 by Abhinav Krishna and Vamshidhar Meda

This work is subject to copyright. All rights are reserved by the Publisher, whether the whole or part of the material is concerned, specifically the rights of translation, reprinting, reuse of illustrations, recitation, broadcasting, reproduction on microfilms or in any other physical way, and transmission or information storage and retrieval, electronic adaptation, computer software, or by similar or dissimilar methodology now known or hereafter developed.

Trademarked names, logos, and images may appear in this book. Rather than use a trademark symbol with every occurrence of a trademarked name, logo, or image we use the names, logos, and images only in an editorial fashion and to the benefit of the trademark owner, with no intention of infringement of the trademark.

The use in this publication of trade names, trademarks, service marks, and similar terms, even if they are not identified as such, is not to be taken as an expression of opinion as to whether or not they are subject to proprietary rights.

While the advice and information in this book are believed to be true and accurate at the date of publication, neither the authors nor the editors nor the publisher can accept any legal responsibility for any errors or omissions that may be made. The publisher makes no warranty, express or implied, with respect to the material contained herein.

Managing Director, Apress Media LLC: Welmoed Spahr
Acquisitions Editor: Celestin Suresh John
Development Editor: James Markham
Coordinating Editor: Kripa Joseph
Copy Editor: Kezia Endsley

Cover designed by eStudioCalamar

Cover image designed by Pixabay

Distributed to the book trade worldwide by Springer Science+Business Media New York, 233 Spring Street, 6th Floor, New York, NY 10013. Phone 1-800-SPRINGER, fax (201) 348-4505, e-mail orders-ny@springer-sbm.com, or visit www.springeronline.com. Apress Media, LLC is a California LLC and the sole member (owner) is Springer Science + Business Media Finance Inc (SSBM Finance Inc). SSBM Finance Inc is a **Delaware** corporation.

For information on translations, please e-mail booktranslations@springernature.com; for reprint, paperback, or audio rights, please e-mail bookpermissions@springernature.com.

Apress titles may be purchased in bulk for academic, corporate, or promotional use. eBook versions and licenses are also available for most titles. For more information, reference our Print and eBook Bulk Sales web page at http://www.apress.com/bulk-sales.

Any source code or other supplementary material referenced by the author in this book can be found here: https://www.apress.com/gp/services/source-code.

If disposing of this product, please recycle the paper

Table of Contents

About the Authors...xi

About the Technical Reviewer xiii

Foreword xv

Introduction xvii

Chapter 1: First Steps in AI and DevOps......................................1

Artificial Intelligence 101 2

    The Evolution of Artificial Intelligence 3

    Types of AI 4

    How Does AI/ML Work? 6

    Benefits of AI/ML 8

What Is DevOps? 11

    Explaining DevOps with an Example 11

    DevOps Principles..12

    DevOps Processes...17

AI Meets DevOps...23

Summary...24

Chapter 2: Understanding Machine Learning 25

Construct of AI and ML...26

    The Structure..26

    Types of Machine Learning...28

Applications of Machine Learning 30

Challenges and Future Directions.. 32

AI Techniques and Algorithms 33

Supervised Learning Algorithms 34

Unsupervised Learning Algorithms.. 35

Reinforcement Learning Algorithms.. 36

Deep Learning Algorithms 36

Evolutionary Algorithms.. 37

Fuzzy Logic... 37

Large Language Models (LLM).. 38

Transformer-Based Models 39

BERT (Bidirectional Encoder Representations from Transformers) 39

XLNet.. 39

T5 (Text-To-Text Transfer Transformer)... 40

BERT-Based Models for Domain-Specific Tasks................................. 40

Multilingual LLMs 41

Summary.. 41

Chapter 3: Software Development and AI Augmentation **43**

Why Use AI in SDLC... 43

Zenith in Efficiency and Productivity 44

Unparalleled Quality 44

Advanced Decision Making 44

Cost Savings and Effective Resource Management 45

Proactive Risk Management... 45

Improved Developer Experience.. 46

Overview of the Software Delivery Lifecycle and AI Infusion................. 46

Planning.. 47

Gathering Requirements... 48

Designing...49

Building 50

Testing 51

Deployment 53

Maintenance...54

Challenges in the Adoption of AI 55

Increased Complexity 55

Data Quality 56

Initial High Cost and Maintenance......................................56

Integration with Existing Systems 57

Ethical and Security Concerns..57

Summary..58

Chapter 4: Planning and Requirements Management in Projects......59

Integrating AI and LLMs in the Planning Phase....................60

Project Initiation 60

Feasibility Study 62

Resource Planning...64

Project Scheduling 65

Budgeting 66

Communication Plan..67

Risk Management...68

Quality Assurance Planning..69

Agile Estimation Techniques Infused with AI.........................70

Benefits of Leveraging AI for Estimation 70

Agile Estimation Techniques...73

Agile Estimation Tools...83

Requirements Gathering Overview 90

The Importance of Requirements Management in IT Projects 92

Requirements Management Process...94

Good Practices in IT Requirements Management...97

Requirements Gathering Infused with AI 99

Summary...104

Chapter 5: Integrating Generative AI in Software Design and Architecture...107

Overview of Software Design..108

Software Design Components...110

System Design...111

Component Design 114

User Interface Design 119

Data Design 122

API Design 124

Infrastructure Design..127

Security Design 132

Summary...135

Chapter 6: AI Infusion in Software Build and Development.............137

How AI Transforms the Developer Workflow 138

Overview of the Software Build and Development Process.........................140

Development Process..140

A Different Perspective..156

The Software Build Process 159

AI-Driven Build Optimization 160

Predictive Build Failure Analysis 164

Intelligent Dependency Management...165

AI-Driven Security and Compatibility...167

CI and CD Pipeline Creation and Optimization 170

    Pros and Cons of AI in CI/CD...177

    Key Challenge for AI in CI/CD Is the Dependence on Data.........................178

Summary..179

Chapter 7: Infusing AI into Software Testing 181

The Evolution of Software Testing...182

    The Automation Era 182

    The Rise of AI in Testing...183

How AI Enhances Software Testing...183

    ML Algorithms 183

    Natural Language Processing (NLP) 184

    Neural Networks...184

    AI's Impact on Software Testing 184

Key Benefits of AI in Software Testing 186

Challenges in Implementing AI in Software Testing...188

How the V-Model Has Evolved with AI Testing 189

AI-Driven Testing Tools...194

    Tool: Appvance...194

    Tool: Testim..195

    Tool: Applitools...196

    Other Testing Tools 201

    Capabilities and Features 201

    Comparison of Tools 203

    Best Practices for Implementing AI in Software Testing.............................204

Challenges with AI-Driven Testing Implementation 207

Future Trends in AI and Software Testing..210

Summary..212

Chapter 8: AI in Continuous Delivery 213

The Role of AI in Continuous Delivery 214

Key Areas Where AI Can Make a Difference 215

AI in Deployment Automation...216

Benefits of Using AI in Deployment Automation 217

Key Use Cases of AI in Deployment Automation 218

Challenges in AI-Powered Deployment Automation 222

Tools and Platforms Leveraging AI in Deployment Automation 224

The Impact of AI in Deployment Automation................................228

Future Trends and the Road Ahead..232

AI-Powered Release Management..233

AI and the Shift Toward Progressive Release Management 233

Key Aspects of Progressive Release Management Enhanced by AI 234

Key AI Use Cases in Release Management....................................234

Tools Currently Focused on Release Management........................243

AI-Driven Infrastructure Management 245

Key Components of Test and Production Environments 245

Traditional Environment Management Challenges 246

Tools for Solving Configuration Challenges 246

AI Technologies Enhancing Test and Production Environments 247

AI-Driven Automated Provisioning and Configuration 248

Intelligent Monitoring and Incident Management............................250

Predictive Analytics for Performance Optimization 251

AI in FinOps (Financial Operations) 252

AI-Driven Cost Optimization...253

AI in Network Management 254

AI for Automated Network Configuration and Optimization..........254

AI in Firewall and Security Management...........................257

AI in Access Management and Identity Governance 258

Automating Access Control 258

AI for Continuous Monitoring and Audit..........................259

AI in Storage Management and Optimization......................260

AI-Driven Storage Allocation.......................................260

Predictive Storage Maintenance....................................261

AI for Database Management...262

Intelligent Database Optimization................................262

Automated Backup and Recovery with AI...........................263

Future Trends in AI-Driven Infrastructure Management.................264

Summary..266

**Chapter 9: Operations, Observability, and Site Reliability
Engineering..267**

The Operations Quagmire 268

Site Reliability Engineering 269

How SRE Works? 271

The Role of AI in SRE 272

Observability 273

Monitoring vs. Observability.......................................274

Observability and AIOps..275

The Role of AI in Observability....................................276

Incident Management 283

The Role of AI in Incident Management.............................284

Change Management..287

The Role of AI in Change Management...............................288

Capacity Planning 292

    Sub-Processes of Capacity Planning 292

    The Role of AI in Capacity Planning 293

Chaos Engineering 296

    Role of AI in Chaos Engineering 297

Summary 299

Index **301**

About the Authors

Abhinav Krishna is a highly accomplished professional working as a partner at a prestigious consulting firm, where he plays a pivotal role in leading digital transformation programs for clients across diverse sectors. He is part of the Distinguished Member of Technical Staff (DMTS) cadre, which represents a select group of best-in-class technologists. With a proven track record in the industry, Abhinav is recognized for his expertise in guiding organizations through complex and innovative changes to stay ahead of the curve in today's dynamic business environment.

He spearheads various digital transformation initiatives, demonstrating a keen understanding of the unique challenges and opportunities presented by different industries. His portfolio includes successfully steering multiple digital transformation programs, showcasing his ability to navigate and drive change in organizations of varying sizes and complexities. His hands-on experience in implementing cutting-edge technologies and methodologies has contributed to the enhanced efficiency and competitiveness of his clients.

In addition, Abhinav is a multifaceted professional with a prolific career as an accomplished writer. He boasts an impressive literary portfolio of six published books, each delving into the intricacies of digital transformation, DevOps, GCP, and ITIL. Abhinav's written works serve as authoritative guides, offering valuable insights and practical solutions to professionals navigating the complexities of modern business and technology landscapes. Beyond his contributions to the written domain, Abhinav is a panel speaker, captivating audiences with his expertise at industry conferences and events. His commitment to knowledge-sharing extends to digital platforms, where he actively engages as a YouTuber and blogger. Through these mediums, he imparts knowledge, shares best practices, and explores emerging trends, reaching a wider audience eager to enhance their understanding of digital transformation, DevOps, GCP, and ITIL.

Vamshidhar Meda is a seasoned partner at a prominent consulting firm, specializing in guiding organizations through digital transformation initiatives. With a wealth of experience in the field, he serves as a trusted advisor to numerous enterprises, helping them identify opportunities for digital innovation and navigate the complexities of implementation.

He has a demonstrated track record of leading complex initiatives in architecture, cloud, GenAI, SRE, AIOps, Agile, and DevOps. He has completed CTO certification from Wharton and holds a bachelor's degree in computer science, blending technical prowess with business acumen.

He is recognized for spearheading digital transformation initiatives across diverse industries, including in the insurance, capital markets, retail, and healthcare markets. Vamshi is skilled in strategic planning, solution implementation, and fostering collaboration to achieve organizational objectives. He is a decisive leader with a knack for problem-solving and a commitment to excellence.

Vamshi is highly regarded as a keynote speaker at industry-leading conferences, where he shares his expertise and insights on driving successful digital transformations.

About the Technical Reviewer

 **Mohammed Ilyas Ahmed** is an industry professional with extensive expertise in security within the DevSecOps domain, where he diligently works to help organizations bolster their security practices. With a fervent dedication to enhancing security posture, Mohammed's insights and guidance are invaluable to those navigating the complex landscape of DevSecOps. In addition to his involvement in industry events, Mohammed is an active speaker and judge, lending his expertise to technical sessions at prestigious conferences. His commitment to advancing knowledge is evident through his research contributions at Harvard University, where he contributes to journal publications, enriching the academic discourse surrounding security practices. As a distinguished member of the Harvard Business Review Advisory Council, he underscores his commitment to advancing knowledge and fostering collaboration between academia and industry. He is also the author of the book *Cloud-Native DevOps*.

Mohammed's influence extends even farther as a member of the global advisory board at VigiTrust Limited, based in Dublin, Ireland. This additional role highlights his international reach and his involvement in shaping global strategies for cybersecurity and data protection.

Mohammed's dedication to excellence is further highlighted by his numerous certifications, which serve as a testament to his proficiency and depth of knowledge in the security domain. Beyond his professional pursuits, Mohammed is a multi-faceted individual with a diverse range of interests, adding richness to his character and perspective.

Foreword

The expedition toward a true digital transformation is one that many organizations strive for, but only a few fully realize. At the heart of this evolution is the integration of Artificial Intelligence (AI), a force that has the potential to redefine how we approach software development, IT and business operations.

In *AI Integration in Software Development and Operations*, Abhinav Krishna Kaiser and Vamshi Meda take us on a detailed exploration of how AI can transform every phase of the Software Development Lifecycle (SDLC) and IT operations, from DevOps to testing and Site Reliability Engineering (SRE).

I have had the privilege of knowing Abhinav and Vamshi for several years, during which time they worked under my guidance. Over that time, I have witnessed their stellar composure, dedication, and unwavering commitment to advancing AI adoption across domains. Their ability to navigate the complexities of digital transformation and AI integration is remarkable, and their contributions have made a significant impact on the customers and organizations they've served.

As a senior leader responsible for leading large deals and programs, I often see customers requesting AI to be part of their solutions. Yet, many still look to service provider organizations for inspiration on how to successfully incorporate AI into their own products and services. This book comes at a pivotal time, offering the guidance and clarity that organizations need to begin their own AI journeys.

As AI becomes an integral component of every organization, it is inevitable that companies must embrace it to stay relevant. Those who embark on this journey earlier will hold a significant advantage as first movers, seizing opportunities to lead in innovation and operational efficiency. This book serves as a critical guide for those who are ready to get ahead of the curve and leverage AI's full potential to transform their operations.

This book reflects the authors' deep expertise and practical experience, providing a thorough examination of how AI can bring transformative change to software development and operations. What sets this book apart is its fusion of theoretical understanding with real-world case studies, demonstrating the tangible benefits AI can deliver—whether it's speeding up development cycles, improving operational resilience, or optimizing overall efficiency.

As the first volume in what promises to be a groundbreaking series, this book lays the foundation for future exploration into AI's applications in software development and operations. Abhinav and Vamshi have masterfully set the stage, offering readers not just knowledge but a roadmap for AI integration that is both practical and visionary. This is a must-read for anyone looking to understand the full potential of AI within the SDLC and beyond.

I am confident that this series will serve as a guiding light for many organizations, helping them navigate the complexities of AI adoption and achieve their digital transformation goals.

Sorabh Singhal
Vice President and Global Practice Head,
Custom Software Development and DevOps

Introduction

Artificial intelligence (AI) has been a topic of fascination and speculation for several decades. It captured many people's imagination as they were growing up—especially with movies such as the *Terminator* series, where AI was both the hero and the villain. We have come a long way from the days of Alan Turing, and AI systems are now integrated into our daily lives. In short, this AI journey has been nothing short of revolutionary. While AI has evolved over the years, the past year has witnessed an unprecedented surge in growth and application, marking it a pivotal moment in the history of technological advancement.

The world of software development, testing, and IT operations is evolving at an unprecedented pace, with the markets more than the technology defining the speed. The digital era has mandated that organizations innovate faster, deliver complex solutions, and maintain impeccable standards of quality—all while navigating an ever-changing technological environment. As the pressure to optimize processes and reduce time-to-market intensifies, a new paradigm is emerging—the integration of AI into the core practices of software engineering.

This book (*AI Integration in Software Development and Operations*) explores how AI can enhance and accelerate the key functions across the SDLC lifecycle and in IT operations. By adopting AI-driven tools, organizations can unlock new levels of automation, precision, and insight, creating more agile and reliable systems that minimize human error and optimize resource use.

AI's role in these fields is not merely hypothetical—it is actively reshaping how businesses approach everything from gathering requirements, creating code, and detecting bugs, to deployment and infrastructure management.

In software development, AI can assist in generating code snippets, identifying potential defects early in the process, and even offering intelligent recommendations to developers. In testing, AI-driven algorithms can generate test cases, perform intelligent regression testing, and improve the speed and accuracy of error detection. When it comes to IT operations, AI can boost observability, automate routine maintenance tasks, and predict outages before they occur, ensuring high availability, great performance, and increased customer satisfaction.

This book presents a collection of real-world use cases in which AI plays a critical role in improving the efficiency, scalability, and quality of these processes. It delves into how AI can help analyze data and help developers with decision points, and it provides the hidden messages in the data. Furthermore, the book highlights how AI can significantly reduce the risks associated with human error, which remains one of the most common causes of downtime, security breaches, and project delays.

This book provides insights into what AI can do and unravels the range of possibilities, making it ideal for digital leaders, customer organizations, IT practitioners, and digital enthusiasts.

For digital leaders especially, the book offers an unprecedented opportunity to achieve better outcomes at scale. It contains the knowledge and strategies needed to drive AI adoption within their organizations. It goes beyond the theoretical benefits and outlines actionable steps for integrating AI in ways that align with business goals, optimize resources, and future-proof operations. By adopting AI practices, businesses can reduce costs through automation, improve product quality by enhancing testing capabilities, and accelerate release cycles without compromising security or reliability. This book demonstrates how these benefits translate into real-world outcomes, enabling customers to make informed decisions about investing in AI-driven technologies.

For those who are practicing IT across the SDLC lifecycle or in operations, the book provides insights into ideas that can transform daily workflows, enhance productivity, and free up valuable time for innovation.

This is a practical guide on how to apply AI technologies in your work, including insights into selecting the right tools, deploying them effectively, and measuring their impact on development speed, quality, and team collaboration.

At its core, this book aims to bridge the gap between the promise of AI and its practical applications in the field of software development, testing, and IT operations. Each chapter offers detailed case studies, expert insights, and a roadmap for integrating AI into your workflows. Whether you're an industry leader, a technical practitioner, or a customer exploring the potential of AI, this book will equip you with the tools and knowledge needed to stay ahead in an increasingly competitive and AI-driven world.

The journey to integrating AI into your organization is not without its challenges. However, the rewards—improved efficiency, enhanced innovation, faster time-to-market, and reduced operational risk—are too significant to ignore. By the end of this book, you will not only have a clear understanding of AI's transformative potential but will also have a concrete strategy for leveraging it in your own software development and IT practices.

The future of software engineering and IT operations is being written today. Let AI be the catalyst that drives your organization forward.

CHAPTER 1

First Steps in AI and DevOps

Artificial intelligence is no longer just a theory or an experiment carried out in the R&D laboratories of large tech firms. It has gone through cycles of evolution and practical testing to become an integral part of our everyday life. The essence of intelligence, once a characteristic only of animals, is now part of machines. Those sinister movie plots where the machines think for themselves has proven to be possible.

The beauty of intelligence is that it finds a need in all domains, applications, and activities. Think about it. Every task we do, be it watering plants or washing a car, has an element of intelligence that drives it. Such mundane activities can be programmed into machines. A car that is handwashed (in our opinion) is always going to be cleaner than a car that goes through an automated car wash. Artificial intelligence in theory can be applied to all areas where intelligence can be applied.

AI by itself, like intelligence, is pretty useless. It needs to be applied to an activity or system. For example, you use it while writing an email or when seeking information. AI can be embedded into all aspects of digital life, be it cybersecurity, data analysis, banking, and others. This book focuses on infusing AI into DevOps.

The digital world has changed for the better with the advent of the DevOps methodology. It has become a force that has propelled organizations toward executing plans on a whim and raising the bar on

© Abhinav Krishna and Vamshidhar Meda 2024
A. Krishna and V. Meda, *AI Integration in Software Development and Operations*,
https://doi.org/10.1007/979-8-8688-1044-2_1

quality. While DevOps by itself is highly regarded, imagine the outcome if developers were to infuse an element of intelligence into DevOps. A new digital order is shaping up, and the powerful combination of DevOps and AI is the future. This will be the new normal in the coming months and years!

The book takes a microscopic view of bolstering DevOps with AI by presenting several use cases across various application stages, including planning and requirements gathering, code collaboration, testing, and monitoring, among others.

This chapter begins by explaining the fundamentals of DevOps and AI. If you are familiar with both topics, feel free to skip to Chapter 2.

Artificial Intelligence 101

There was a time when we argued that repetitive activities were best handled by machines and anything that required cognitive ability was best handled by humans. We used to provide examples of tasks triggered through events best done by the machines, while an activity like coding could only be done by humans. We did not realize that we would be eating our words with a humble pie. Machines can now do nearly what humans can, except for showing emotions. This too may be possible in coming years.

Artificial intelligence is essentially the process whereby machines perform activities that require intelligence. Think of a task that you perform today, and possibly that machines can do as well as or better than you can! For example, AI could write this book, but it cannot match our experience or the writing style (at the time of writing).

AI can do everything that humans can—in theory. Examples include writing a letter to your manager, researching a paper, driving a car, translating languages, generating images, and writing code. In fact, every solution that humans work with has an element of AI embedded in it. Phone calls on Samsung phones can be translated into different languages in real-time. A water heater can conserve energy in the summer by limiting the temperature. There are a handful of devices today that have AI in them. AI is a nascent territory that is waiting to be conquered. The early starters have an edge.

The Evolution of Artificial Intelligence

Our first experience with AI was through the movies, most famously with the *Terminator* series. Those machines (collectively called Skynet) were capable of strategizing, thinking and most importantly, protecting their own survival. They enslaved the human race to do their bidding. This image of AI as the villain and the current AI are polar opposites, and we embrace AI in its version today, in hopes that the AI of the fantasy world will remain what it was meant to be—a fantasy.

Humans have imagined inanimate objects having a brain of their own for a number of centuries. But the fantasy turned a corner with the invention of the computer. The term *artificial intelligence* was coined by John McCarthy at the Dartmouth Conference in 1956. As technology advanced, there were multiple attempts to bring intelligence to computers, but it wasn't until the Internet boom and cloud computing that it became practically possible.

With the Internet, collaboration fueled sweeping improvements to the logic and the art of possibilities. In 1997, for the first time a computer beat the world chess champion Gary Kasparov in a game of chess. IBM's Deep Blue succeeded where previous generations had tried and failed. The game of chess was not just a domain of humans anymore, and Deep Blue proved that it had a better showcase of intelligence.

In the 2000s, deep learning and neural networks moved research and development toward artificial intelligence. The emergence of Big Data and advancements in deep neural networks led to machine learning, providing the ability for computers to learn from large amounts of data.

AI applications started to appear during this era, with text-to-speech engines, translation, computer vision, and personal assistant engines opening the floodgates.

More recently, AI has become capable of driving cars, designing posters, and writing volumes of content. Products like ChatGPT and DALL-E bring AI closer to the everyday user.

Types of AI

Artificial intelligence is an emerging field and several organizations and universities across the globe are investing heavily in this technology. Figure 1-1 shows the various AI categories that are active at this point in time. In years to come, these categories will likely take on a different shape.

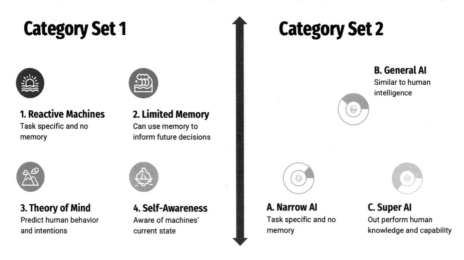

Figure 1-1. *AI categories*

Reactive Machines/Narrow AI

This is the most basic form of artificial intelligence. It responds to the logic that is designed, and there is no learning and no memory embedded in this category of AI. In many ways, it is typical of the logic being executed on the back of defined scenarios.

The famous IBM Deep Blue computer that beat Garry Kasparov in chess in 1997, as well as Apple's Siri, fall in this category. Based on the current scenario, they can make predictions but do not necessarily learn from experience. In the truest sense, they are not AI, but they sowed the seeds to what it is today and might become tomorrow.

Limited Memory/General AI

Limited memory or General AI refers to the capability of AI to understand, learn, and apply knowledge across a wide variety of tasks. It implies a level of cognitive ability that's close to humans.

This category of AI is not a bridge that we have crossed quite yet, but this technology is in research and production.

Self-driving cars are a classic example of limited memory AI. The system can store pertinent information like the speed and distance of cars and then make appropriate driving decisions to navigate the road. Open AI's ChatGPT is another example whereby unabated learning has led it to understanding our natural language and responding in a meaningful manner.

Theory of Mind

Theory of mind is the ability of AI to socialize with humans by understanding emotions, state of mind, and circumstances. This is the next step in the AI evolution. There are ongoing efforts (such as Fujitsu's K computer) to build this capability with a super computer that is working toward simulating the human brain's neural activities.

Self-Awareness/Super AI

This category of AI is as far as the human mind can imagine. Super AI's goal is to think and do what humans do and more—to surpass human knowledge and capabilities. This AI goes beyond understanding our emotions and beliefs and evokes emotions, desires, and beliefs of its own. This sounds a lot like Skynet from the *Terminator* movie series.

The thinking behind this category of AI implies that AI would have its own conscience, through which it gets its own sense of needs, beliefs, emotions, and desires. It's self-aware. It sees itself as what it is, and, based on its interactions with humans, desires to become something else.

How Does AI/ML Work?

At a macro level, AI/ML takes shape through six steps, as defined in Figure 1-2.

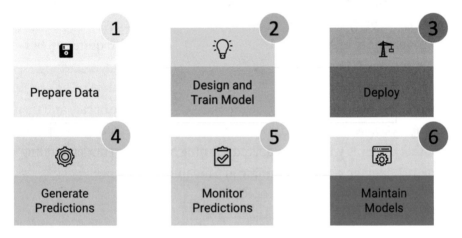

Figure 1-2. *Steps to building artificial intelligence/machine learning*

Prepare Data

Organizations need to ensure that the data is available, free from error, and in a format that is standardized and digestible by machines.

For example, if AI is expected to identify car models, the data must essentially be made up of different sets of car models. Also, the data needs to be clean, without any clutter, duplicates, and other redundancies.

Design and Train Model

If the prepared data is considered the foundation, then developers have a good base to build the rest of the AI logic. They then design the AI model and put it through a training exercise. Python, Java, C++, and LISP are some of the programming languages used to develop AI programs. Python is the most common, and the preferred framework is TensorFlow.

Note   *TensorFlow was created by Google in 2015, and it is an open source library for numerical computation and machine learning.*

You can train neural networks with other frameworks as well, including PyTorch and Pandas.

Using the framework, the machine learning model is created and the attributes from the data are labeled and fed into the model. For example, data used to identify car models is labeled with the appropriate car models, such as Chevrolet Optra, Tata Safari, and Audi A7.

After the data is fed into the system, tests are carried out by machine learning developers and data scientists to ensure that the program can identify the right car models.

Deploy

Upon successful testing in lower environments, the artificial intelligence program is deployed into production.

Generate Predictions

With the AI program online, real data can be fed into the program, and the program will be capable of carrying out what it is meant to do.

The car model images can either be fed by exposing the APIs to the sources of data or they can be batch-fed into the system. Based on the images that are fed into the program, the AI program should be able to identify the correct car models.

Monitor Predictions

Although data that is prepared and fed during the development and training stages is cleaned and sanitized, the same cannot be expected from live data. And yet, the AI program is expected to work accurately with the inputs that it can recognize and maybe throw out a message if it's outside the scope. The predictions must always be monitored to ensure that the program is working as expected.

Maintain Models

Monitoring serves as a feedback loop back to the developers to identify any shortcomings and areas for improvement. With AI, there is always scope for improvement since the inputs can come in any shape, size, and format. Developers need to use the feedback to fix bugs or enhance the program.

For example, let's say that a car model that was trained to the AI program receives an upgrade in the form of body uplift. This is new data that the program needs to learn, and depending on the source of data, the developers need to ensure that the program is trained and tested before deploying the upgrade into production.

Benefits of AI/ML

There was a time when IT was seen as a supporting character, and businesses realized that costs had to be cut in order to remain competitive and relevant in the market. As network connectivity between continents strengthened, activities were offshored toward the East. For several decades, this meant cost savings. With the economies in the offshoring countries picking up along with the competition to retain good talent, the cost factor between onshore and offshore became negligent.

Businesses can no longer rely on offshoring services to cut costs. IT is no longer a supporting character but a partner for business' growth and success. The solution to cutting costs lies in being more effective and efficient in their operations, and they have gone through several cycles of optimization. Still there is a need to cut costs further and be more efficient. The path to this perceived efficiency lies in the success of AI programs. This is one of the primary reasons that several organizations, research institutions, and universities have taken initiative to improve AI.

Apart from the obvious improvement in efficiency and productivity gains, the other benefits of adopting AI include:

- Humans are looking at AI to make the right decisions for them. With vast amounts of data being generated, humans cannot digest the information quickly enough to make an effective decision. A well-trained AI program can be much more efficient at ingesting data and suggesting a good decision. For example, a stock market trader may not have sufficient people on the team to analyze the company records, news, and sector performance in a matter of minutes and hours. An AI program fed with all the relevant will be a good aide in reading the data and coming up with suggestions.

- A vast amount of data is being generated, the majority of which is unstructured. This includes images, videos, and audio. There are valuable insights hidden in such data, and its analysis requires intelligence rather than just logic. For example, a program that scours social media for brand perception may read a post like "this burger is bad..." as negative, while in the natural language the poster is referring to it as *great* colloquially. A well-trained AI program that distinguishes context and colloquialism can differentiate and eliminate such errors.

– The market is changing at the speed of light. Therefore, businesses have to pivot faster than ever before. Earlier, companies used Agile and DevOps methodologies to support quick pivoting, but with the pace picking up, there needs to be a surge through AI to support in churning out market-ready solutions in short order. For example, a tool like GitHub Copilot can accelerate the development of custom applications.

– No two customers are the same. While the best organizations put their best foot forward to please their customers, they may end up only serving 80% of them. With AI and ML, programs can analyze user behavior, history, and styles, among other aspects, to serve particular customers, which can help such organizations reach all their customers successfully.

– AI can replace rule-based applications with intelligence. This capability will boost the applications to support any scenario that may come up. Further, AI can help automate businesses processes through the employment of Robotic Process Automation (RPA) to enhance and accelerate processes.

What Is DevOps?

When you ask an average IT professional what DevOps is, they will say that it has something to do bringing together the development and operations teams. Well, this does not tell the entire story.

There are multiple perceptions about DevOps in the core. In fact, if you Google the web, you will be surprised to find multiple definitions for DevOps, no two of which converge on common aspects and elements.

During the beginning of the DevOps era, to amuse my curiosity, I spoke to a number of people to learn what DevOps is. Most bent toward automation, some spoke of that thing they do in startups, and there were very few who spoke of it as a cultural change. Interesting! A particular example made me sit up and start joining the DevOps dots, and it all made sense eventually.

Explaining DevOps with an Example

Say that you are a project manager of an Internet banking product. The past weekend you deployed a change to update a critical component of the system after weeks of development and testing. The change was deployed successfully; however, during post-implementation review, the program threw an error which forced you to roll back the change.

The rollback was successful, and all the artifacts pertaining to the release were brought to the table to examine and identify the root cause the following Monday. The root cause was identified, and a developer was pressed into action to fix the bug. The code went through the scrutiny of various tests, including the tests that were not originally included that could have caught the bug in the functional testing stage rather than in production. All the tests run okay, a new change is planned and approved by the change advisory board, the change is then implemented, tested, got the green light.

These are the typical activities that are undertaken when a deployment fails. The moment things go south, what is the first thing that comes to a project manager's mind? Do they think about what they should do next or do they start thinking about the developer or the person responsible for the bug in the first place? Or do they think about the tester who identified the scenarios, wrote the scripts, and performed exploratory testing? We work in a culture where we typically think about the people responsible for the problem. This culture blames people and tries to pass the buck.

DevOps is about culture. Instead of a culture that blames the people or the processes, DevOps follows a blameless culture. We are all human after all. We are not perfect. We make mistakes. What's the point in blaming people? In fact, we expect that people will make mistakes. This acceptance leads to a system where mistakes are identified and rectified before they reach the production. The DevOps system brings the development and operation teams together and develops processes that embed automation within the concept of a single team.

DevOps Principles

DevOps principles are in a state of constant evolution. In fact, there are multiple versions of these principles. The most widely followed principles are represented by the CALMS acronym. Figure 1-3 shows a mug from a marketing campaign for DevOps featuring CALMS.

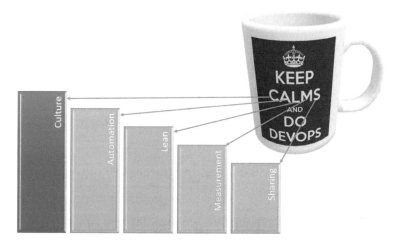

Figure 1-3. *DevOps principles(mug image credit: devopsnet.com)*

CALMS stands for:

- Culture

- Automation

- Lean

- Measurement

- Sharing

Culture

There is a popular urban legend that the late Peter Drucker famously said that culture eats strategy for breakfast. This essentially means that, if you want to make a massive mind-boggling earth-shaking change, start by changing the culture that can make it happen and then adapt to the new way of working. Culture is something that cannot be changed easily and quickly. It is embedded into human behavior and requires an overhaul of the people's behavior and ideas.

Some of the behavioral traits that DevOps seeks to change are:

- Take responsibility for the entire product and not just the work that you perform.

- Step out of your comfort zone and innovate.

- Experiment as much as you want, because there's a safety net to catch you if you fail.

- Communicate, collaborate, and develop affinity with the involved teams.

- For developers especially—you build it, you run it.

Automation

Automation is a key component of the DevOps methodology. It is a massive enabler for faster delivery and also crucial for providing rapid feedback. Under the culture principle, I talked about a safety net with respect to experimentation. This safety net is made possible through automation.

The objective is to automate whatever is possible in the software delivery lifecycle. The kind of activities that can be efficiently automated are those that are repetitive and that don't require human intelligence. For example, building infrastructure was a major task that involved hardware architects and administrators, and most importantly building servers took a significant amount of time. This time was added to the overall software delivery timeline. Thanks to technology, we now have the cloud infrastructure and servers can be spun up through code. We don't need hardware administrators to do it. Developers can do it themselves. Once the environment provisioning script is written, it can be automated to spin up servers. Automation has changed the way we see infrastructure.

Tasks such as running a build or a test script can also be automated. Activities that involve human cognizance are hard to automate. Writing code or test scripts requires human intelligence and machines, as of today, cannot do this.

Lean

DevOps has borrowed heavily from the Lean methodology and the Toyota Production Systems (TPS). The thinking behind it was to keep things simple. With the advent of automation, architecture became more complex and workflows became more complicated. The Lean principle helps developers develop processes that are easy to comprehend and simple to work with.

There are two parts to the Lean principle:

- **Do not bloat the logic or the way you do things; keep them straightforward and minimal.** An example is the use of microservices, which do not overcomplicate the architecture. Developers no longer build monolithic architectures that are cumbersome when it comes to enhancements, maintenance, and upgrades. Microservice architectures are easier to upgrade, troubleshoot (maintain), and enhance.

- **Reduce waste from the methodology.** One of the key wastes are defects. Defects are a nuisance. They delay the overall delivery and the amount of effort that goes into fixing them is just sheer waste of time, effort, and money. The next type of waste pinpoints convoluted processes. If something can be done by passing the ball from A to B, why does it have to bounce off C? There are many such wastes that can be addressed when making the software delivery more efficient and effective.

Measurement

If you aim to automate everything, then you need a system to provide feedback whenever something goes wrong. Feedback is possible if you know what the optimum results should be. The only way you can find out if the outcome is the optimum is by measuring it. So it is key that you measure everything if you are going to automate everything!

The measurement principle indicates which measures to implement and how to monitor the overall software delivery. It is not a simple task to measure everything. Many times, developers don't even know what they should measure. A good DevOps process architect can help solve this problem. For example, if you are running static analysis on your code, the extent of passable code must be predetermined. This is not a random number; there needs to be scientific reasoning behind it. A number of companies allow unit tests to pass when 90% of the code is error-free. Ideally, it should be 100%, so why should anybody compromise for 90%? That's the kind of logic that must go into measuring everything.

Operations, applications, infrastructure, performance, and other parameters fall under this principle. With automation in place, it is extremely important that all the critical activities, and the infrastructure that support them, be monitored and optimized.

Sharing

The final principle is sharing, which hinges on the need for collaboration. If developers aim to significantly hasten the process of software delivery, they cannot work in silos any more. Their knowledge, experience, thoughts, and ideas must be shared for others to join in the process of making the end result better, enhanced, and profound.

One of the key takeaways of this principle is to put everyone who works on a product or service on a single team and promote knowledge sharing. This will lead to collaboration rather than competition and skepticism.

There are a number of collaboration tools on the market today that can help support this cause. Workers don't even have to co-located to share and collaborate. Tools such as Microsoft Teams and Slack help get information across to entire teams. When information is transparent, there is no reason for others to worry or be skeptical about the dependencies or the outcome.

DevOps Processes

Processes are a key component in ensuring the success of any project. However, many DevOps implementations focus more on automation and technology, and the processes that are supposed to be the basis for automation take a backseat. It is important that processes are defined first along with a functional DevOps architecture, and then translated into tooling and automation. The process must always drive the tools and never the other way around.

Waterfall project management methodologies (such as PMI backed project management and PRINCE—projects in controlled environments) are not favored in the IT field anymore. There are various reasons for this—mainly due to the rigidity these processes bring to the project management structure. Most IT projects are run on Agile project management methodologies due to the flexibility they offer in ever-changing market conditions. According to PMI's *Pulse of Profession* publication, 71 percent of organizations are now leveraging Agile. Another study by PricewaterhouseCoopers, in a study named *Agile Project Delivery Confidence,* reports that Agile projects are 28 percent more successful than their waterfall counterparts. This is huge considering that Agile is still new and emerging whereas the waterfall methodology has existed since the 1960s.

When we talk about Agile project management, there are a number of methodologies to pick from—Scrum, Kanban, Scrumban, Extreme Programming (XP), Dynamic Systems Development Method (DSDM), Crystal, and Feature Driven Development (FDD) are some examples.

Regardless, these methodologies all follow a manifesto that was formulated in a ski resort in Utah in 2001. There are a set of 12 Agile principles that provide guidance in setting up project management processes.

This book does not go into the Agile project management processes. These processes are similar regardless of the DevOps implementation. The specific DevOps processes that are introduced on top of the Agile processes are:

- Continuous integration

- Continuous delivery

- Continuous deployment

Continuous Integration

A number of developers work together on the same piece of code, which is referred to as the *mainline* in software development lingo. When multiple developers are at work, conflicts arising due to changes performed on pieces of code is quite common. Software developers generally integrate their pieces of code into the mainline once a day.

When conflicts arise, developers discuss and sort them out. This process of integrating code manually at a defined time slows down the development process. Conflicts can have drastic results, with hundreds of lines of code having to be rewritten. Imagine the time and effort lost due to manual integration. Suppose I could integrate code in almost real-time with the rest of the developers. In that case, the potential amount of rework can be significantly reduced. This is the concept of continuous integration.

To be more specific, *continuous integration* is a process where developers integrate their code into the source code repository (the mainline) on a regular basis, usually multiple times a day. When the code is integrated with the mainline, any conflicts will be evident immediately. Resolving conflicts is no longer an affair where all the developers sit across the codebase and brainstorm together. Only those who have conflicts need to sort them out manually. By doing this conflict resolution multiple times a day, the negative effects that conflicts have are drastically minimized.

Note   *The best definition of continuous integration was coined by Martin Fowler from ThoughtWorks, who is also one of the founding members of the Agile Manifesto, created at a ski resort in Utah.*

Continuous integration is a software development practice where members of a team integrate their work frequently, usually each person integrates at least daily—leading to multiple integrations per day. Each integration is verified by an automated build (including test) to detect integration errors as quickly as possible. Many teams find that this approach leads to significantly reduced integration problems and allows a team to develop cohesive software more rapidly (Source: `https://www.martinfowler.com/articles/continuousIntegration.html`).

Integrating the code with the mainline is just the beginning. Continuous integration is not just about integrating the code; it goes beyond that. Whenever the code is integrated, the entire mainline is rebuilt, and other quality checks such as unit testing and code-quality checks (static and dynamic analysis) also are carried out.

Note   *Build is a process where the human-readable code is converted into machine-readable language (executable code), and the output of a build activity is a binary.*

Unit testing is a quality check where the smallest testable parts of an application are tested individually and in a componentized manner.

Static analysis is an examination of the source code against the coding standards set forth by the industry/software company. Examples: naming conventions, blank spaces, and comments.

Dynamic analysis is an examination of the binary during runtime. Such an examination helps identify runtime errors such as memory leaks.

An Illustration

Say that a particular project has three developers, and each developer integrates their code three times a day. On a daily basis, this equates to nine integrations. As per the illustration in Figure 1-4, code that is integrated gets unit tested first, followed by software build and code quality checks. All this happens automatically whenever any code is integrated.

With nine integrations on a daily basis, that means nine unit tests, twelve builds on the entire mainline, and nine code quality checks.

Suppose one of the builds, unit tests, or code quality checks fails? The flow is interrupted, and the developer gets down to work to fix the defect. This ensures that the code flow isn't hampered and that other coders can continue coding and integrating their work onto the mainline.

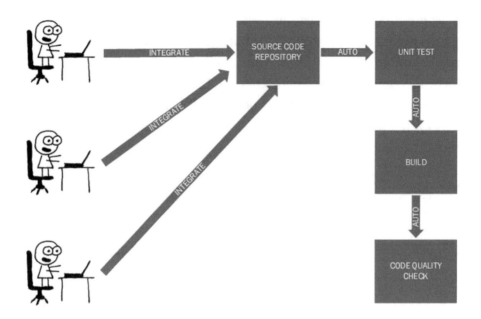

Figure 1-4. *Continuous integration*

Continuous integration allows for the fast delivery of software, and any roadblocks are avoided or identified as early as possible, thanks to rapid feedback and automation. The objective of continuous integration is to hasten the coding process and generate a binary without bugs.

Continuous Delivery

With continuous integration, you achieve two things:

- Binary is generated successfully

- Code level and runtime checks and analyses are complete

The next item in the software delivery lifecycle (SDLC) is to test the generated binary from various angles, aspects, and perspectives. This includes system tests, integration tests, regression tests, user acceptance tests, performance tests, security tests, and more. When you are done with the agreed number of tests, the binary is deemed to be acceptable and deployable into production. The qualified binary can be deployed into production with the push of a button. The qualification of any of the binaries as releasable into production is called *continuous delivery*. It is generally referred to as a natural extension of the continuous integration process. See Figure 1-5.

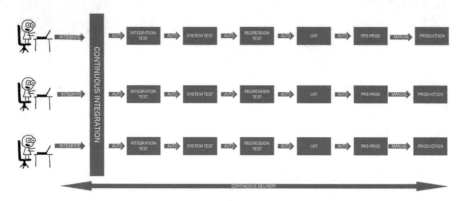

Figure 1-5. *Continuous delivery*

Figure 1-5 shows an illustration of a continuous delivery pipeline. After every successful cycle of continuous integration, the binary is automatically subjected to an integration test. When the integration test is successful, the same binary is automatically system tested. The cycle passes on up to the pre-production environment as long as the tests (the regression and UAT tests in this illustration) are successful. When the same binary is successfully deployed in the preproduction environment (in this illustration) or any other environment that comes before the production environment, the binary becomes qualified to be deployed on to production. The deployment into the production environment is not done automatically but requires a trigger. The entire cycle, starting from the code push into the source code repository up to the manual deployment into the production environment, is referred to as continuous delivery.

Figure 1-5 shows three developers integrating their code and three deployable binaries. Continuous delivery does not dictate that all the three binaries have to be deployed into production. The release management process can make a decision to deploy only the latest binary every week. Remember that the latest binary will include the code changes performed by all the developers up until that point in time.

The sequence of automation for the activities beginning with the continuous integration process up until the production environment is referred to as a *pipeline* or *continuous delivery pipeline* in this case.

AI Meets DevOps

DevOps is the present and the future. It is the bedrock on which solid software development is carried out, and this is a prime reason why organizations are sprucing up their DevOps capabilities and strengthening their ability to deliver software rapidly.

The essence of DevOps is to build an environment that is safe for the development and operation teams to experiment and innovate. This requires the power of automation to ensure that the necessary checks and balances act as a safety net.

While traditionally, the automation included in DevOps was based on workflows, logic, and triggers, AI has introduced several new avenues for DevOps to evolve. At every stage of SDLC, maintenance and observability, AI has a key role to play and sets the bar far higher in the race for rapid development. Think a new feature can be developed in the morning, and it be rolled out into production by the afternoon. This is not a dream but a reality that's possible with the components of AI.

This book is about unravelling the possibilities of speeding up software development further, and building software with the highest possible quality. DevOps is well understood by the majority of organizations today and AI has shown that it can match human intelligence in most cases. This is a perfect storm that companies can ride to create a new beginnings for software development.

Summary

Artificial intelligence is the new kid in town. It's standing up to human intelligence and is challenging us every step of the way. Its ability to decipher hidden meanings in the underlying data and generate outcomes is the gateway to innovation. DevOps, the software development methodology that is in vogue, infused with AI is a perfect foil to innovate more quickly.

This is a 101 chapter for AI and DevOps. On the AI side of the fence, the chapter explained its beginnings, types, and how it works. On the DevOps side, the chapter explained the reason for its existence, principles, and processes—continuous integration and continuous delivery.

CHAPTER 2

Understanding Machine Learning

For about a century, writers and filmmakers dreamt of machines having their own mind and thoughts. It began with invading aliens. More recently, in *I, Robot,* featuring Will Smith, android robots served humans. One of the robots, Sonny, was able to think on its own, have emotions, and even dream. This 2004 movie was my first experience with artificial intelligence (AI) that did not involve aliens. Twenty years on, that science fiction movie might become a reality very soon. We are in a period where the difference between the imaginary and the real world is becoming blurry. Technology can now learn and improvise on its own. In some ways, it is chilling to think of a future in which we are not in complete control. However, the reality is that we are building and improving this technology, because the true path to achieving unparalleled productivity, top notch quality, and scales of economy is through artificial intelligence and machine learning.

This chapter focuses on machines learning from humans, which forms the basis for AI taking shape.

© Abhinav Krishna and Vamshidhar Meda 2024
A. Krishna and V. Meda, *AI Integration in Software Development and Operations,*
https://doi.org/10.1007/979-8-8688-1044-2_2

Construct of AI and ML

Artificial intelligence development involves teaching machines to learn and to use those lessons to generate certain outcomes.

While artificial intelligence involves learning and delivering expected outcomes, the learning phase is referred to as machine learning (ML). Similar to how we teach kids about apples and bananas by displaying pictures, we teach machines by exposing them to data. Learning is accelerated through spider crawlers (like Google crawlers), which enable machines to learn from the information that is available on public forums, apart from what is manually fed to them. ML is the driver that makes AI relevant because the knowledge the mahcines receive is enriched by the day, and the outcomes are dynamic based on the current situation.

The Structure

The terms artificial intelligence and machine learning are often used in conjunction or interchangeably. However, machine learning is a subset of the artificial intelligence, as illustrated in Figure 2-1.

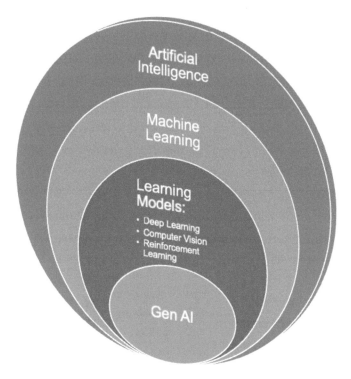

Figure 2-1. *Artificial intelligence and its components*

Machine learning is the process or activity where machines learn from the data provided to them. This learning improves over time, with new datasets replacing existing ones, so machine learning is a continuous process. Machine learning was once a topic of interest only to scientists, but now has become an integral part of various sectors, including finance, healthcare, marketing, and technology. It's revolutionizing the way we interact with data and make decisions.

Note   *Machine learning is the science of building algorithms that can learn from and make predictions or decisions based on data. In the traditional computing model, developers wrote programs that provided predictive output for specific inputs. However, in machine learning, algorithms are designed to learn from patterns and relationships within the data and make decisions or predictions based on those patterns.*

There are several learning models, including deep learning, computer vision, and reinforcement learning, among others. Generative AI (Gen AI) is a technology that can produce content, including videos, images, text, and audio.

Big Data plays a pivotal role in shaping AI and ML. The amount of clean data that is fed into the machines makes the AI smarter. Machines can identify patterns and trends and predict the future course of action. This is particularly useful for predicting weather patterns, supply and demand, and customer's buying behavior, as well as detecting fraud.

Types of Machine Learning

Just as human learning can happen through books, classroom teaching, or experience, machines can learn in a number of ways too. This learning however is restricted by the exposure that humans provide.

Figure 2-2 illustrates the three most common types of machine learning.

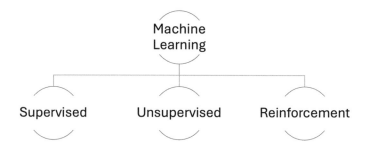

Figure 2-2. *Types of machine learning*

Supervised Learning

Supervised learning is like sending machines to school. Machine schools are the instruments for training machines. In this case, we employ labeled datasets to train machines.

The training involves input-output pairs, where each input is associated with a specific output. Machines are taught to read the input and, with a lookup table of sorts, machines can provide a predictable output.

A classic example of this is image classification, where images of cats and dogs are labeled and fed to machines. Machines learn to distinguish between cats and dogs based on specific features, such as posture, shape of the ears and eyes, among other attributes. Then, when the machine is presented with new photographs of cats and dogs, it can distinguish and classify them correctly.

Unsupervised Learning

Unsupervised learning involves training algorithms on unlabeled data. The algorithm learns to find patterns or structure in the data without explicit guidance. Common tasks in unsupervised learning include clustering similar data points together or dimensionality reduction.

Amazon's shopping recommendations are a result of unsupervised learning. Based on your browsing and buying behavior, the machine identifies a pattern—in this case your preferences—and it recommends products in the same or related category. For example, when I look for whey protein powder, Amazon recommends other supplements like creatine monohydrate and protein shaker bottles.

Reinforcement Learning

Machines are spoon fed information with supervised learning and are left to learn from nature with unsupervised learning. While the former is time consuming and expensive, the latter's outcomes are unpredictable. This is where reinforcement learning comes into play.

Reinforcement learning is a type of machine learning where an agent learns to make decisions by interacting with an environment. The agent receives feedback in the form of rewards or penalties based on its actions, allowing it to learn an optimal behavior through trial and error.

It is employed widely in the gaming industry, where machines try to outmaneuver a human player or try to introduce dynamic play. Take the example of chess, where the machines are rewarded every time they make a right move and penalized for every wrong move. This encourages the machines to make the right moves and avoid the wrong ones. The learning happens in the environment and through interactions. The rewards and penalties ensure that the learning moves in the right direction.

Applications of Machine Learning

Machine learning finds focus in areas where decision making is done on the back of data analysis. In fact, all sectors and areas of technology use a wide variety of data for decision making. A good leader relies on the data, which impacts decision making. Machine learning does the same. It reads and analyzes data that will help it determine the best course of action, and depending on the processing engines used, decisions are made accordingly.

Some common applications of machine learning include:

- **Shopping and content recommendations.** We are in the period of impatience, and the lack of time has made us highly dependent on the Netflixes and Amazons of the world to recommend shows to watch and products to buy. These recommendations have a personal touch because they are built on our browsing and purchase history.

- **Reading X-rays, ECGs, and MRIs.** Humans can make mistakes, depending on the experience of the medical practitioner, fatigue, and social context. Many people also want a second opinion, especially if the outcomes are adverse. Machines have learned to read these charts as they involve patterns and data, and more often than not, their readings are good at identifying conditions such as tumors and fractures.

- **Helping the finance and investment sectors.** Machine learning is still picking up speed in the finance sector, and once it fully does, we don't know the implications of who stands to benefit. However, machines are effectively fighting fraud by dissecting millions of transactions within a span of minutes.

- **Translating audio in real-time for seamless conversations.** Google translate is perhaps the first machine to employ natural language processing (NLP) to translate text seamlessly between languages. The technology has deepened with the machines understanding spoken text, including colloquial speak.

- **Assessing people's skills and developing dynamic training content.** The educational sector is seeing an inflow of machines getting into the ring with tools such as Stackfactor. The days of trainers, classroom trainings, and old school assessments are likely numbered.

Challenges and Future Directions

With any new technology comes accompanying challenges. These are challenges not only to machine learning directly but they also have ripple effects on current technologies, technologists, and processes. Keeping the focus solely on machine learning, the following are challenges that will potentially alter the fabric of AI.

- **Machines learn from data and data alone.** People can influence the quality of data, and the amount of data that can be exposed to machines. Good, clean data ensures that machines are learning the right things. However, real-world data is not clean and often not complete. If the intention is to build a good machine that can replicate human decisions, additional effort needs to be factored to preprocess the data and label it.

- **Decisions should be questioned by nature, whether made by people or machines.** With machines, there should be a traceable lineage leading to the data source. However, many machine learning models, such as deep neural networks, are black boxes, making it difficult to interpret their decisions. The problem with black boxes is that no matter how good the decisions are, we don't know why they were made.

- **As machine learning is done by data provided by people, there is a possibility that the data could be biased.** Machine decisions are only as good as the data they receive. Bad data can exacerbate biases, leading to ethical concerns in areas such as hiring, lending, and criminal justice. It is the developer's ethical responsibility to ensure that the machines are used ethically and there are sufficient checks and balances to ensure that biases do not creep in.

Despite these challenges, the future of machine learning is promising. Ongoing research aims to address these challenges while pushing the boundaries of what is possible with artificial intelligence. As technology continues to evolve, machine learning will undoubtedly play a central role in shaping the future of society and industry.

Machine learning represents a powerful paradigm shift in computing, enabling computers to learn from data and make intelligent decisions autonomously. Its wide-ranging applications and transformative potential make it one of the most exciting and impactful fields in modern technology.

AI Techniques and Algorithms

An *algorithm* is a set of instructions to be followed in calculations or other operations. It provides the workflows for the identified scenarios. You might have worked with algorithms in school and at work, typically developing programs and processes for the intended purposes. Artificial intelligence algorithms are several hundred/thousand times more complex. They are not merely trying to find possible outcomes but are building a system to think like humans.

To provide machines with human-like intelligence and perform analysis and processing, several artificial intelligence techniques and algorithms are employed, each suited to different types of problems and data. Every algorithm has a specific purpose and leads to a range of outcomes.

Integrating AI techniques and algorithms into DevOps and MLOps workflows enables automation, optimization, and decision making in various aspects of software development, deployment, and operations. These techniques help streamline processes, improve efficiency, and enhance the reliability of software systems in production environments.

Figure 2-3 shows an overview of some of the key AI techniques and algorithms.

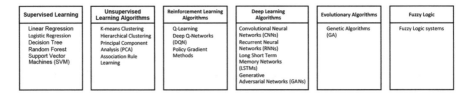

Figure 2-3. *Key artificial intelligence algorithms*

Supervised Learning Algorithms

Linear Regression: A simple regression algorithm used to predict a continuous variable based on one or more input features. Widely used in DevOps and MLOps for tasks like forecasting resource utilization and predicting system performance based on historical data.

Logistic Regression: A classification algorithm used to predict the probability of a binary outcome based on one or more input features. Employed in MLOps for binary classification tasks, such as determining whether a software release will lead to system downtime.

Decision Trees: A treelike model where each node represents a decision based on the value of a feature, leading to the prediction of a target variable. Useful in DevOps for identifying optimal paths in deployment pipelines based on various parameters like test results or code quality metrics.

Random Forest: An ensemble learning method that constructs multiple decision trees during training and outputs the mode of the classes (classification) or mean prediction (regression) of the individual trees. Applied in MLOps for ensemble learning, where multiple models can predict deployment success rates or identify potential bottlenecks in the development process.

Support Vector Machines (SVM): A supervised learning algorithm used for classification and regression tasks by finding the hyperplane that best separates the classes. Utilized in DevOps for anomaly detection in system logs or monitoring for security breaches.

Unsupervised Learning Algorithms

K-means Clustering: A clustering algorithm that partitions data into K clusters based on similarity, with each cluster represented by its centroid. Employed in MLOps for grouping similar deployment patterns or identifying clusters of users with similar system usage behavior.

Hierarchical Clustering: A method that builds a hierarchy of clusters by either merging or splitting them recursively based on their similarity. Useful in DevOps for organizing and categorizing system logs or identifying hierarchical dependencies in software components.

Principal Component Analysis (PCA): A dimensionality reduction technique that transforms high dimensional data into a lower dimensional space while preserving most of the variance in the data. Applied in MLOps for reducing the dimensionality of feature vectors extracted from software metrics or system logs.

Association Rule Learning: A method used to discover interesting relations between variables in large databases, often applied in market basket analysis. Utilized in DevOps for analyzing patterns in configuration management databases or identifying correlations between deployment practices and system stability.

Reinforcement Learning Algorithms

Q-Learning: A model free reinforcement learning algorithm used to find the optimal action selection policy for a given Markov Decision Process. Employed in MLOps for optimizing resource allocation strategies or automating decision making processes in deployment pipelines.

Deep Q-Networks (DQN): An extension of Q-learning that uses deep neural networks to approximate the Q-value function, enabling it to handle high dimensional state spaces. Useful in DevOps for optimizing continuous integration and continuous deployment (CI/CD) workflows or for automating error resolution procedures.

Policy Gradient Methods: Algorithms that directly learn the policy function that maps states to actions, such as the REINFORCE algorithm and Actor Critic methods. Applied in MLOps for dynamic resource provisioning or optimizing workload distribution in distributed computing environments.

Deep Learning Algorithms

Convolutional Neural Networks (CNNs): Deep learning models designed for processing structured grid data, commonly used in image and video recognition tasks. Widely used in MLOps for image recognition tasks, such as identifying anomalies in infrastructure monitoring data or analyzing system architecture diagrams.

Recurrent Neural Networks (RNNs): Deep learning models capable of processing sequential data, making them suitable for tasks such as natural language processing and time series prediction. Employed in DevOps for timeseries forecasting tasks, such as predicting future system loads or estimating future resource requirements.

Long Short Term Memory Networks (LSTMs): A type of RNN with memory cells that can learn long-term dependencies, often used in sequence prediction tasks. Useful in MLOps for analyzing sequential system logs or predicting future software release cycles.

Generative Adversarial Networks (GANs): Deep learning models consisting of two neural networks—the generator and the discriminator—competing against each other, commonly used for generating synthetic data. Applied in DevOps for generating synthetic data for testing purposes or simulating various deployment scenarios.

Evolutionary Algorithms

Genetic Algorithms (GA): Optimization algorithms inspired by the principles of natural selection and genetics, often used to find optimal solutions in complex search spaces. Employed in MLOps for optimizing hyperparameters of machine learning models or tuning the configuration of deployment environments.

Fuzzy Logic

Fuzzy Logic Systems: A computational approach based on fuzzy set theory that deals with reasoning that is approximate rather than exact. Utilized in DevOps for handling imprecise or uncertain information in system monitoring or decision making processes.

Large Language Models (LLM)

A *Large Language Model* (LLM) refers to a machine that understands our natural language, in the manner that we speak, including the words, grammar, and style. While AI systems understanding our language is one part of the equation, LLMs are trained and designed to produce output of human-like text at scale. AI models have undergone massive lengths of training with vast amounts of text data. They use sophisticated algorithms to learn the nuances of the language, including grammar, syntax, semantics, and context. The primary objective of an LLM is to perform numerous natural language processing (NLP) tasks, such as text generation, translation, summarization, sentiment analysis, and question answering.

OpenAI's GPT (Generative Pre-trained Transformer) is a popular LLM, and there are multiple models, such as GPT-2 and GPT-3. They have been trained for several days, with massive datasets containing diverse text, generally gathered through web spiders from the Internet. The model is quite mature and is capable of generating contextually relevant text depending on the given prompt or input.

LLMs are used in various sectors and have a wide range of applications across industries, including content generation, customer service automation, language translation, and virtual assistants, among others. They have taken AI capabilities to greater heights in understanding and generating natural language and they are paving the way to innovative solutions in various fields.

By leveraging the capabilities of different types of LLMs in DevOps contexts, organizations can automate routine tasks, improve communication and collaboration, and enhance overall productivity and efficiency in software development and operations. LLMs come in various types, each with its own architecture, training methods, and applications. The following sections describe some common types of LLMs.

Transformer-Based Models

Transformer-based models, such as OpenAI's GPT series, are characterized by their self-attention mechanism, which allows them to efficiently capture dependencies between words in a sequence. They excel at generating coherent and contextually relevant text based on input prompts.

DevOps Applicability: Within a DevOps environment, a transformer-based model like GPT-3 can be employed for automated incident response. When alerted about a system issue, the model can analyze logs, suggest potential root causes, and recommend troubleshooting steps, enabling faster incident resolution.

BERT (Bidirectional Encoder Representations from Transformers)

BERT models utilize bidirectional context to capture the full context of words in a sentence, enabling them to understand nuances in language and perform well across various NLP tasks.

DevOps Applicability: In DevOps, a BERT-based model can be utilized for automated ticket triage. By analyzing the description of incoming tickets, the model can categorize and prioritize them based on urgency and severity, facilitating efficient ticket management and resource allocation.

XLNet

XLNet combines autoregressive and autoencoding approaches, allowing it to capture bidirectional context effectively and generate high-quality text representations. It achieves state-of-the-art performance in various NLP benchmarks.

DevOps Applicability: Within a DevOps pipeline, an XLNet model can be applied for automated release notes generation. By analyzing code changes and commit messages, the model can summarize key updates and enhancements, assisting in the documentation of software releases.

T5 (Text-To-Text Transfer Transformer)

T5 adopts a unified text-to-text framework for various NLP tasks, simplifying model architecture and training. It can handle diverse tasks by framing them as text-to-text transformations, where inputs and outputs are represented as text strings.

DevOps Applicability: In a DevOps setting, a T5 model can be deployed for automated code review. Developers provide textual descriptions of proposed code changes, and the model evaluates them against coding standards and best practices, providing feedback and suggestions for improvement.

BERT-Based Models for Domain-Specific Tasks

BERT-based models are fine-tuned for domain-specific tasks, leveraging transfer learning techniques to adapt pretrained representations to specialized domains, such as biomedicine or law.

DevOps Applicability: Within a healthcare-focused DevOps team, a BioBERT model can be used to automate the analysis of medical records and diagnostic reports. By extracting key medical terms and diagnoses from text data, the model supports clinical decision-making and facilitates data-driven healthcare operations.

Multilingual LLMs

Multilingual LLMs, like mBERT and XLM, are designed to handle text in multiple languages, making them valuable for cross-lingual applications. They can understand and generate text in different languages, facilitating communication and collaboration in multicultural environments.

DevOps Applicability: In a multinational DevOps team, an XLM model can be deployed for multilingual chatbot development. The model can understand inquiries and provide responses in multiple languages, enabling seamless communication and knowledge sharing among team members across different language backgrounds.

Summary

This chapter provided a high-level overview of artificial intelligence and machine learning concepts. While AI is the overarching umbrella, machine learning describes that way machines learn. Generative AI is the latest kid on the block and can generate text, video, and audio content.

Training AI models involves several methodologies, each for a distinct use case. Supervised learning, unsupervised learning, reinforcement learning, deep learning, evolutionary algorithms, and fuzzy logic are some of the algorithms that were covered in this chapter.

The ability to communicate in a natural language is possible through LLMs. The chapter briefly explored several LLMs, including transformer based, BERT, XLNet, T5, and multi-lingual options from a DevOps standpoint.

CHAPTER 3

Software Development and AI Augmentation

The ability to develop software at record speed, with useful features and enhanced stability, separates the leaders from the flock. That's why we see the likes of Netflix and Amazon running ahead, with substantial market saturation. To this capability, add artificial intelligence, and imagine the force of power that can dominate the market. If it's done right, the combination is spellbinding and hard to beat.

This chapter explains the software development lifecycle (SDLC) and explores how AI can augment it. Of course, when I talk of software development, that includes DevOps, with its set of tools, the automation process, and the whole gamut.

Why Use AI in SDLC

DevOps in SDLC was a game changer. It automated the entire pipeline based on triggers and logic. This accelerated development in conjunction with the Agile methodology. The next level of transformation through AI will change the way we perceive software development, including its timelines, the acceptable bugs, and allowance for maintenance. It's as though we are entering a world of perfection, where creation happens at the snap of a finger and the result is perfection.

© Abhinav Krishna and Vamshidhar Meda 2024
A. Krishna and V. Meda, *AI Integration in Software Development and Operations*,
https://doi.org/10.1007/979-8-8688-1044-2_3

Zenith in Efficiency and Productivity

As AI takes center stage and takes control of task automation, the focus of the development teams tend toward developing and improving features, while leaving the rest for machines to manage.

AI can automate code generation, testing, bug fixing, deploying, and upgrading, among other tasks. Unlike the current crop of code review tools like SonarQube and Crucible, AI-driven tools can conduct holistic code reviews faster, and can do a better job than human reviewers, identifying potential issues and suggesting improvements in real-time.

Unparalleled Quality

AI can make a significantly marked difference in predictive analytics. History may not always be an indication of the future, but with software development, past errors are prone to hinder development. AI can analyze historical data to predict potential issues and proactively address them, reducing the chances of errors and defects in the final product.

An area in which developers often fall short is comprehensiveness, because it's hard to cover every single feature in functional test cases. When AI is integrated during the initial requirements gathering phase, it can generate comprehensive test cases and perform thorough testing, including regression and non-functional cases. This comprehensive testing—at breakneck speeds—ensures higher quality software with fewer bugs and vulnerabilities.

Advanced Decision Making

Artificial intelligence's strength lies in its analysis of huge loads of data, making sense of that data, and using those lessons to arrive at sane decisions. This provides valuable insights and recommendations, helping stakeholders make informed decisions about all aspects of the program including program planning, resource allocation, and risk management.

The aspect of software development where we are generally left wanting of a good decision is which features we need to develop ahead of the rest. AI can help in gathering and analyzing requirements more accurately, and in prioritizing the features. AI can also ensure that the final product aligns closely with user needs and business objectives.

Cost Savings and Effective Resource Management

Every company aims to build software more cheaply, since building software is a perennial process involving maintenance and adding new features. AI can be leveraged to optimize resource allocation and utilization, be it the infrastructure and licenses or humans who are a part of the program. By effectively utilizing program resources, costs are contained. As an added benefit, humans involved in the program get better opportunities to work on creative aspects of software development.

AI's automation contribution further ensures that routine tasks get taken care by the machines, thus leading to further cost savings.

Proactive Risk Management

Risks and opportunities are like the threads of a fabric—they are intertwined. The ability of great leaders to turn risks into opportunities separates the exceptional from the common. While teams and specialists analyze the program for risks, the result may not often be comprehensive and they are not always successful at predicting risks. AI can predict potential risks and issues in the entire SDLC based on historical data, current configurations, and the plans, which will allow the team to take proactive measures to mitigate them.

In the area of IT security, AI has been a great addition, with its ability to identify vulnerabilities based on patterns. AI-driven security tools can be deployed to continuously monitor the software for vulnerabilities and threats, ensuring robust security throughout the SDLC.

Improved Developer Experience

Developer onboarding is the process of integrating new developers into a team or organization. Effective onboarding helps new hires become productive quickly and ensures that they are familiar with the tools, processes, and culture of the organization. The onboarding experience can significantly impact a developer's job satisfaction, productivity, and retention.

AI can transform developer onboarding by providing tailored learning experiences, automating repetitive tasks, and offering real-time support.

Overview of the Software Delivery Lifecycle and AI Infusion

The software delivery lifecycle (SDLC) is a structured mechanism that produces high-quality software that meets the client's needs. The structure exists to ensure that the software delivered is of quality, and the development is efficient and is consistent across the lifecycle. This methodology is composed of several key phases, each integral to the successful creation and maintenance of a software product. It includes planning, gathering requirements, designing, building, testing, deployment, and maintenance, as indicated in Figure 3-1. This cycle consequently provides a methodical approach for developing software through processing of specified activities and deliverables within phases. While the phases indicate a sequential flow, in reality this process is carried out in parallel and in iterations. So, at any juncture, all the phases could be active for different parts and releases of the software.

We discuss the specific challenges and concerns, like security and risk, in the next set of chapters.

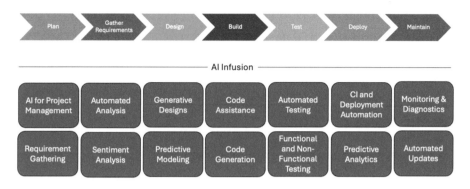

Figure 3-1. *AI infused SDLC*

By integrating with artificial intelligence, the face of conventional methodology changes by making the entire process of SDLC more efficient, accurate, and innovative. AI can make a difference in each of these SDLC phases, as indicated in Figure 3-1. The upcoming sections examine each of the SDLC phases and the AI infusion areas. Further, the rest of the chapters in this book focus on peeling the DevOps onion across these phases.

Planning

The first logical activity/phase is to plan, which builds the foundation for the entire software. During this phase, the customer, the development teams, and all other stakeholders get together to establish clear, achievable objectives—what the software intends to do.

These objectives are generally drawn from a business need or a market opportunity. Planning stems from pragmatism, which is determine through the feasibility study, which assesses the project's viability from technical, operational, and economic perspectives. This study helps determine whether the project makes sense and should indeed proceed and identifies any potential challenges. Further, the requisite resource allocation is another crucial aspect, involving the identification and assignment of necessary resources, such as skilled personnel, budget, and technology.

Generally, businesses conduct a high-level risk assessment to anticipate possible risks and develop strategies to mitigate them. The outcome of this phase is a detailed project plan, which outlines timelines, milestones, and deliverables, serving as a roadmap for the entire project.

AI Infusion in Planning

AI for Project Management: AI tools can forecast the timelines, resource requirements, and potential risks involved in a project based on analysis of historical data from various projects.

Requirements Gathering: The AI technique called Natural Language Processing (NLP) will analyze the communication among stakeholders to automatically derive and prioritize requirements.

There are significant benefits of using AI for planning, like providing comprehensive insights, which helps with data-driven decision making, reviewing past scenarios, and providing realistic recommendations across numerous elements like budgeting, resourcing, stakeholder engagement, and scheduling.

Using AI also has challenges. For example, the historical data may not be relevant to the project's current ecosystem, and it might also overlook some unique project specific requirements or changes in resourcing or budgeting.

Gathering Requirements

Once the plan is ready, the Gathering Requirements phase is instrumental in understanding and documenting what the software should achieve.

The requirements are obtained from customers and other related stakeholders through various methods, including interviews, surveys, and workshops. Requirements come in two forms—functional and non-functional. *Functional requirements* describe the specific behaviors or functions of the software, and non-*functional requirements* outline the performance standards, security measures, and usability criteria.

The requirements are thoroughly documented in Word and Spirit, to ensure they are clear, complete, and consistent. They are further validated to confirm that they accurately reflect the stakeholder needs and expectations. Once the requirements are in place, they need to be prioritized, to ascertain the critical parts that need to be developed and tested ahead of the rest.

The output of this phase is a comprehensive requirements specification document, which acts as a reference for the subsequent phases.

AI Infusion in Gathering Requirements

Automated Analysis: AI can help analyze and check the requirements against business goals and other existing documentation for their completeness and consistency.

Sentiment Analysis: NLP tools that assess the stakeholder's feedback and sentiments can prioritize features in view of user needs and preferences.

AI infusion in requirements management can provide key insights, automate specific or repetitive tasks, and research key features being built or implemented. They also facilitate better decision making, which will ultimately lead to more successful project outcomes and goals.

Designing

Just as a building architect develops blueprints for a house with all the construction specifications, the Designing phase in SDLC translates requirements into a blueprint for building the software. Software architects are primarily involved in this phase to create and validate the designs.

This includes the overall system architecture, which defines the structure and interaction of hardware and software components. The architecture serves as a reference artifact and is the backbone of the system, and it is meant to include provisions for scalability, reliability, and performance.

Along with the software, there are several accompanying designs that are included, such as database design (schema, tables, relationships) and UI design (intuitive and user-friendly interfaces), among others.

Component design involves detailing the internal workings of individual software modules and specifying how they will interact and function. All design elements are thoroughly documented in design specifications, providing a clear and consistent guide for developers.

AI Infusion in Design

Generative Design: AI algorithms can provide suggestions on design patterns and architectures that are best-practices-based and based on earlier successful projects.

Predictive Modeling: AI can help in predicting design issues and potential failures by simulating various scenarios and identifying weak points in the design.

Bringing AI in designing elements of SDLC helps with speed, consistency, best practice implementation , clear visualization, and parallel testing. This is very useful for projects being implemented as MVP (Minimum Viable Products).

There are challenges in which outputs are generic and work should be done for customization, as well as review of the design to meet overall specification. In addition, some tools provide output that is specific to a provider, like AWS or GCP.

Building

The Building phase represents the majority of the development that happens in SDLC. Software developers write the source code within the guardrails of the design documents, adhering to established coding standards and guidelines to maintain code quality and established rules.

One of the key activities in this phase is unit testing. It involves testing individual components, and it is carried out by developers. The developers leverage source version control tools for enabling collaboration and managing code changes. Further, code reviews are conducted regularly to ensure that the code meets quality standards and to identify potential issues early. The objective of this phase is to provide a robust, error-free software product.

AI Infusion in Building

AI-Powered Code Assistance: AI pair programmers are tools that can help a developer by recommending code snippets, pointing out possible bugs, and performing real-time code reviews.

Automated Code Generation: AI can generate boilerplate code, letting the developers focus on more complex tasks. They can help write unit test cases as well.

Infusing AI in the Building phase will help with coding efficiency, increase the speed of development, and generate unit test cases covering all of the code. We have seen tools help fast-track some key migration or technology currency programs.

There are drawbacks like security and privacy concerns and over reliance on AI, which might hinder Software Developers skills. There is a broader need for AI-augmented software developers within each of the teams.

Testing

Unit tests conducted in the Build phase check the components individually, but they don't test the system as a whole, and not in a production-like environment. The objective of the Testing phase is to ensure that the software product conforms to quality standards, is free from defects, and meets the business requirements.

In this phase, a comprehensive test plan is developed, detailing various test cases and scenarios that the software must pass. The testing environment that mirrors the production setup is spun to ensure realistic testing conditions.

There are multiple types of testing carried out to ensure that all facets of a software product are thoroughly vetted. *Functional testing* checks the software product against the functional requirements to ensure it works as it is supposed to. *Integration testing* checks for the connections and handshakes between different parts of the system to ensure they work well together as one system. The *holistic test* verifies if the entire software product works well. *Performance testing* is a test of the software performance against non-functional parameters. In this, the software is put to test under different conditions, such as varying loads and stress situations. One of the final tests is *user acceptance testing* (UAT), which is conducted by the end users to validate that the software meets their needs and expectations. Most of these tests are generally automated through various testing tools.

Any defects identified during testing are meticulously tracked, prioritized, and resolved to ensure a polished final product.

AI Infusion in Test

Automated Testing: AI-led testing tools can generate test cases, run the tests, detect bugs, and even recommend how to fix them. Machine learning models can pinpoint areas in the code that likely contain defects.

Non-functional tests: AI enables non-functional tests like performance and security tests to identify any reliability or security issues.

AI infusion in quality engineering or testing will help create more comprehensive and faster testing across functional and non-functional areas. This also helps reduce production defects and reduce operational or support costs and any downtime issues for the software.

Challenges include initial setup, integration with several components, test design, and the data being used. Some defects may not be identified if the LLM models are not well trained.

Deployment

The Deployment phase refers to the activity of releasing the software product to the production environment, wherein the software product moves from development to operational use. This is a critical phase, since it modifies the existing live product with a new release (in majority of the cases unless it is a new product). The deployment planning's objective is to release the software to product with minimal impact to end users—the intricate activities include creating a detailed schedule and procedure for the release.

The production environment is prepared in accordance with the design to run the software optimally. The software product is installed and configured on the environment. If a new system is being set up, deployment includes migrating data from old to new, with necessary data transformation and checks, thus ensuring data integrity.

Once the software is configured and the data is migrated, a series of sanity checks and deployment verification measures are conducted to ensure that the software functions correctly, post-installation. The accompanying tasks of getting the end users and support personnel trained is a responsibility of the phase.

AI Infusion in Deployment

Continuous Integration and Deployment: AI optimizes end-to-end CI/CD pipelines due to process automation, which in turn improves build times and deployment efficiency. AI tools can handle all the processes of deployments and, in case of failures, perform the rollbacks automatically.

Predictive Analytics: AI can tell the optimum deployment time based on historical data, which would reduce downtime and user disruption.

By using AI in the Deployment phase, deployment can be faster by identifying patterns, reducing deployment issues, and monitoring deployment activities with no human intervention. Increased dependency of AI may infuse additional challenges, like unable to resolve issues when AI malfunctions. Sometimes, the recommended fix may be inaccurate.

Maintenance

Maintenance is the final phase, which ensures the software works as it should and remains relevant over time. Following deployment of a software release, it is common for bugs to crop up, which are addressed in this phase over a period of time.

To keep the software stable and functional, regular software updates are released to improve functionality, enhance security, and boost performance.

Non-functional aspects such as performance and security, among others, are updated through continuous monitoring and subsequent fixes and improvements.

Maintenance of a software product also involves keeping the documentation up-to-date to reflect any changes made to the software. This ongoing process ensures that the software adapts to changing needs and continues to deliver value to its users.

Monitoring and Diagnostics: AI systems can continuously monitor the performance of software, detect anomalies, and diagnose them on the spot.

Automated Updates: AI can patch and update through identification of the updates required and their deployment with less human intervention.

Maintenance is one area where AIOps has been used for the last few years. It has helped in self-healing issues, helping to increase the availability and reliability of applications.

There are limitations, including how complex the software design is, and how the models are trained to handle errors.

Challenges in the Adoption of AI

The prospects of artificial intelligence boosting software development through unparalleled efficiency, high quality, and effecting cost savings are mouthwatering. But there are many bumps in the way of getting to that stage. For instance, training AI to analyze requirements for identifying risks is a complex process that takes ample time and effort. This section examines some of the critical challenges faced when infusing AI into SDLC.

Increased Complexity

If you consider the software development process as it existed a decade earlier, it was sequential and straightforward. We started with a project charter, followed by planning (requirements gathering), software development, testing, and project closure. Although it was not efficient or even effective, it was not complex.

The introduction of DevOps added a fair degree of complexity depending on the level of desired automation. With AI, the complexity is bound to go a couple of notches higher. More importantly, it demands resources with special knowledge of building and training AI models. At this juncture, there is a notable skill gap in the AI domain. Finding and retaining skilled professionals capable of developing, implementing, and maintaining AI solutions is difficult. Existing staff may also need extensive training to understand and effectively use AI tools, which can be time-consuming and costly as well.

Data Quality

The effectiveness of AI is directly proportional to the quality of data that is used in its training. An AI system needs high-quality data to operate effectively. Bad data is bound to produce wrong predictions and recommendations. AI models commonly use supervised learning. Such models require labeled data. The process of accurately and consistently labeling data is often labor-intensive and expensive. AI systems also require large volumes of high-quality data for training and optimization. Collecting sufficient, relevant, and clean data can be challenging, especially for organizations lacking historical records.

One of the risks involving AI is its ability to handle sensitive data. Yes, AI models can be trained on this too, but the cost of mishandling such data can be expensive. It is imperative that sufficient guardrails are established to ensure data privacy and security while complying with regulations such as GDPR and HIPAA. The task of handling sensitive data responsibly adds another layer of complexity to AI implementation.

Initial High Cost and Maintenance

In the long run, the cost savings are promising, but getting started can be an expensive affair. Implementing AI solutions requires substantial upfront capital investment for the AI models, skilled people to train the AI, and the hardware to host the data and the AI. This is in addition to the cost associated with building the software product.

Setting up the AI program is one part of the equation, while its ongoing maintenance is another. AI systems require continuous monitoring, periodic updating, and ample maintenance, all of which add to existing operational costs.

Integration with Existing Systems

It is widely understood that building something from scratch is usually easier than trying to change something that already exists. Likewise, integrating AI with existing systems, especially legacy ones, can be challenging, owing to compatibility issues. This may also demand significant modifications and upgrades to the existing infrastructure.

As an organization grows, its data and software footprint expand along with it. With AI in tow, ensuring that AI tools can scale to meet growing organizational needs and handle increasing data volumes and complexity is a significant challenge.

Ethical and Security Concerns

The integration of AI into application development also raises ethical and security concerns. These include the potential for bias in AI models, the risk of data breaches, and the need to ensure that AI-driven decisions are transparent and accountable. The following list expands on each of these concerns:

- **Bias in AI models:** AI models can inherit biases present in the data they are trained on. This can lead to biased decision-making, particularly in areas such as automated code generation and performance monitoring. We have seen models that recommend services of a specific cloud provider, for example.

- **Data security:** AI models often require access to sensitive data, raising concerns about data security and privacy. Ensuring that data is securely handled and that AI models are compliant with data protection regulations is critical.

- • **Transparency and accountability:** AI-driven decisions should be transparent and accountable. Developers need to understand how AI models make decisions and be able to explain these decisions to stakeholders.

Summary

The chapter provided an overview of the SDLC model and how AI can be infused in each of its phases. AI infusion into SDLC has its pros and cons, with benefits such as improved efficiency, high quality, and better decision making. It comes with demanding challenges that can hinder adoption in the short term, such as an increase in complexity, the need for quality data for training needs, and the initial high cost.

CHAPTER 4

Planning and Requirements Management in Projects

"If you don't know where you are going, you'll end up someplace else."

—Yogi Berra

There are two types of people. Those who plan meticulously, spending ample time brainstorming, whiteboarding, and preparing for a desired outcome. And there are those who are adventurous and dynamic, and who like to live life in the moment and see where it takes them. While they may seem adventurous, is it often very foolish to do anything without planning. They say that planning is only half the battle, but imagine that you could win half the battle before you even start to do something. That's a massive advantage that should never be missed.

© Abhinav Krishna and Vamshidhar Meda 2024
A. Krishna and V. Meda, *AI Integration in Software Development and Operations*,
https://doi.org/10.1007/979-8-8688-1044-2_4

Planning can take a long time. We can't put my finger on how long you need to plan, but whatever that number is, it is never enough. Every project, activity, and initiative requires sound planning to be successful. As Abraham Lincoln said, "Give me six hours to chop down a tree and I will spend the first four sharpening the axe," a good solid plan is critical to any project.

This chapter digs deep into the initial two phases of SDLC—planning and requirements management. While the focus remains on integrating AI with the planning and requirements gathering phases, this chapter provides a broad-based view of the phases, discusses various LLM techniques that can be used in each of the phases, and dives into the pros and cons of each activity. Further, the chapter looks at how AI can be used to analyze Agile requirements and come up with planning and estimation.

Integrating AI and LLMs in the Planning Phase

The beauty of planning a project is that you conceive all the possible areas of study and start planning for them. For example, if we were to sell clothes door-to-door, we would need to plan for what to wear, which neighborhoods to visit, what we will say, how much clothes to carry with us, where to park our car, and so on. There are many more areas that we could plan, just for a simple door-to-door campaigning activity. No matter how many plans we develop, it is never enough; there is way to over-plan.

In SDLC projects as well, there are plans and sub-plans. We could write a separate book just to cover the various plans of SDLC, but for the scope of this chapter, let's restrict the topic to key areas of planning, beginning with project initiation.

Project Initiation

Project initiation is the foundation of SDLC. A project has a scope, length of time to execute, and a cost associated with it (referred to as the triple constraints). During project initiation, the first of the triple constraints comes into play with the project's scope and objectives being clearly defined to ensure alignment with the overarching business goals. This involves outlining what the project aims to achieve and specifying the boundaries within which it will operate.

AI can be integrated into the project initiation activity as follows:

Define the Project's Purpose and Scope

An AI tool can gather and synthesize information from various sources like research papers, industry news, and market analysis reports to provide a comprehensive understanding of the current market landscape. It can identify gaps, opportunities, and competitive advantages to help shape the project's purpose and scope.

AI Application: GPT-4 can be used to analyze market trends, industry reports, and competitor analysis to define the project scope and purpose.

Pros: Provides comprehensive insights and data-driven decision making, leading to a well-defined project purpose and scope.

Cons: Potential bias if the input data is not comprehensive or contains biases, which could skew the project's initial direction.

Identify Stakeholders and Their Expectations

Based on the analysis of the stakeholders' communications, AI can identify key themes, concerns, and expectations. This helps in understanding stakeholder priorities and aligning project goals accordingly.

AI Application: LLMs can be employed to perform sentiment analysis on stakeholder communications and feedback from emails, surveys, and meetings.

Pros: Efficiently identifies key stakeholder concerns and expectations, ensuring that the project aligns with their needs from the outset.

61

Cons: Privacy concerns regarding the analysis of personal communications. The accuracy of sentiment analysis might not always capture nuanced stakeholder sentiments.

Establish Project Objectives and Goals

AI can review past project successes and failures to set benchmarks and define SMART (specific, measurable, achievable, relevant, and timebound) goals.

AI Application: Analyze historical project data to set realistic and achievable objectives and goals.

Pros: Sets realistic and achievable project goals based on data-driven insights.

Cons: Historical data may not always be relevant or available, particularly with innovative or unprecedented projects.

Feasibility Study

The feasibility study is a key activity to complete before initiating full-blown projects. This study assesses the project's viability from multiple perspectives, including technical, financial, and operational aspects. The goal is to determine whether the project is not only possible but also worthwhile in terms of the resources required and the potential benefits.

AI can be integrated into the feasibility study activity as follows.

Technical Feasibility

AI can analyze large datasets from tech industry reports and forums to predict which technologies will remain viable and innovative.

AI Application: Use AI to evaluate the suitability and future viability of different technology stacks by analyzing current usage trends and projecting future technological developments.

Pros: Provides a detailed analysis of technological options, reducing the risk of choosing obsolete or less supported technologies.

Cons: Potential inaccuracies in long-term predictions, especially in fast evolving tech landscapes.

Operational Feasibility

AI can create detailed simulations to determine how the new system will integrate with existing processes and what operational challenges might arise.

AI Application: AI simulates the operational impact of the project on current business processes and resource utilization.

Pros: Identifies potential operational challenges early, allowing for proactive planning.

Cons: Simulations may not capture all real-world complexities, especially in dynamic environments.

Economic Feasibility

AI can model various financial scenarios, including best case, worst case, and most likely outcomes, helping stakeholders understand financial viability.

AI Application: AI-driven financial models analyze cost benefit scenarios and return on investment (ROI) based on historical financial data and market conditions.

Pros: Provides a more precise economic feasibility analysis, aiding in better financial decision making.

Cons: Dependence on accurate financial data and assumptions, which might be volatile or uncertain in some markets.

Resource Planning

Resource planning also takes place during the project planning phase. It involves estimating the resources required for a project, including personnel, technology, and budgetary needs. At this stage, the project budget is often roughly estimated, providing a framework for the financial resources that will be allocated.

Identify Required Resources

AI can cross-reference current project needs with past projects of similar scope to predict resource requirements accurately.

AI Application: AI analyzes project requirements and historical data to suggest necessary resources, including human resources, equipment, and software.

Pros: Optimizes resource allocation by predicting accurate needs.

Cons: May overlook unique project specific requirements or changes in resource availability.

Allocate Roles and Responsibilities

AI tools can create detailed profiles of team members and suggest optimal role assignments to maximize efficiency and performance.

AI Application: AI matches team members to roles based on their skills, experience, and past performance metrics.

Pros: Enhances team efficiency and utilization by ensuring the right people are assigned to the right tasks.

Cons: Potential resistance from team members and oversight of human factors such as team dynamics and individual preferences.

Project Scheduling

Project scheduling is a key activity in any project and one of the triple constraints. The activity involves organizing tasks, resources, and timelines to ensure a project is completed on time and within budget. It provides a detailed plan that outlines when the tasks will start, how long they will take, when they need to be completed, and any dependencies. The schedule serves as a roadmap for the project, guiding the project team through the execution phase.

Timeline Development

AI tools can simulate different scheduling scenarios to find the most efficient timeline that meets project deadlines and resource constraints.

AI Application: AI generates optimized project schedules by analyzing task dependencies, resource availability, and historical project timelines.

Pros: Creates efficient and realistic timelines, reducing the risk of delays.

Cons: Complexity in integrating AI generated schedules with existing project management tools and processes.

Use Project Management Tools

AI continuously monitors project progress and provides real-time updates and alerts for potential delays, along with recommended actions to stay on track.

AI Application: AI integrates with project management software (like Jira, Asana) to predict delays and suggest corrective actions.

Pros: Proactive delay management and increased ability to stay on schedule.

Cons: Possible over-reliance on AI predictions and the need for continuous data input for accuracy.

Budgeting

The final constraint in project management, budgeting, is the process of estimating, allocating, and controlling the financial resources that are required for a project. The activity ensures that the project has the requisite finances to cover people, infrastructure, licenses, and so on. The project budget serves as a financial blueprint, guiding how resources are used throughout the project's lifecycle.

Estimate Costs

AI tools can create detailed cost models, including fixed, variable, and unforeseen costs, to provide comprehensive budget estimates.

AI Application: AI predicts project costs using historical project data, market analysis, and resource cost trends.

Pros: Provides accurate cost estimates, reducing the risk of budget overruns.

Cons: Requires comprehensive and up to date financial data. Potential inaccuracies in dynamic market conditions can skew the data.

Prepare a Detailed Budget Plan

AI tools can generate dynamic budget plans that adjust as actual costs are incurred, helping to manage the budget effectively.

AI Application: AI monitors expenditures in real-time and forecasts future budget needs, adjusting for unexpected costs.

Pros: Real-time budget tracking and adjustment lead to better financial control.

Cons: Potential inaccuracies if the market or project conditions change rapidly.

Communication Plan

Communications is estimated to account for more than 50 percent of the overall project effort. It is a key component of a project, and it guides how information is shared and exchanged among project stakeholders throughout the lifecycle of a project. Its objective is to ensure that all concerned stakeholders are kept informed, engaged, and aligned with the project's goals and progress, and of potential issues that arise. At the core, a mature communication plan helps prevent misunderstandings, keeps the project on track, and fosters collaboration among team members and stakeholders.

Establish Communication Channels

AI tools can analyze past communication data to determine the most effective channels and methods for different stakeholders.

AI Application: AI recommends optimal communication channels based on stakeholder preferences and communication patterns.

Pros: Enhances communication efficiency and effectiveness.

Cons: Risk of impersonal communication if AI recommendations are followed too rigidly.

Plan Regular Meetings and Status Updates

AI can manage calendars, send reminders, and create meeting agendas based on project milestones and progress.

AI Application: AI schedules regular meetings, generates automated status updates, and identifies key points for discussion.

Pros: Reduces administrative overhead and ensures timely communication.

Cons: Dependence on AI for accurate scheduling and updating content.

Risk Management

How well a project can manage risks is a critical success factor. A project must ensure that it identifies, assesses, prioritizes, and mitigates risks that could potentially derail a project. It involves planning how to handle potential problems before they occur, with the goal of minimizing negative impacts on the project's objectives, such as scope, time, cost, and quality. Effective risk management is essential for ensuring that a project stays on track and achieves its goals despite uncertainties.

Identify Potential Risks

AI tools can create risk profiles and predict the likelihood and impact of various risks, allowing for proactive risk management.

AI Application: AI analyzes historical data, market conditions, and project specific variables to identify and predict risks.

Pros: Early and accurate risk detection helps prepare mitigation strategies.

Cons: High dependence on the accuracy of historical data and potential for missing unforeseen risks.

Develop Risk Mitigation and Contingency Plans

AI can model different risk scenarios and provide recommendations on how to avoid or minimize their impact.

AI Application: AI suggests risk mitigation strategies based on similar past projects and simulates potential scenarios to develop contingency plans.

Pros: Effective risk mitigation planning reduces the project's vulnerability to risks.

Cons: Simulations may not account for all real-world complexities and potential rare events.

Quality Assurance Planning

The quality of a product needs to be based on a design, and not on probability. Quality Assurance (QA) planning lays the foundation for stability and reliability. It involves defining the processes, standards, and activities that will ensure the project's deliverables meet the required quality standards. The idea of this plan is to ensure that defects are prevented. Quality assurance planning is a critical component of project management, as it ensures that the final product is fit and meets all specified requirements.

Define Quality Standards

AI can analyze successful projects within the industry to define quality metrics and standards for the current project.

AI Application: AI benchmarks quality standards against industry best practices and past project successes.

Pros: Establishes robust quality criteria, ensuring high standards are maintained.

Cons: Initial setup and integration of AI tools can be complex and time consuming.

Plan for Quality Control and Assurance Activities

AI tools can generate test cases, execute tests, and analyze results to ensure that quality standards are met throughout the project lifecycle.

AI Application: AI automates testing processes, identifies potential quality issues, and recommends improvements.

Pros: Faster testing cycles and reduced human error lead to higher quality outcomes.

Cons: Overreliance on automated tools may overlook nuanced quality issues that require human judgment.

Agile Estimation Techniques Infused with AI

In Agile project management, estimating the length and breadth of a project is not straightforward. For starters, in the waterfall method, the scope is frozen and the development, testing, and other activities take place one after another. This provides a semblance of stability in terms of determining project estimates.

Agile in comparison is quixotic. You bundle all the requirements into a product backlog and freeze the scope for a sprint, which is anywhere between two to four weeks. So, while you know what you are going to achieve in a particular sprint, you don't know how long the entire project will take. In fact, the project ends up being open ended, as new requirements are added and redundant ones are retired. Therefore, you employ certain Agile estimation techniques to estimate the effort, time, and resources required to complete tasks, user stories, and features in the project. Contrary to the traditional estimation (waterfall) methods, Agile estimation focuses on flexibility, adaptability, and collaboration, allowing teams to make more accurate and dynamic estimates as the project evolves. These techniques are particularly useful in environments where requirements change frequently, and detailed upfront planning is not feasible.

Benefits of Leveraging AI for Estimation

Estimation is an art, and it is based on past performance. AI is best suited whenever there is data that can be analyzed and applied to the decision-making process. Incorporating Agile estimation techniques into AI projects enhances the ability to manage complexity, adapt to changes, and deliver high-quality outcomes efficiently. Each technique contributes uniquely to the planning and execution process, ensuring AI projects are well structured, resource efficient, and aligned with stakeholder needs. AI technologies further enhance these techniques by providing data-driven insights, predictive analytics, and automation, thereby improving accuracy and efficiency.

Better Predictability

The accuracy of estimates is bound to be higher, as AI can efficiently analyze historical project data to identify patterns and trends, which is a better way to estimate as opposed to relying on intuition. Further, AI models can look at the data objectively, which reduces cognitive biases that humans may subconsciously exhibit.

A typical example uses a three point estimation technique, where a team can anticipate potential delays in data labeling for a supervised learning project, adjusting timelines and resources accordingly.

Enhanced Collaboration

Collaboration succeeds when there is rationale behind the claims, and this eventually leads to agreement. By providing data-backed estimates, AI can facilitate more informed discussions among team members, leading to better decision-making. Also, AI tools can facilitate remote collaboration by providing real-time data insights and historical context during discussions. It can generate visual representations of estimates, trends, and potential risks, making it easier for stakeholders to understand and engage with the estimation process.

For example, during a *planning poker* (a technique discussed later in this section) for a machine learning project, data scientists, engineers, and product managers discuss potential data quality issues, ensuring everyone is aware and can contribute solutions.

Improved Resource Allocation

Employing AI in Agile estimation can ensure efficient use of resources, optimizing team productivity and project efficiency. AI-driven tools can suggest optimal resource allocation based on task complexity and historical performance, thereby improving efficiency. A common challenge that developers encounter in Agile projects is that some team members have more work than others. AI can help balance workloads across team members by providing accurate estimates of task complexity and duration, leading to a more even distribution of work.

With the Agile estimation technique of *affinity mapping* (a technique discussed later in this section), an AI project manager can identify whether data preprocessing requires significant effort and allocate more resources to this phase to avoid bottlenecks.

Flexibility

The name of the Agile game is flexibility, and AI enhances flexibility in Agile estimation by enabling dynamic re-estimation, supporting scenario analysis, handling uncertainty, and facilitating personalized and adaptive estimation processes. AI can provide real-time feedback on project progress and highlight areas needing adjustment, thereby enhancing the team's ability to adapt quickly.

For example, during a sprint review, the team revisits their T-shirt size estimates and adjusts it based on new findings about the complexity of integrating a new AI model with a legacy system.

Focus on Value

AI can be trained to keep a constant eye on meeting objectives, where AI can focus on value in Agile estimation by prioritizing tasks that deliver the highest business and customer impact, optimizing resource allocation, enabling data-driven decision-making, and ensuring continuous alignment with evolving project goals. AI can analyze user feedback and engagement metrics to help prioritize features that deliver the most value, aligning development efforts with user needs.

The *dot voting* technique (a technique discussed later in this section) helps prioritize a feature that improves user engagement in an AI-based personalized learning platform, ensuring the team focuses on high-impact work.

The impact of AI on each Agile estimation technique and relevant use cases for AI projects are explained in the following section.

Agile Estimation Techniques

Since Agile focuses on the need to pivot as and when needed, there are specific Agile estimation techniques that are in vogue. These techniques are particularly useful in environments where requirements change frequently, and detailed upfront planning is not feasible. This section goes in depth into some of the common techniques, explains how AI supports the estimations, and looks at how these techniques impact AI projects.

Planning Poker

Planning poker involves team members estimating the effort of a user story using cards with values (typically a Fibonacci sequence: 1, 2, 3, 5, 8, 13, 21, etc.). Each member selects a card privately and reveals it simultaneously. If there are major variances in the estimates, the team discusses the reasoning behind the estimates and then re-estimates until consensus is reached. Figure 4-1 illustrates the planning poker Agile estimation technique.

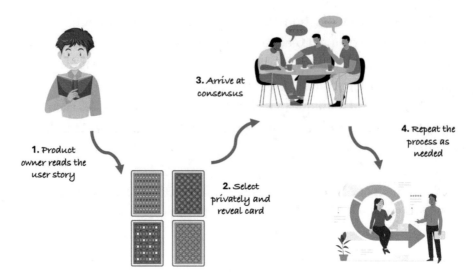

Figure 4-1. *Planning poker Agile estimation technique*

Example: Estimating the effort to develop a feature for an AI-based recommendation system:

- **User Story:** "As a user, I want the recommendation system to suggest products based on my purchase history."

- **Discussion:** The team discusses potential complexities, such as data preprocessing, model selection, and integration with the existing system.

- **Estimation:** Team members reveal their cards. If estimates range from 5 to 13, the team discusses further and aligns on a final estimate, say 8.

Impact of AI in estimation:

- **Enhanced Decision Support:** AI tools can analyze historical estimation data to provide recommendations during planning poker sessions, making the process more data-driven.

- **Build Consensus**: AI can automatically highlight when the estimation variance is bigger, or when the estimates diverge significantly from historical data or predictive models. This provides a suitable nudge toward conducting focused discussions on areas of disagreement and facilitating quicker consensus.

- **Providing Suggestions**: When there are significant variances in estimates, AI can suggest a median estimate based on historical data or statistical analysis, to help the team arrive at a decision.

- **Knowledge Sharing:** Facilitates discussions that can uncover hidden aspects of AI projects, such as potential biases in data or algorithmic limitations.

- **AI Use Case:** Using an AI tool to analyze past sprint data and suggest likely effort estimates, thereby improving accuracy and reducing the time spent in estimation meetings.

T-shirt Size Estimation Technique

Tasks are categorized into sizes (XS, S, M, L, XL) based on their relative effort, time required, and complexity. The t-shirt size estimation technique is illustrated in Figure 4-2.

Figure 4-2. *T-shirt sizing Agile estimation technique*

Example: Estimating various tasks for an AI chatbot project:

- **Small (S):** Implementing a basic keyword recognition module.

- **Medium (M):** Developing a natural language processing (NLP) model for intent detection.

- **Large (L):** Integrating the chatbot with an external API for real-time data fetching.

- **Extra Large (XL):** Designing a conversational AI capable of handling complex queries and providing contextual responses.

Impact of AI in estimation:

- **Automated Complexity Analysis:** AI can assist in categorizing tasks by analyzing code complexity and historical performance, suggesting appropriate T-shirt sizes.

- **Reduce Variation in Estimates:** The sizes of the t-shirts in the market are not standardized. We need to refer to the size chart of every brand before we order one. But with AI, it is possible to normalize the sizes by providing objective, data-backed size recommendations. This will ensure varied interpretation of t-shirt sizes.

- **Continuous Learning:** AI not only derives analysis from past data but can also learn from the outcomes of past estimations, by refining their T-shirt size recommendations over time based on how accurate previous estimations turned out to be. This continuous learning helps improve the accuracy of future estimations.

- **AI Use Case:** Implementing an AI tool that evaluates the codebase and suggests T-shirt sizes based on code complexity and past project data.

Dot Voting (Multi Voting)

Dot voting is democracy in action. Team members vote with dots on tasks that are written on stickers. The task with the most votes is considered the highest priority or has the highest effort. It is an effective estimation technique which invokes the wisdom of the crowd.

Example: Prioritizing features for an AI-driven fraud detection system:

- **Features:** Anomaly detection algorithm, real-time monitoring dashboard, user alert system, and transaction analysis module.

- **Voting:** Each team member places dots next to the features they believe are most critical. If "anomaly detection algorithm" receives the most dots, it is prioritized for development.

Impact of AI in estimation:

- **Democratized Decision Making:** Ensures that diverse perspectives from data scientists, engineers, and domain experts are considered, leading to a more balanced and comprehensive prioritization.

- **Prioritization:** Helps quickly identify the most critical tasks, ensuring that high-impact features are developed first.

- **Enhanced Voting Insights:** AI can analyze past voting patterns and project outcomes to provide insights on which features tend to deliver the most value.

- **AI Use Case:** Utilizing an AI system to recommend feature priorities based on historical success metrics and team voting patterns.

Affinity Mapping

Description: Affinity mapping is a pattern recognition estimation technique. It involves organizing and categorizing tasks into meaningful groups based on their natural relationships. The estimation is done collectively for each of the groups rather than individual tasks.

Example: Grouping tasks for an AI image recognition project:

- **Categories:** Data collection, model training, validation, and deployment.

- **Tasks:** Collecting labeled images, developing a convolutional neural network (CNN), validating the model on a test dataset, and deploying the model to a cloud service.

- **Estimation:** The team estimates the effort for each category, ensuring all related tasks are considered together.

Impact of AI in estimation:

- **Pattern Recognition:** Aligns well with teams' skills in clustering and pattern recognition, aiding in logical task grouping and comprehensive effort estimation.

- **Effort Distribution:** Helps in distributing effort across various phases of development, like data preprocessing, model training, and validation, ensuring balanced resource allocation.

- **Automated Task Clustering:** AI can automatically group similar tasks using machine learning algorithms, making the affinity mapping process faster and more accurate.

- **AI Use Case:** Implementing an AI-driven tool to analyze and group tasks for an AI project, enhancing the accuracy and efficiency of effort estimation.

Bucket System

The bucket system is similar to affinity mapping. Similar tasks are placed into "buckets" representing different effort levels, complexity, or size. The team discusses and moves tasks between buckets until they agree on estimates. This estimation technique is employed when a team needs to estimate a number of tasks in a short period of time.

Example: Estimating efforts for a speech-to-text AI system:

- **Buckets:** 1 hour, 2 hour, 4 hour, 8 hour, and 16 hour.

- **Tasks:** Developing a speech recognition module (8 hour), fine-tuning the model (4 hour), integrating with a transcription service (2 hour), and testing the system (4 hour).

- **Discussion:** The team discusses and agrees on the bucket placements for each task.

Impact of AI in estimation:

- **Scalability:** Effective for large development projects with numerous tasks, allowing for a structured and scalable estimation process.

- **Categorization:** Supports categorization of tasks based on complexity, such as simple feature extraction versus complex model tuning, ensuring appropriate allocation of time and resources.

- **Historical Analysis:** AI can analyze historical data to suggest initial bucket placements for tasks, reducing the time required for manual categorization.

- **AI Use Case:** Using an AI tool to analyze past project data and recommend initial bucket assignments for tasks in a new AI project, streamlining the estimation process.

Three-Point Estimation

The three-point estimation technique is a traditional waterfall project management method that is used to estimate the time, effort, or cost required to complete a task by considering three possible scenarios: the optimistic (best-case), pessimistic (worst-case), and most likely outcomes. The final estimate is calculated as (O + 4M + P) / 6.

Example: Estimating effort for creating a sentiment analysis AI:

- **Optimistic (O):** Two days (if everything goes smoothly).

- **Most Likely (M):** Four days (based on typical scenarios).

- **Pessimistic (P):** Six days (if significant issues arise).

- **Final Estimate:** (2 + 4*4 + 6) / 6 = 4 days.

Impact of AI in estimation:

- **Risk Management:** Helps account for uncertainties in projects, such as data quality issues or unexpected algorithmic challenges.

- **Balanced Estimates:** Provides a balanced view of effort, incorporating best- and worst-case scenarios, which is particularly useful in complex projects where variance is high.

- **Predictive Analytics:** AI can predict optimistic, pessimistic, and most likely scenarios based on historical data, providing more accurate three-point estimates.

- **AI Use Case:** Implementing an AI tool to generate three-point estimates for AI tasks by analyzing historical project performance and outcomes.

Use Case Points

The use case points estimation technique measures the effort required to build software in realizing use cases. The estimates are based on the complexity of use cases, considering actors, scenarios, and technical/environmental factors.

Example: Estimating effort for an AI-driven customer support system:

- **Actors:** Customers, support agents, and system administrators.

- **Scenarios:** Query resolution, escalation handling, and feedback collection.

- **Complexity Factors:** NLP model sophistication, integration with CRM, and real-time response capability.

- **Estimation:** Each use case is evaluated for complexity, and effort is estimated accordingly.

Impact of AI in estimation:

- **User Centric:** Ensures projects are aligned with user needs and real-world use cases, leading to higher relevance and user satisfaction.

- **Complexity Accounting:** Helps in estimating the effort required for different use cases, from simple automation to complex predictive analytics, ensuring comprehensive planning.

- **Automated Complexity Assessment:** AI can evaluate the complexity of use cases by analyzing similar past projects, streamlining the estimation process.

- **AI Use Case:** Using an AI tool to assess the complexity of new use cases in an AI project, providing more accurate and efficient effort estimates.

Agile Estimation Tools

Agile estimation techniques—such as planning poker, T-shirt sizing, and story points—are crucial for predicting the effort required to complete tasks in a project. Integrating AI into these estimation techniques can enhance their accuracy and efficiency by leveraging historical data, predictive analytics, and real-time adjustments.

Integrating AI into Agile estimation techniques through popular project management/application lifecycle management tools like JIRA, Azure DevOps, Trello, GitHub, and Asana can significantly enhance the estimation process. AI-powered plugins and extensions can analyze historical data, predict effort, facilitate real-time adjustments, and help teams reach consensus more efficiently. By leveraging AI capabilities, teams can improve estimation accuracy, reduce discussion time, and ensure more reliable sprint planning and execution.

The following sections cover specific examples of how AI can be infused into Agile estimation techniques using popular project management tools.

JIRA with AI Integration

AI-Powered Estimation Plugins

JIRA users can use AI-powered plugins like "Agile Poker for JIRA" or "Planning Poker AI" to assist with various Agile estimation techniques. Figure 4-3 shows the Agile Poker for JIRA plugin in action.

Figure 4-3. *Agile Poker for JIRA plugin (Source:* `https://marketplace.atlassian.com`)

Functionality:

—   **Historical Data Analysis:** These plugins analyze past sprint data and user stories to provide initial estimates.

—   **Predictive Analytics:** AI algorithms predict the complexity of new user stories based on historical patterns and similar tasks.

Example Workflow:

1.   **Setup:** Team members log in to JIRA and start an estimation session using the AI-powered plugin.

2.   **AI Suggestions:** The plugin analyzes historical data and suggests estimates (e.g., story points, T-shirt sizes) for each user story.

3.   **Team Review:** Team members review the AI's suggestions and provide their own estimates.

4. **Consensus Building**: The AI plugin adjusts its
   suggestions in real-time based on the team's input,
   helping the team reach a consensus more quickly.

Azure DevOps with AI Estimation

AI-Based Estimation Tools

Azure DevOps users can use AI tools like "Azure DevOps Extensions for Estimation" integrated with machine learning models to assist with Agile estimation techniques. Figure 4-4 shows the Azure DevOps Estimate plugin.

Figure 4-4. *Azure DevOps Estimate plugin (Source:* `https://marketplace.visualstudio.com/`*)*

Functionality:

- **Effort Prediction:** The AI tool predicts the effort required for user stories based on past project data and similar tasks.

- **Pattern Recognition:** The tool identifies patterns in past estimations and outcomes to refine its predictions for new user stories.

Example Workflow:

1. **Initiate Session:** The team initiates an estimation session within Azure DevOps.

2. **AI Estimates:** The AI tool provides initial estimates for each user story based on historical data and pattern recognition.

3. **Team Estimates:** Team members compare their estimates with the AI's predictions and discuss any discrepancies.

4. **Final Estimates:** The AI tool helps facilitate discussions and adjusts its estimates based on team feedback to reach a consensus.

Trello with AI Assistance

AI-Powered Automation Tools

Trello users can use power-ups like "Butler" combined with AI capabilities to enhance Agile estimation sessions.

Functionality:

- **Automated Estimations:** AI algorithms provide initial estimates for Trello cards (user stories).

- **Historical Insight:** The AI analyzes past project cards to refine its estimation model continuously.

Example Workflow:

1. **Planning Session:** Team members open an estimation session using Trello and the AI-powered power-up.

2. **AI Insights:** The AI analyzes the current board and provides initial estimates for each card.

3. **Member Input:** Team members review the AI's estimates and provide their own, discussing any differences.

4. **Refinement:** The AI adjusts its estimates in real-time based on team feedback, helping the team reach a consensus efficiently.

GitHub Projects with AI Estimation

AI-Enhanced Project Management Tools

GitHub users can leverage AI-enhanced project management tools like "ZenHub" with integrated AI features for Agile estimation. Figure 4-5 shows the ZenHub board that it is integrated with GitHub.

Figure 4-5. *ZenHub board (Source:* `https://blog.zenhub.com/`*)*

Functionality:

- **Predictive Analysis:** AI models predict estimates for issues based on similar past issues.

- **Real-Time Collaboration:** The AI facilitates real-time collaboration and estimation adjustments during the estimation session.

Example Workflow:

1. **Session Start:** Team members start an estimation session within GitHub using ZenHub.

2. **AI Predictions:** The AI tool analyzes historical issues and provides initial predictions.

3. **Team Discussion:** Team members provide their estimates, compare them with the AI predictions, and discuss any differences.

4. **Consensus Building:** The AI tool helps adjust estimates based on team feedback, aiding in reaching a consensus.

Asana with AI Estimation

AI-Powered Estimation Integrations

Asana users can use AI-powered integrations like "Forecast" or "Effort Estimator" that use machine learning to assist with Agile estimation techniques. Figure 4-6 shows Asana with an AI-generated workflow.

Figure 4-6. *Asana with an AI-generated workflow (Source:* `https://zapier.com`*)*

Functionality:

- **Effort Estimation:** AI models analyze historical task data to predict complexity and assign estimates.

- **Task Similarity:** The tool identifies similar tasks from past projects to provide more accurate estimates for new tasks.

Example Workflow:

1. **Initiate Session:** The team initiates an estimation session within Asana.

2. **AI Estimates:** The AI tool provides initial estimates for each task based on historical data and task similarity.

3. **Team Input:** Team members review the AI's estimates, provide their own estimates, and discuss any differences.

4. **Final Estimates:** The AI tool facilitates discussions and adjusts the estimates based on team feedback, helping to reach a consensus.

Requirements Gathering Overview

Figure 4-7 shows a popular cartoon on project management, where all the customer wanted was a tire swing. It's like the game of Chinese whispers (or telephone), where the requirements are passed from one person to another, distorted along the way. The end result is something completely different and wrong.

Figure 4-7. *Requirements management gone wrong*

In the SDLC lifecycle, the requirements for the product/project serves as the genesis for what is to be built. Therefore, gathering requirements is the most critical phase of any project. It sets the foundation for a product. It goes without saying that if the customer's mind is well understood, the product will be usable, align with customer needs, feasible under the given constraints, and most importantly, deliver value. I am not going into quality just yet, because there is a lot that can go wrong between accurately capturing requirements and deploying them.

Requirements gathering is when the product owners and business analysts identify, capture, and document the specific needs, objectives, and expectations of the stakeholders, including clients, end users, and other parties who have an interest in the project's outcome.

Requirements serve as the blueprint for what the project will ultimately deliver. Yes, the requirements can and will change along the way. Yet, the requirements that are in place at the time of development serve as the North Star.

The requirements gathering process is essentially about understanding what the customer intends to build, what problems need solving, and the opportunities. These requirements must be translated into unambiguous instructions that can be further translated into actions, leading to build and test phases. Requirements are not just functional. There are unstated non-functional requirements as well, such as performance, security, usability, and compliance with the local laws.

Effective requirements gathering helps prevent misunderstandings, miscommunications, and scope creep—common challenges that can derail projects, lead to cost overruns, and result in a product that fails to meet user expectations.

The Importance of Requirements Management in IT Projects

While requirements management needs to tick a number of boxes to lead to a successful project, its goals are broadly based on the following key performance indicators.

Aligning Business and IT Goals

Business Objectives: Effective requirements management ensures that IT projects align with the strategic goals and objectives of the organization. For instance, a financial institution developing a new online banking platform would prioritize security and user experience to align with its goal of providing safe and convenient services.

Stakeholder Satisfaction: Properly managed requirements ensure that all stakeholders' needs and expectations are met, leading to higher satisfaction and acceptance of the final product. For example, in the development of a new customer relationship management (CRM) system, sales teams, marketing, and customer service representatives' needs must be considered and met.

Reducing Project Risks

Scope Management: Clearly defined requirements help manage the project scope, preventing scope creep and ensuring that all necessary features are included without adding unnecessary complexity. For example, during the development of an e-commerce website, defining the scope to include only essential features such as product listings, a shopping cart, and a checkout process can prevent unnecessary additions like an integrated blog or forum.

Risk Mitigation: Identifying and addressing potential issues early in the project lifecycle can mitigate risks and prevent costly rework. For instance, in a healthcare software project, early identification of regulatory compliance requirements can prevent significant legal and financial risks later.

Cost and Time Efficiency

Avoiding Rework: Capturing accurate requirements reduces the likelihood of changes during the development phase, saving time and costs associated with rework. For example, in software development, clear requirements can prevent the need for redesigning and redevelopment of features.

Resource Allocation: Proper requirements management allows for better planning and allocation of resources, ensuring that the project is completed within budget and on time. For instance, in a project to develop a new mobile app, understanding the requirements upfront allows for proper scheduling of development, testing, and deployment resources.

Requirements Management Process

The process of gathering requirements opens the communication pathway between the project, customer, and other involved stakeholders. It has to be a collaborative approach and iterative in nature. It requires a variety of skills, including technical expertise, analytical thinking, and interpersonal communication. As mentioned earlier in this section, the product owners and business analysts, along with the architects, work closely with stakeholders to elicit requirements through various techniques such as interviews, workshops, surveys, observation, and document analysis.

While requirements gathering is about getting the communications right to align with the customer needs, it indeed goes beyond that. Requirements gathering is also about understanding what the customer intends to do rather than what customer needs (want over need). Many times, customers may want something entirely different than what they are able to communicate. Therefore, it is crucial for the project stakeholders to study the requirements and seek out information that is intended and unstated. Requirements gathering is also about validating and prioritizing requirements to ensure that they are accurate, complete, and aligned with the project's goals, which is more efficient because it prevents the need for rework at a later stage.

The process of requirements gathering, although it happens at the start of the SDLC cycle, is not a one-time activity. In a market that shifts often, requirements tend to change often, so it is imperative that the requirements be validated regularly.

The requirements gathering process is illustrated in Figure 4-8.

Requirements Management Process

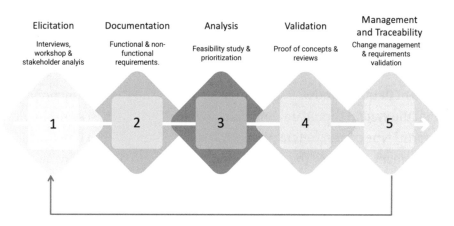

Figure 4-8. *Requirements management process*

Gathering Requirements

Techniques: Various techniques such as interviews, workshops, surveys, and observation are used to gather requirements from stakeholders. Effective communication skills are crucial during this phase to ensure that all needs are met. For example, in developing an enterprise resource planning (ERP) system, workshops with different departments (finance, HR, supply chain, and others) can provide a comprehensive view of the system requirements.

Stakeholder Analysis: Identifying and understanding the roles and interests of different stakeholders helps in gathering comprehensive and relevant requirements. For instance, in a project to develop a new customer support system, stakeholders might include customer service representatives, managers, and IT staff.

Requirements Documentation

Documentation Standards: Requirements are documented in a structured format, using templates and standards such as IEEE 830 to ensure consistency and clarity. For example, using a standard template for functional requirements documentation helps in maintaining clarity and completeness.

Types of Requirements: Requirements are categorized into functional (what the system should do) and non-functional (how the system should perform) types. In an online payment system, for example, a functional requirement could be "the system should process credit card payments," while a non-functional requirement could be "the system should process payments in three seconds."

Requirements Analysis

Feasibility Study: Analyzing the feasibility of requirements in terms of technical, financial, and operational aspects ensures that they are realistic and achievable. For instance, when developing a new software product, a feasibility study might reveal that certain desired features are too costly or technically challenging to implement within the project timeline.

Prioritization: Prioritizing requirements based on factors such as business value, risk, and cost help identify the most critical aspects first. For example, in a project to develop a new website, core functionalities like user logins and content management might be prioritized over less critical features like social media integration.

Requirements Validation

Review and Approval: Requirements are reviewed and validated by stakeholders to ensure accuracy and completeness. This phase may involve formal reviews, walkthroughs, and inspections. For example, in developing a new inventory management system, requirements might be reviewed by the warehouse staff and IT specialists to ensure accuracy.

Prototyping: Creating prototypes or mockups can help validate requirements by providing a visual representation of the final product. For instance, when designing a new user interface for a software application, prototyping can help in gathering feedback from users before the final development stage.

Requirements Management and Traceability

Traceability Matrix: A traceability matrix is used to track the relationships between requirements and other project artifacts, such as design, development, testing, and implementation. This ensures that all requirements are addressed throughout the project lifecycle. For example, in a software development project, a traceability matrix can ensure that each requirement is tested and validated before release.

Change Management: A formal process for managing changes to requirements is essential to control scope and ensure that any changes are documented, assessed, and approved. For instance, in an IT infrastructure upgrade project, any changes to hardware or software requirements need to go through a formal change management process.

Good Practices in IT Requirements Management

This section looks at some of the good practices that developers should employ in IT requirements management.

Continuous Stakeholder Engagement

Engaging stakeholders throughout the project lifecycle ensures that their needs and expectations are consistently addressed, leading to higher satisfaction and successful project outcomes. For example, when developing a new mobile banking app, continuous feedback from end users and bank employees can ensure that the app meets user needs.

Clear and Concise Documentation

Using standardized templates and clear language helps avoid misunderstandings and ensures that all stakeholders have a common understanding of the requirements. For instance, using a clear and concise template for documenting user stories in an Agile project can help the development team understand and implement the requirements accurately.

Effective Communication

Regular communication with stakeholders, project teams, and other involved parties is crucial for ensuring that requirements are understood and correctly implemented. For example, in a project to implement a new CRM system, regular meetings and updates can ensure that all stakeholders are on the same page.

Using Requirements Management Tools

Utilizing tools such as IBM Rational DOORS, JIRA, or Microsoft Azure DevOps can help developers manage, track, and document the requirements more efficiently. For instance, using JIRA to track user stories and their implementation status can improve transparency and accountability in Agile projects.

Regular Reviews and Audits

Conducting regular reviews and audits of requirements and related project artifacts ensures that issues are identified and addressed promptly, maintaining the quality and accuracy of the requirements. For example, regular audits of requirements in a software development project can ensure that all critical requirements are being met and any deviations are corrected.

Requirements Gathering Infused with AI

Gathering, analyzing, and validating requirements can be efficiently handled and accurately documented with the help of AI. Since requirements are essentially data that can be analyzed against market trends and other conditions, AI has the potential to significantly enhance the requirements management process in IT projects. By leveraging AI technologies, organizations can improve accuracy, efficiency, and effectiveness in capturing, analyzing, and managing requirements. The following sections outline several ways that AI can be infused into requirements management, along with examples of Large Language Model (LLM) techniques.

Enhancing Requirements Elicitation

Natural Language Processing (NLP)

Automated Requirement Extraction: AI can analyze large volumes of textual data (such as emails, meeting notes, and documents) to extract relevant requirements. For example, NLP algorithms can be used to scan customer feedback and automatically identify common requests or issues that need to be addressed.

   Example: Using NLP techniques, a project manager can deploy an AI system to analyze customer feedback on a new software product. The AI system can extract recurring themes, such as requests for new features or reports of bugs, and compile them into a list of requirements.

Chatbots for Stakeholder Interaction: AI-driven chatbots can interact with stakeholders to gather requirements through conversations. These chatbots can ask clarifying questions, provide examples, and ensure that all necessary information is collected.

   Example: A software company can deploy an AI chatbot to engage with users and gather requirements for a new feature. The chatbot can ask users about their specific needs, preferences, and pain points, and then compile the information into a structured format for further analysis.

Large Language Models (LLMs)

Contextual Understanding: LLMs, such as GPT-4, can understand the context and nuances of stakeholder communications, making it easier to extract accurate requirements from unstructured data.

Example: Using GPT-4, a business analyst can input transcripts of stakeholder meetings. The model can generate a summary of key points and requirements, highlighting critical needs and concerns discussed during the meetings.

Improving Requirements Analysis

Predictive Analytics

Feasibility and Impact Analysis: AI can predict the feasibility of requirements by analyzing historical data from past projects. It can also assess the potential impact of new requirements on the project's timeline, budget, and resources.

Example: In a project to develop a new e-commerce platform, AI can analyze past projects' data to predict the likely challenges and resource needs to implement specific features. This can help project managers prioritize features that provide the most value with the least risk.

Prioritization: AI algorithms can prioritize requirements based on factors such as business value, risk, and stakeholder input. Machine learning models can analyze past project data to identify patterns and suggest optimal prioritization strategies.

Example: In a software development project, AI can analyze the historical data to determine which features have provided the most business value. The model can then prioritize new requirements based on their potential impact.

Large Language Models (LLMs)

Requirement Clarification: LLMs can help clarify ambiguous requirements by generating questions that need to be answered to achieve a clear understanding.

Example: An LLM like GPT-4 can analyze a vague requirement such as "improve user experience" and suggest specific questions, like "Which aspects of the user experience need improvement?" or "What metrics will be used to measure improvement?"

Enhancing Requirements Documentation

Automated Documentation

Template Generation: AI can automatically generate requirement documentation templates based on the project type and industry standards. This ensures consistency and saves time for project teams.

Example: An AI tool can generate a standardized template for documenting functional requirements in a healthcare IT project, ensuring compliance with regulatory standards.

Real-time Updates: AI-driven tools can automatically update requirement documents in real-time as new information is gathered or changes are made, ensuring that all stakeholders have access to the most current information.

Example: In an Agile software development project, AI tools can automatically update user stories and requirement documents based on sprint reviews and feedback, ensuring that the documentation is always up to date and accurate.

Large Language Models (LLMs)

Enhanced Documentation: LLMs can generate detailed and coherent requirement documents based on brief inputs, ensuring thorough documentation.

Example: Using GPT-4, a project manager can input bullet points describing a feature. The model can generate a comprehensive requirements document, including functional and non-functional requirements, user stories, and acceptance criteria.

Facilitating Requirements Validation

AI-based Prototyping

Interactive Prototypes: AI can generate interactive prototypes based on the gathered requirements, allowing stakeholders to visualize and interact with the proposed solution. This helps validate requirements and gather additional feedback.

    Example: For a new mobile application, AI can create interactive prototypes that stakeholders can test on their devices. The feedback collected from these interactions can be used to refine and validate the requirements.

Simulation and Testing: AI can simulate various scenarios and test the requirements against them to identify potential issues early in the process.

    Example: In a project to develop an automated trading system, AI can simulate different market conditions to test if the requirements for risk management and transaction speed are met.

Large Language Models (LLMs)

Requirement Validation: LLMs can assist in validating requirements by generating test cases and scenarios that ensure all aspects of a requirement are covered.

    Example: An LLM like GPT-4 can analyze a requirement for a new software feature and generate a comprehensive list of test cases to ensure the feature meets all specified criteria.

Enhancing Requirements Management and Traceability

Intelligent Traceability

Automated Traceability Matrix: AI can automatically create and maintain a traceability matrix, linking requirements to design, development, and testing artifacts. This ensures that all requirements are accounted for and tracked throughout the project lifecycle.

Example: In a complex software development project, AI can maintain a traceability matrix that links requirements to code changes, test cases, and deployment scripts. If a requirement changes, AI can quickly identify all affected components and provide recommendations for managing the impact.

Change Impact Analysis: AI can analyze the impact of requirement changes on the overall project and suggest mitigation strategies to manage these changes effectively.

Example: In an IT infrastructure upgrade project, any changes to hardware or software requirements would need to go through a formal change management process. AI can assess the potential impact of these changes on project timelines and budgets.

Large Language Models (LLMs)

Dynamic Traceability: LLMs can dynamically update traceability matrices by analyzing project artifacts and identifying links between requirements and other project elements.

Example: Using GPT-4, a project manager can input new requirements or changes, and the model can update the traceability matrix, linking requirements to relevant design documents, test cases, and code modules.

Leveraging AI for Continuous Improvement

Continuous Learning and Improvement

Feedback Loops: AI can continuously gather feedback from stakeholders and analyze project outcomes to improve the requirements management process. Machine learning models can learn from past projects to identify best practices and areas for improvement.

Example: A project management office (PMO) can use AI to analyze data from completed projects and identify trends and patterns. This information can be used to refine the requirements management process, improving accuracy and efficiency in future projects.

Performance Metrics: AI can track and analyze key performance metrics related to requirements management, such as requirement stability, stakeholder satisfaction, and project success rates.

Example: AI can analyze project data to measure the stability of requirements over time, identifying patterns that indicate potential areas for improvement in the requirements gathering process.

Large Language Models (LLMs)

Continuous Improvement Insights: LLMs can provide insights and recommendations for continuous improvement based on the analysis of project data and stakeholder feedback.

Example: Using GPT-4, a project manager can input historical project data and receive recommendations on how to improve the requirements management process, such as identifying common sources of requirement changes and suggesting strategies to mitigate them.

Summary

This chapter focused on the first two phases of SDLC—planning and requirements gathering.

The planning phase, no matter how long it takes, is a critical construct and a critical success factor. During this phase, the developer delves into initiating projects with feasibility studies, budgeting, scheduling, resource allocation, communication, and risks and quality control plans. Each of these activities can be bolstered by integrating AI into the system.

Estimating project resources, schedule, and budget in an Agile project can be challenging. Estimation looks at the past data, and with AI, developers can analyze past data and help arrive at the best possible estimates through the various Agile estimation techniques and tools that are plugged into AI.

Requirements management that follows planning is a critical piece of the SDLC puzzle and it is the foundational phase on which the entire project sits. There are multiple techniques to elicit requirements from customers and other stakeholders, including conducting workshops and surveys. Integrating with AI, the gathered requirements are wholly validated and ensured that they are in line with the wants and needs of the customers.

CHAPTER 5

Integrating Generative AI in Software Design and Architecture

> *"The function of good software is to make the complex appear to be simple."*
>
> —Grady Booch

This quote succinctly captures the goal of software design—to hide the complexities of technology behind an intuitive and accessible interface. It can only get better using AI.

Software design is critical. As with requirements gathering, you need to get the design right since it determines how the product stands the test of time. Software design in the SDLC is a framework for ensuring that the software is robust, stable, scalable, and efficient. During this phase, the building blocks (including architecture, components, infrastructure, interfaces, and data, among others) are designed to satisfy specified requirements. This process acts as a link between the customer's need/problem to the solution, transforming abstract requirements into concrete plans that can be implemented through coding. This is a quintessential phase, as it influences the functional aspects as well as the non-functional ones.

© Abhinav Krishna and Vamshidhar Meda 2024
A. Krishna and V. Meda, *AI Integration in Software Development and Operations*,
https://doi.org/10.1007/979-8-8688-1044-2_5

A good software design is meant to provide guidance and point toward true north for the development teams. It should provide clarity and direction, ensuring that developers have a clear understanding of what needs to be built. The aim should be to build a functional system with reduced complexity, achieved by breaking the system into manageable components, thus making it easier to understand, develop, and test.

As an architect, leveraging AI tools and LLM can enhance the overall software design and architecture process across various components. This chapter explains what a good software design looks like, digs into key software design components, including data, security, and user interface (UI), discusses some of the pros and cons, and includes examples for how AI can be infused along with available tools in the industry.

Overview of Software Design

A good software design ensures that the parts of the software can be reused. This allows for efficient development. A solid design foundation includes setting up DevOps pipelines and embedded automation. This helps identify potential issues early in the development process, saving time and resources by avoiding costly revisions at later stages. It also true that this foundation plays a critical role in ensuring that the software is flexible and scalable, capable of adapting to changing requirements and growing with the needs of the users. Building modular designs that can flexibly decouple/integrate with other modules facilitates collaboration among developers, enabling teams to work in parallel and integrate their work seamlessly.

A building design could be a one-time thing, but software design should be looked at as an iterative process. As new technology and requirements flow in, the design may need to be revisited and refined to accommodate those new requirements or to address unforeseen challenges. Software can remain relevant through continuous improvement, which is possible only on the back of a solid design.

The process of developing software design starts with the analysis of requirements, where the stated and unstated needs of the customer and other stakeholders are thoroughly understood. A high-level design (HLD) is produced, which indicates the direction of travel—such as building a bespoke application, employing microservices, using a COTS platform such as Salesforce, the choice of design patterns, and so on. The architectural design serves as a roadmap that guides the development process, outlining how different components will interact and how data will flow through the system.

After the HLD is in place, the design process moves on to a detailed design, where individual components are defined in greater depth. This is referred to as the low-level design (LLD). This includes specifying the internal structure of modules, defining algorithms and data structures, and detailing how components will interact with each other through interfaces.

There are the design principles and best practices that need to be followed during the design process to ensure that the software is efficient and maintainable. This includes building *modular software,* which focuses on dividing the system into smaller, self-contained units; *abstraction,* which focuses on hiding the complex details of components behind simple interfaces; and *encapsulation,* which ensures that the internal workings of a component are not exposed to other parts of the system. Alongside these principles are principles like *cohesion*, which promotes the grouping of related functionalities within a single module; and *coupling*, which seeks to minimize dependencies between modules. These principles all play a crucial role in creating a robust design.

Software Design Components

There are several questions that developers need to answer during the software architecture and design phase, notable questions include these:

- What is the system's functionality?
- Can the system be protected from external threats?
- Can we deploy the system with zero downtime?
- How should data integration work?
- Should it be a microservices or monolithic architecture?
- How will the system respond to various elements like performance?

This chapter focuses specifically on seven key software design components to help answer these questions and dives deep into how AI can be infused into each component. The seven software design components that must be considered during the Design phase are listed here and illustrated in Figure 5-1:

- System design
- Component design
- User interface (UI) design
- Data design
- API design
- Infrastructure design
- Security design

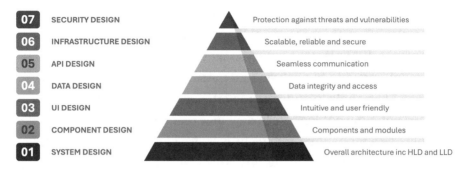

Figure 5-1. *Software design components*

System Design

System design is the process of defining the key architecture, components, modules, interfaces, and data for a system to meet specific requirements. It involves creating a blueprint that outlines how different parts of the system will interact and work together. Effective system design ensures that the system is scalable, maintainable, and meets performance and security standards. It serves as a crucial step in translating business needs into technical solutions. The design process includes both high-level and low-level design. High-level design focuses on the system's overall structure and low-level design outlines individual components.

You can infuse AI-driven design tools to simulate various types of architectures and predict their performance when deployed to production. For example, AI can help you decide if a microservices or a monolithic structure is the best for a particular case scenario.

AI can explore a wider range of designs; it optimizes for performance, scalability, accessibility, and reliability.

The recommendations of AI may require end-to-end human validation before providing any signoffs and requires customization based on business and technical specifications.

Consider an online retail system example. Two sets of architecture were developed—one was a monolith while the other employed microservices. IBM's Watson was brought in to weigh in on the architectures, provide an analysis, and possibly rule in favor of one of them. The AI was able to understand both high-level designs, and it identified potential bottlenecks in data flow that one might encounter by employing a monolithic architecture. It also highlighted the potential scalability challenges. The analysis was well received by the stakeholders, and it helped the online retailer choose the optimal design.

AI Intervention for High-Level Design

For a high-level design, the system is broken into smaller, more manageable pieces, like detailing the rooms within a blueprint. AI can help by modeling data flows and interactions between modules. For instance, it can simulate how data will travel from the frontend to the backend and suggest improvements. This process will help improve accuracy and predict integration challenges. Setting up these models can be complex and may not cover all scenarios.

We have seen Google's AutoML, which can assist in modeling the interaction between different modules of a healthcare application, predict potential data flow issues and optimize the interactions.

OpenAI Codex is capable of translating the high-level requirements into detailed design documents. We used the tool to create a detailed design document, so that the time and effort saved could be used in refining the design. The other advantage that we witnessed was that the tool generated a consistent approach to design, which helped in forging the final designs with minimal rework.

Here is another use case for Codex: if you are designing an inventory management system, you can input the description into the tool console, which then generates a comprehensive set of design documents, including architecture diagrams, component interactions, and data flow models based on the generic parameters or conditions.

While AI tools can help greatly during the design phase, there are a few challenges that you must be aware of as well. The designs can be generic and there will be further work needed to customize them to fit specific project needs. The designs generated by the tools more often than not require thorough review and refinement to ensure that the design is in line with the requirements. So, while the AI tools may act as an accelerator, they do not eliminate human involvement.

AI for Low-Level Design

In the low-level design stage, elements from the HLD are broken into components and modules. This could be a host of things like classes, methods, algorithms, data structures, and database schemas. This is analogous to an interior designer specifying the details of each room.

AI tools can assist in optimizing algorithms used in low-level design. AI-based profilers or performance analyzers can suggest more efficient ways to implement a particular algorithm or function. Tools such as Google AutoML, OpenAI Codex, and Intel AI Analytics can profile the algorithms and codes for performance and stability improvement.

AI can generate class diagrams and detailed specifications. For instance, We have seen it used for the development of a streaming service, where the tool created pseudo-code for complex algorithms based on the high-level design. This streamlined the development process, because it provided a solid starting point for developers.

We have seen AI used to recommend design patterns as well. For example, in IBM Watson, the tool provides recommendations on design patterns based on project requirements. For example, when designing a notification system, Watson might suggest the Observer pattern for handling real-time updates. The recommendations could be based on best practices or from the learning that it has gathered from previous implementations. Using AI with design patterns ensures adherence to proven design patterns and improves robustness, which is extremely helpful for large enterprises.

The recommendations also depend on the quality of the input. Incomplete details can lead to less relevant suggestions, and recommendations might need to be adapted to fit specific project constraints.

Other use cases of system design include automatic generation of diagrams by using a tool like Lucidchart with AI Integration. This tool helps generate architecture diagrams from textual descriptions. For example, if you describe the architectural details of a microservices based application, Lucidchart creates detailed diagrams such as component and sequence diagrams. This is a productivity booster, as the tool can quickly generate professional diagrams, facilitating communication and speeding up the design process. This will also help produce a clear visual representation of the system architecture.

By infusing AI, the design output increases precision and reduces the time spent on manual design, but the AI-generated designs might lack the creativity and contextual understanding a human designer would bring.

The diagrams of complex systems often need manual adjustments in order to accurately represent all interactions. The quality of the diagrams depend on how clear the initial descriptions are.

Component Design

Component design is the design stage where developers define the individual components or modules, specifying their interfaces and interactions. It's similar to assigning roles on a team.

AI can generate component specifications and predict integration issues. For instance, AI can suggest how different microservices should communicate based on their functions. This helps reduce manual effort and foresees integration challenges early. We have seen that some of the recommendations from the AI tool require human validation. It is also true that the quality of the design is dependent on the quality of initial data.

LLMs like OpenAI Codex can suggest optimal interfaces for the different services in a microservices-based architecture for an e-commerce application, ensuring they communicate efficiently and reduce integration problems.

Consider an example of designing an e-commerce application using a microservices architecture. One of the key challenges is ensuring that the different microservices can communicate efficiently. Each microservice typically handles a specific business function (e.g., User Management, Product Catalog, Order Processing, Payment Processing, etc.). The interfaces between these services are crucial because they define how data is exchanged, how services interact, and ultimately, how well the system functions as a whole.

LLMs have a significant role in the interface design stage. The following section takes a closer look at how AI significantly accelerates and supports the interface design stage.

Understanding Microservice Responsibilities

LLMs can analyze descriptions of each microservice's responsibilities and suggest appropriate interface definitions. For instance, if you describe the Order Processing service, which handles order creation, validation, and status updates, the LLM can understand that this service needs to interact with several other services, such as User Management, Product Catalog, and Payment Processing.

Example: Suppose you input a description of the Order Processing service's role in an e-commerce application. The LLM might identify that the service needs to:

- Retrieve user information (from User Management).

- Validate product availability and prices (from Product Catalog).

- Handle payment transactions (through Payment Processing).

- Update order status (possibly requiring a communication interface with a Shipping service).

Suggesting API Endpoints and Methods

Once the LLM understands the roles of the microservices, it can suggest specific API endpoints and methods for each service. This is critical because it ensures that each service exposes the necessary functions while keeping the interface simple and efficient.

Example: For the Order Processing service, the LLM might suggest:

- POST /orders to create a new order.

- GET /orders/{orderId} to retrieve order details.

- PUT /orders/{orderId}/status to update the status of an order.

- GET /orders/user/{userId} to fetch all orders from a specific user.

These endpoints are designed to encapsulate the functionality required by other services to interact with Order Processing, ensuring that only necessary data is exposed and that the service interactions are efficient.

Optimizing Data Exchange Formats

LLMs can also suggest the optimal data exchange formats (e.g., JSON and XML) and structures (e.g., payload schema) to ensure efficient communication between services. By optimizing the data formats, LLMs help reduce the payload size and parsing time, thereby improving overall system performance.

Example: For the POST /orders endpoint, the LLM might suggest a JSON payload structure like this:

```
{
  "userId": "string",
  "items": [
    {
      "productId": "string",
      "quantity": "integer"
    }
  ],
  "paymentMethod": "string",
  "shippingAddress": {
    "street": "string",
    "city": "string",
    "postalCode": "string",
    "country": "string"
  }
}
```

This structure is comprehensive (covering all necessary information) and efficient (avoiding unnecessary data, thus reducing payload size).

Ensuring Efficient Communication

By suggesting well-defined interfaces and efficient data formats, LLMs help minimize integration problems. They ensure that each service's interface is designed with the consumer services in mind, reducing the chances of miscommunication or data inconsistencies between services.

Example: In a scenario where Order Processing interacts with Payment Processing, the LLM might recommend that the POST /payments endpoint in the Payment Processing service return a standardized response format that includes a transaction ID, status, and timestamp. This ensures that Order Processing can easily parse and handle the payment response, reducing the likelihood of integration issues.

Facilitating Service Versioning and Compatibility

LLMs can suggest versioning strategies for APIs, ensuring backward compatibility when interfaces evolve. This is critical in microservices architectures, where different teams might update their services independently.

Example: If a new version of the Order Processing service needs to introduce a new field in the order creation payload (e.g., `discountCode`), the LLM might suggest versioning the endpoint as `POST /v2/orders` and providing clear documentation on how it differs from `POST /v1/orders`. This approach allows existing consumers to continue using the older version without disruption while enabling the new functionality.

Benefits of Using LLMs for Interface Design

- **Efficiency:** LLMs speed up the design process by providing suggestions based on best practices and existing knowledge, thereby reducing the need for manual brainstorming.

- **Consistency:** Ensures that all service interfaces follow a consistent design pattern, which is crucial in large systems where multiple teams work on different services.

- **Error Reduction:** By suggesting well-defined interfaces and data formats, LLMs help reduce the chances of integration errors, leading to smoother service interactions.

- **Scalability:** Facilitates easier scaling of the application, as new services can be added with interfaces that align well with existing ones.

Potential Challenges

- **Context Awareness:** While LLMs are powerful, they rely on the context. If the initial input lacks detail, the suggested interfaces might not fully meet the project's needs.

- **Customization Needs:** The generated interfaces might need further customization to align with specific project requirements, especially in complex or domain-specific applications.

- **Evolving Requirements:** As business needs evolve, the LLM-generated interfaces may require updates, which could involve significant rework if the changes are substantial.

By leveraging LLMs in the component design phase, developers can ensure that the microservices in an e-commerce application have well-optimized interfaces that promote efficient communication and reduce integration challenges. This results in a more robust and maintainable architecture.

User Interface Design

The focus of user interface (UI) design is to develop the visual and interactive aspects of the software product, with the goal of ensuring an intuitive and user friendly design. The scope of UI design is to ensure that the software is attractive (aesthetics) and the software can interact with users efficiently.

119

Integrating AI into UI design is transformative, enhancing efficiency, personalizing user experiences, and ensuring the interface remains intuitive and responsive. By leveraging AI tools and models, designers can create innovative, user-centric interfaces that adapt and improve continuously, meeting the evolving needs and preferences of users.

Provided with the user behavior and interaction data, AI can predict user preferences and optimize usability. AI-driven prototyping tools and automated usability tests can refine the UI design.

Integrating AI into user interface (UI) design offers numerous advantages that streamline the design process and significantly enhance user experiences. The next section takes a closer look at how AI can be applied in various aspects of UI design.

Analyzing User interaction

AI can analyze user interactions with prototypes to identify areas for improvement.

This results in user-friendly interfaces that can quickly adapt to feedback, whereas AI might not fully capture the subtle aspects of human intuition and creativity.

The analysis by AI can potentially reveal patterns that might not be obvious through traditional analytics, and this help designers understand user pain points and identify areas where the UI can be improved.

For example, Adobe XD's Auto-Animate feature, powered by AI, helps create interactive prototypes that can be tested with real users. The AI analyzes user interactions and provides insights into how the interface can be improved for better usability.

Personalized User Design

AI can personalize the UI based on individual user behaviors and preferences, creating a more tailored and engaging user experience.

For example, Adobe Sensei analyzes user data to personalize the UI. If a user frequently accesses certain features, the AI can make those features more prominent and accessible, adjusting layouts, color schemes, and content dynamically based on user interactions.

Personalized interfaces increase user engagement and satisfaction. Users are more likely to stay engaged with a UI that feels customized to their needs. UI can be very dynamic and adapt in real-time to changing user behaviors.

Personalization requires extensive user data to function effectively and raises potential privacy concerns that need to be managed.

Enhanced Accessibility Like Voice-Activated Interfaces

A popular AI application that has found feet is the development of voice-based and conversational user interfaces. The Natural Language Processing (NLP) models allow users to interact with voice assistants and chatbots. These chatbots interact with users using voice commands similar to a natural conversation, thereby enhancing accessibility and convenience.

For example, Amazon Alexa Voice Service (AVS) can be integrated into applications to allow voice commands for tasks like searching for information, controlling smart devices, or navigating through the application. This is great for users with disabilities or those who prefer hands-free interaction. It offers a seamless, intuitive way to interact with the system. This also adds a modern, innovative feel to the application.

However, the challenge that AI developers face is that there are multiple languages, as well as multiple dialects and accents. For the AI to work efficiently across the board requires accurate voice recognition technology to train the AI with different datasets. It should also be noted that implementing and testing voice interfaces can be complex.

Data Design

Data design is a process of structuring and organizing data within a system to ensure that it is stored, managed, and utilized efficiently. It involves defining how data is represented, relationships between different data entities, and the rules governing data integrity and access. Effective data design aims to create a logical and physical model of data that supports the requirements of applications and users, facilitates data integration and retrieval, and ensures data consistency and quality. Key components of data design include data modeling, data schema design, normalization, and the implementation of data governance practices to maintain data accuracy and security.

AI can optimize data structures and database schemas for performance and scalability. AI tools can design and normalize database schemas, ensuring efficient data access patterns. For example, AI can suggest the best ways to index and partition large datasets. By using AI, it will enhance data integrity and performance.

The following sections look at a few use cases for data design.

Automated Data Documentation

AI can automatically generate documentation for data models, databases, and datasets, providing clear and comprehensive descriptions.

DataRobot can analyze a dataset and produce detailed documentation, including descriptions of each field, data types, relationships, and sample data. This documentation is essential for data governance and understanding.

This documentation will help increase efficiency, providing clear, standardized documentation that is easy to understand. The tool can also support data governance by ensuring all data is well-documented.

As data structures become more complex, the difficulty of generating accurate and comprehensive documentation increases. Complex data models, especially those involving nested objects, relational databases with multiple foreign keys, or NoSQL databases with flexible schemas, require precise documentation that captures the intricate relationships and constraints. There is a constant need for providing sufficient context so that AI can produce the accurate data.

Consider a data structure of an e-commerce platform. It might involve multiple related entities like Users, Orders, Products, Payments, and ShippingDetails. Each of these entities could have nested fields (e.g., Address inside User, LineItems inside Order). AI might struggle to accurately document these relationships and the interactions between them without additional context.

We have observed that incomplete or inaccurate documentation can lead to misunderstandings in how data should be handled, leading to potential errors in implementation, data retrieval, and integration across different systems.

Automated Data Modeling

AI can assist in creating data models that define how data is structured and related within a system. This includes designing tables, fields, and relationships in a database.

IBM's Watson Studio can analyze existing data and business requirements to automatically generate data models. It can recommend the best structure for relational databases or NoSQL databases based on usage patterns and data characteristics.

There are other tools, like dbdesigner.AI and SQLPrompt, that are quite popular. Dbdesigner.AI helps generate database schemas from data models and SQLPrompt helps with schema normalization and optimization. It provides suggestions for improving schema design and query performance.

Data Anomaly Detection

AI can identify anomalies in data, such as unusual patterns or outliers, which could indicate errors or important trends.

Tools like Anodot use AI to monitor data streams in real-time, detecting anomalies that might indicate issues, like fraud, system failures, or significant shifts in user behavior.

This helps in real-time identification of issues as they occur, allowing for quick responses, detecting subtle anomalies that might be missed by traditional methods. This also helps in handling large volumes of data efficiently.

Anodot may sometimes flag false positives, such as marking normal variations as anomalies, which mandates the necessary intervention of humans. The initial setup is complex and requires ongoing training to maintain accuracy.

API Design

API design involves creating a structured and efficient way for software applications to communicate. A well-designed API allows developers to access the functionality of a service or application seamlessly. Key aspects of API design include:

- **Endpoint Definition**: Specifying the URLs through which the API can be accessed.

- **Request Methods**: Defining the HTTP methods (GET, POST, PUT, DELETE) for different operations.

- **Data Formats**: Deciding on the format (typically JSON or XML) for requests and responses.

- **Authentication and Authorization**: Implementing security measures to control access.

- **Error Handling**: Designing a consistent approach for reporting and managing errors.

- **Documentation**: Providing detailed documentation to help developers understand how to use the API effectively.

The following sections look at some of the use cases where AI can be infused in API design.

Automated API Documentation Generation

AI can automatically generate comprehensive and interactive documentation for APIs, ensuring consistency and reducing the time spent by developers on manual documentation.

For example, SwaggerHub integrates with Swagger/OpenAPI specifications to generate documentation directly from the API code. By analyzing annotations and comments in the code, SwaggerHub produces interactive documentation that developers can use to explore and test API endpoints.

Say that you have an e-commerce platform with numerous endpoints for products, orders, and customers. SwaggerHub can analyze your API code, generate detailed descriptions for each endpoint, include request and response examples, and provide an interface for testing these endpoints directly from the documentation.

This saves developers significant time by automating the documentation process, ensures that all API endpoints are documented uniformly, and allows developers to interact with the API directly from the documentation.

We have seen challenges with initial setup when it requires proper annotations. Documentation and code comments may need manual review to ensure completeness and correctness.

API Design Validation

AI can validate API designs by checking for common issues such as naming inconsistencies, missing endpoints, and security vulnerabilities, ensuring that the API follows best practices and standards.

A tool like Stoplight uses AI to analyze API specifications written in OpenAPI, Swagger, and RAML. It provides real-time feedback on potential issues, including security vulnerabilities, naming conventions, and adherence to design standards.

Consider an API designed for a banking application. Stoplight can analyze the API's security measures, ensuring endpoints are protected and data is encrypted. It can also verify that naming conventions are consistent across all endpoints, enhancing readability and maintainability.

This helps with error reduction, ensures the API follows industry best practices, and highlights potential security issues that need addressing.

Intelligent API Design Assistance

AI can assist in designing APIs by suggesting endpoints, request methods, and data formats based on the desired functionality and existing patterns in similar APIs.

Postman uses AI to suggest optimal API designs by analyzing existing APIs and usage patterns. It can recommend the best structure for new endpoints, appropriate HTTP methods, and data formats that align with industry standards.

For a social media platform developing a new messaging feature, Postman can analyze existing messaging APIs and suggest endpoints for sending, receiving, and deleting messages. It can also recommend using WebSockets for real-time message updates and provide examples of JSON payload structures.

AI provides helpful suggestions and best practices, accelerates the design process with intelligent recommendations, and maintains a consistent design across different APIs.

The recommendations may need to be tailored to specific business needs. Also, users need to understand how to leverage AI's suggestions effectively.

Natural Language Interface for API Queries

AI can enable natural language queries to interact with APIs, making it easier for non-technical users to access the data and use the interface.

Dialogflow by Google allows users to interact with APIs using natural language. It translates user queries into API calls and returns the results in a user-friendly format.

A customer service application could use Dialogflow to allow customers to inquire about their order status using natural language. When a customer asks, "Where is my order?," Dialogflow translates this query into an API call to the order management system and returns the status of the order, making the interaction seamless and intuitive.

Tools like Dialogflow make APIs more accessible to non-technical users by simplifying the process of querying APIs and supporting multiple languages and complex queries.

Software developers may struggle with very complex or ambiguous queries, and they require training and refinement to improve accuracy.

By integrating AI into API design, developers can significantly enhance efficiency, consistency, and performance. These use cases illustrate how AI tools and models can be applied to various aspects of API design, from documentation and validation to code generation, predictive analysis, and natural language interaction.

Infrastructure Design

Infrastructure design involves creating the foundational systems and networks that support the operations of an organization's IT environment. This includes physical and virtual resources such as servers, storage systems, networking components, and the necessary software to manage these resources. Effective infrastructure design ensures scalability, reliability, security, and performance, aligning with the organization's current and future needs. Key components of infrastructure design include:

- **Network Architecture**: Designing the layout of networks, including LANs, WANs, and cloud networks.

- **Server and Storage Design**: Determining the specifications and configurations for servers and storage solutions.

- **Virtualization and Cloud Services**: Implementing virtual machines, containers, and cloud services for flexibility and efficiency.

- **Security Architecture**: Ensuring robust security measures to protect data and systems.

- **Disaster Recovery and Backup**: Planning for data backup and recovery in case of failures or disasters.

- **Monitoring and Management**: Implementing tools for monitoring performance and managing infrastructure resources.

By integrating AI into infrastructure design, organizations can significantly improve efficiency, scalability, security, and performance. These detailed use cases demonstrate how AI tools and models can be applied to various aspects of infrastructure design, from capacity planning and provisioning to load balancing, security monitoring, disaster recovery, and network optimization.

The following sections look at some use cases for infusing AI in infrastructure design.

Predictive Capacity Planning

AI can analyze usage patterns and predict future capacity needs, helping organizations scale their infrastructure efficiently.

A tool like Turbonomic uses AI to continuously analyze application demand and automatically adjust resources in real-time to ensure optimal performance. It predicts future needs based on historical data and trends, allowing for proactive resource planning.

A retail company uses Turbonomic to manage its e-commerce platform infrastructure. During holiday seasons, the platform experiences spikes in traffic. Turbonomic predicts these spikes based on past data and automatically scales the servers and network capacity to handle the increased load, ensuring a seamless shopping experience for customers.

Advantages of using Turbonomic include efficiency by ensuring resources are available when needed, avoiding downtime, optimizing resource allocation, reducing unnecessary expenses, and helping to anticipate future infrastructure needs.

We have seen challenges with initial setup, as it requires integration with existing systems and historical data, As always, predictions are only as good as the data they are based on.

Automated Infrastructure Provisioning

AI can automate the provisioning of infrastructure resources, reducing manual intervention and speeding up deployment times.

Tools like HashiCorp Terraform can be integrated with AI models to automatically provision infrastructure based on defined policies and real-time demand. AI can analyze the current workload and trigger Terraform to deploy additional resources as needed.

A tech startup leverages Terraform with AI to manage its cloud infrastructure. As user activity increases, the AI model predicts the need for more computational power and triggers Terraform to provide additional virtual machines and storage. This automated process ensures that the application remains performant without manual intervention.

Using AI with Terraform helps quickly provision resources to meet demand, ensuring infrastructure is deployed consistently according to predefined templates. It can also easily scale resources up or down based on real-time needs.

The initial setup and integration can be complex. Continuous monitoring and adjustments may be required to ensure that the AI is working as expected.

Intelligent Load Balancing

AI can optimize load balancing by predicting traffic patterns and distributing requests more efficiently across servers.

We have seen platforms like Avi Networks use AI-driven analytics to predict traffic patterns and optimize load balancing across application servers. It can adjust routing decisions in real-time to ensure even distribution and optimal performance.

An online streaming service uses Avi Networks to manage its load balancing. The AI model analyzes user traffic patterns, predicting peak viewing times. During these periods, Avi Networks adjusts the load balancing algorithms to distribute traffic evenly across servers, preventing any single server from becoming overloaded and ensuring a smooth streaming experience for users.

Using AI will help ensure efficient distribution of traffic, thereby reducing latency and adapting to changing traffic patterns dynamically. It will also help enhance the reliability and availability of applications.

Getting the AI to work correctly is an iterative process, since the level of complexity is quite high. AI must be constantly tuned to the application needs. Identifying traffic patterns is not a straightforward ask. The geography and other contextual factors come into play, and getting to the optimal state can be grind.

Automated Disaster Recovery

AI can automate disaster recovery processes, ensuring quick and efficient recovery of systems and data in case of failures.

The Zerto platform integrates AI to monitor system health and automatically trigger disaster recovery procedures when necessary. It ensures data integrity and minimal downtime during recovery.

An e-commerce company uses Zerto to manage its disaster recovery. During a data center outage, Zerto's AI detects the issue and automatically initiates the recovery process. Virtual machines and databases are restored from backups to a secondary data center, ensuring that the online store remains operational with minimal downtime.

The AI tool helps reduce business impact by reducing the downtime through restoring services automatically. One of the key focuses during recovery is to ensure that data integrity is accurate and current. This will also help increase efficiency as it automates complex recovery processes, saving time and resources.

We have seen challenges in setting up automated recovery plans. This can be a complex process, and it requires regular updates and testing to ensure effectiveness.

Intelligent Network Optimization

AI can optimize network performance by analyzing traffic patterns and adjusting configurations to enhance speed and reliability.

Platforms like Cisco DNA Center use AI to monitor network traffic and optimize configurations in real-time. They adjust bandwidth allocation, prioritize critical applications, and identify potential issues before they impact performance.

An esteemed university uses Cisco DNA Center to manage its campus network. AI analyzes student and faculty network usage, identifying peak times and adjusting bandwidth allocation accordingly. During exam periods, it prioritizes access to learning management systems and online resources, ensuring smooth and reliable connectivity for all users.

The integration with AI helps increase performance by enhancing network speed and reliability, identifying and addressing issues before they affect users, and optimizing resource usage and reduces bottlenecks.

Initial setup requires detailed configuration and integration, and there is a major dependency on getting data continuously for optimal performance.

Security Design

Security design involves creating a comprehensive framework to protect an organization's information systems from threats, vulnerabilities, and breaches. This framework encompasses policies, procedures, and technologies that safeguard data integrity, confidentiality, and availability. Effective security design addresses various aspects, including:

- **Access Control**: Defining who can access which resources and under what conditions.

- **Data Encryption**: Protecting data in transit and at rest using cryptographic techniques.

- **Network Security**: Implementing firewalls, intrusion detection/prevention systems, and secure network configurations.

- **Endpoint Security**: Securing individual devices like computers, smartphones, and IoT devices.

- **Identity Management**: Managing user identities and ensuring secure authentication and authorization.

- **Incident Response**: Establishing protocols for detecting, responding to, and recovering from security incidents.

The following use cases show how AI can be infused as part of security design.

Threat Modeling and Risk Assessment

The Microsoft Threat Modeling tool is leveraged by developers to identify, analyze, and mitigate potential security threats and vulnerabilities during the software development process. It is a great aid in designing secure systems, as it offers a structured approach to threat modeling.

The tool integrated with AI is capable of identifying potential threats and of providing strategic recommendations to mitigate them. For example, if you are designing a web application, this tool might highlight risks like SQL injection and recommend using parameterized queries.

The key to the application of the tool is to incorporate it during the development stages and to address potential threats and vulnerabilities before they occur.

While the tool works well for systems with limited integrations, an enterprise-wide application requires further refinement, and it is to be noted that the accuracy of threat modeling depends on the quality of input data about system components and interactions.

Security Design Recommendations

OpenAI Codex is a handy tool for integrating security best practices into design. For example, when developing authentication mechanisms, Codex might suggest using OAuth 2.0 for secure authorization based on best practices. Integrating Codex ensures that the best practices of IT security are integrated into the design, and it allows developers to accelerate the integration of security features by providing relevant recommendations.

On the downsides, the tool at times offers generic recommendations, and it requires adaptation to the application by a security consultant.

Anomaly Detection and Security Monitoring

AI can enhance security by detecting anomalies and potential threats in real-time, providing proactive protection against attacks.

Tools like Darktrace use machine learning to detect anomalies in network traffic and user behavior that could indicate security threats. It provides real-time alerts and automated responses to mitigate risks.

Darktrace helps provide proactive security by detecting threats early and reducing the risk of breaches, and it also automatically responds to potential threats by minimizing response insights. Such tools provide detailed insights into network and user behavior.

Darktrace may occasionally flag activities as threats (Flag Positives), which will require integration with existing security systems.

By integrating AI into security design, organizations can significantly enhance their ability to detect, prevent, and respond to threats. These detailed use cases illustrate how AI tools and models can be applied to various aspects of security design, from threat detection and policy management to authentication, phishing prevention, incident response, and vulnerability management.

Infusing AI into these phases of software design and architecture significantly enhances efficiency, accuracy, and consistency. By using AI tools, developers can streamline processes, improve documentation, and integrate best practices more effectively. However, it is essential to be aware of the potential challenges and limitations, ensuring that AI generated outputs are carefully reviewed and refined to meet the project's specific needs.

Summary

This chapter looked at the design phase in particular and broke down software design into seven distinct design areas—component, system, user interface, data, API, infrastructure, and security. For each of these design areas, the chapter identified the potential areas where AI can support them by bringing consistent structure to the design process. Further, some of the limitations of the AI tool were also highlighted.

CHAPTER 6

AI Infusion in Software Build and Development

The advent of AI has heralded a new era in application development, fundamentally changing how software is conceived, built, tested, and maintained. Today, AI is not merely an auxiliary tool; it is a cornerstone of modern software engineering practices, enhancing every phase of the development lifecycle. As organizations strive for agility, efficiency, and innovation, AI emerges as a powerful ally, enabling developers to build robust, scalable, and intelligent applications at an unprecedented pace.

This chapter explores the profound impact of AI on application development, detailing how AI-driven tools and techniques are reshaping the build process. It also delves into the role of AI in application modernization, a critical aspect for organizations looking to transition from legacy systems to modern, cloud-native architectures. By the end of this chapter, you will have a comprehensive understanding of how AI is infusing new life into application development, driving innovation and paving the way for the future of software engineering.

© Abhinav Krishna and Vamshidhar Meda 2024
A. Krishna and V. Meda, *AI Integration in Software Development and Operations*,
https://doi.org/10.1007/979-8-8688-1044-2_6

Historically, software development has relied on manual processes, with limited automation. The advent of machine learning and AI has marked a significant shift, enabling the automation of tasks such as code completion, testing, and even deployment. This chapter traces this evolution and discusses how AI has grown from simple scripts to advanced tools like GitHub Copilot and ChatGPT.

AI in application development refers to the integration of machine learning algorithms, natural language processing (NLP), and other AI technologies into the software development process. The scope of AI's influence spans from automating repetitive coding tasks to optimizing complex build pipelines and ensuring seamless deployment. AI is also increasingly being used to enhance software quality through intelligent testing, predictive analytics, and automated refactoring.

AI's infusion into application development is not a one-size-fits-all approach. It varies based on the application type, development environment, and specific challenges faced by development teams. However, the common thread is AI's ability to learn from data, make informed decisions, and improve processes over time, making it an invaluable asset in the modern developer's toolkit.

How AI Transforms the Developer Workflow

AI transforms the developer workflow by automating mundane tasks, providing intelligent suggestions, and enabling faster decision-making. Here's how:

- **Automated Code Generation**: Developers can use AI to automatically generate code for repetitive tasks, such as creating data models or API endpoints, saving time, and reducing errors.

- **Intelligent Code Reviews**: AI tools can review code in real-time, providing feedback on potential bugs, security vulnerabilities, and adherence to coding standards. This not only improves code quality but also accelerates the review process.

- **Predictive Analytics**: AI can predict the impact of code changes on the overall system, helping developers understand the potential risks before merging code into the main branch. This includes information on dependency analysis, compatibility issues, security, and vulnerabilities.

- **Optimized Testing**: AI-driven testing tools can automatically generate and execute test cases, ensuring comprehensive test coverage and identifying edge cases that might be missed by manual testing.

- **Deployment Automation**: AI can automate deployment processes, selecting the best strategies based on historical data, monitoring deployment in real-time, and triggering rollbacks if any issues are detected.

- **Improve Developer Experience**: AI can help improve the developer experience (DevEx) and developer onboarding by providing tailored learning experiences, automating repetitive tasks, and offering real-time support.

- **Application Modernization:** AI facilitates application modernization by analyzing legacy codebases, identifying outdated patterns, and suggesting modern alternatives. AI can automatically refactor code, improving its structure, readability, and performance. Also, AI can predict the impact of modernization efforts on performance, scalability, and maintainability, helping teams make informed decisions.

Overview of the Software Build and Development Process

The software build and development process—specifically coding, testing, building, and deploying applications—includes critical steps in the creation of a functional and reliable software product.

Development Process

At the heart of software development is the coding phase, where developers implement features and functionality using programming languages, libraries, and frameworks that suit the project's requirements. This phase is more than just writing code, it is about ensuring that the code is modular, scalable, and maintainable. Developers break down complex tasks into smaller, manageable modules, making the code easier to understand and test.

A key aspect of modern software development is version control, typically using tools like Git. Version control enables developers to collaborate effectively, track changes in the codebase, and revert to previous versions if necessary. Branching and merging strategies are critical in maintaining a clean codebase while allowing multiple developers to work on different features simultaneously.

Testing is integral to the coding phase. Unit testing is often employed to validate the smallest parts of an application, ensuring each individual unit (like functions or methods) works as intended. Integration testing follows, verifying that different modules or components of the application interact correctly. Automated testing frameworks like JUnit, pytest, and Mocha allow developers to continuously run tests, catching errors early and improving code quality.

Another essential part of the development phase are code reviews. These peer reviews help maintain coding standards, improve readability, and catch potential bugs or issues before they reach production. Developers use platforms like GitHub or GitLab for submitting and reviewing pull requests, facilitating collaboration, and ensuring that only high-quality code is merged into the main branch.

This part of the chapter looks at several use cases where AI is being infused into the development phase of SDLC. Figure 6-1 identifies six key use cases, covering automated code generation, legacy code refactoring, code reviews, unit testing, documentation, and bug detection and prediction. This chapter dives into each of these use cases

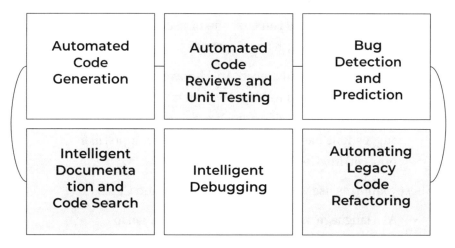

Figure 6-1. *Key AI use cases*

Automated Code Generation and Refactoring

One of the most visible impacts of AI in application development is automated code generation and refactoring. AI tools use machine learning models to understand context, generate relevant code snippets, and even refactor existing code for better performance and readability.

Some of the tools being used for automated code generation are described here:

- **GitHub Copilot:** This tool, powered by OpenAI's Codex, offers real-time code suggestions as developers type. Whether developers are writing boilerplate code or implementing complex algorithms, Copilot assists by generating code based on natural language prompts.

- **Tabnine**: An AI-driven code completion tool that supports multiple programming languages and IDEs. Tabnine uses deep learning models to predict the most likely code completions, enhancing developer productivity.

- **Kite:** Kite provides AI-powered code completions and documentation as you code, helping developers write code faster and with fewer errors.

- **Amazon CodeWhisperer:** An AI-powered coding assistant designed to help developers write code faster and with fewer errors. It provides real-time code suggestions based on natural language prompts, like how GitHub Copilot works.

These platforms use various LLMs like GPT-4 and Codex:

- As a language model, GPT-4 can be fine-tuned to understand and generate code in various programming languages. It can be integrated into development environments to provide context-aware code suggestions.

- A specialized variant of GPT, Codex is trained specifically on code repositories and is the backbone of tools like GitHub Copilot.

- Amazon SageMaker primarily uses Hugging Face Transformers and AWS's proprietary LLMs to provide natural language processing (NLP) capabilities. SageMaker allows you to use a variety of LLMs from these sources to build, train, and deploy machine learning models.

Here are some scenarios in which AI based tools can be used in application development:

- **API Development**: A developer working on an API can use GitHub Copilot to generate boilerplate code for handling HTTP requests, input validation, and error handling. This saves time and ensures that the API adheres to best practices.

- **Data Models**: When building a new application, developers can use AI tools to generate data models based on database schemas or UML diagrams. For example, Tabnine can suggest class structures, relationships, and methods based on the project's context.

- **Legacy Code Refactoring**: AI tools can help refactor legacy code by suggesting modern, efficient alternatives to outdated or inefficient code patterns. Kite, for instance, can suggest better ways to handle data-processing tasks, improving performance and maintainability.

Table 6-1 shows the differences between tools currently in the code generation space.

Table 6-1. *AI Tool Comparison for Tool Generation*

Feature	Amazon CodeWhisperer	GitHub Copilot	Tabnine	Kite
Primary Use Case	AWS service integration, general coding	General coding, multi-language support	General coding with custom model training	General coding, documentation assistance
Integration	Deep integration with AWS services	Integrates with GitHub, VS Code, etc.	Compatible with major IDEs like VS Code, JetBrains, and Sublime Text	Supports multiple IDEs including VS Code, Atom, and PyCharm
Supported Languages	Python, JavaScript, Java, and others	Python, JavaScript, TypeScript, and more	Python, JavaScript, TypeScript, Java, C++, and others	Python, JavaScript, Java, and more
Security Features	Built-in security and compliance checks	Code suggestions without specific security checks	Local or cloud-based models	No specific security features
IDE Support	Visual Studio Code, JetBrains, AWS Cloud9	Visual Studio Code, JetBrains IDEs	Visual Studio Code, IntelliJ IDEA, Sublime Text, etc.	Visual Studio Code, Atom, PyCharm, etc.

(continued)

Table 6-1. (*continued*)

Feature	Amazon CodeWhisperer	GitHub Copilot	Tabnine	Kite
Model Customization	Pre-trained models optimized for AWS	No customization, uses OpenAI Codex	Custom model training on proprietary codebases	Uses pre-trained models with no customization
Documentation and Learning	Limited contextual help	Provides inline comments and doc strings	Limited to code completions	Offers inline documentation and code examples
Pricing	Free tier available, with some limits	Available as part of GitHub subscription	Free and paid versions, with different feature sets	Free version with some limitations, paid options available

Pros:

- **Timesaving**: AI tools significantly reduce the time it takes to write code, especially for repetitive tasks.

- **Consistency**: AI ensures that code adheres to established standards and patterns, reducing the likelihood of errors.

- **Learning Assistance**: AI tools can serve as a learning resource for less experienced developers, providing real-time suggestions and explanations.

Cons:

- **Context Limitations**: AI-generated code might lack a deep understanding of the project's overall architecture, leading to code that may not fit perfectly within the existing codebase.

- **Overreliance**: Developers might become too reliant on AI tools, potentially stifling their creativity or understanding of the underlying logic.

- **Security Risks**: If not carefully reviewed, AI-generated code can introduce security vulnerabilities or performance issues.

AI in Code Reviews

The Importance of Code Reviews in Development

Code reviews are a critical part of the software development process. They ensure that code is of high quality, adheres to coding standards, and is free from bugs or security vulnerabilities. Traditionally, code reviews are done manually by peers, which can be time-consuming and subject to human error.

How AI Enhances Code Reviews

AI enhances code reviews by automating the detection of potential issues, providing intelligent suggestions, and ensuring that code adheres to best practices. AI-driven code review tools analyze the codebase, identify common errors, and flag potential issues before they are merged into the main branch.

Tools and technologies that are currently available with AI infusion in peer review include these:

- **DeepCode**: An AI-powered code review tool that analyzes code to detect bugs, security vulnerabilities, and performance issues. It uses machine learning to understand the context of the code and provides actionable suggestions for improvement.

- **Snyk**: A tool focused on security, Snyk integrates with code review processes to identify vulnerabilities in dependencies and suggest fixes.

- **CodeGuru**: Amazon's AI-powered code review tool provides recommendations on improving code quality, security, and performance.

Some of the examples and use cases are as follows:

- **Security Audits**: A development team working on a financial application can use Snyk during code reviews to ensure that all dependencies are secure and up to date. Snyk will automatically flag any vulnerabilities and suggest the necessary updates.

- **Performance Optimization**: An e-commerce platform looking to optimize its backend performance can use CodeGuru to review its codebase. CodeGuru will analyze the code and provide suggestions on improving performance, such as optimizing database queries or reducing memory usage.

- **Bug Detection**: A team maintaining a large codebase can use DeepCode to automatically detect common bugs, such as null pointer exceptions or off-by-one errors, before they are merged into the production branch.

Pros and Cons of AI in Code Reviews
Pros:

- **Efficiency**: AI tools can review code much faster than humans, allowing for more frequent reviews and quicker feedback.

- **Consistency**: AI ensures that all code is reviewed against the same set of rules and standards, reducing the variability that can occur with human reviewers.

- **Focus on High-Level Issues**: With AI handling routine checks, human reviewers can focus on more complex issues, such as architecture and design.

Cons:

- **False Positives/Negatives**: AI might flag issues that are not actually problems (false positives) or miss problems (false negatives).

- **Contextual Understanding**: AI tools may lack the context to understand certain design decisions, leading to suggestions that are not appropriate for the specific project.

- **Overreliance**: Developers might become too reliant on AI tools, potentially overlooking issues that require human intuition or experience.

AI in Bug Detection and Prediction

AI-based bug detection and prediction tools aim to identify issues in code before they occur, improving overall software quality. These tools rely on historical data, code patterns, and machine learning models to detect likely problem areas early in development.

Tools:

- **Amazon CodeGuru:** Leverages AI to provide performance recommendations and identify potential security vulnerabilities.

- **Factory.AI:** This new AI tool is designed to detect bugs and enhance code quality by predicting potential issues, automating bug tracking, and offering insights based on historical data.

- **DeepCode:** Uses AI to analyze code in real-time, flagging errors and vulnerabilities by learning from millions of open source projects.

We have seen scenarios in which a development team is working on a time-sensitive release. They use Factory.AI to analyze their codebase. It flags a potential performance issue related to database queries, allowing the team to refactor and improve the code before testing. Similarly, DeepCode identifies a possible security vulnerability in an API call, ensuring that the team can address it early, thus preventing future downtime or breaches.

The code snippet shown in Figure 6-2 represents a simplified Ruby on Rails controller action for creating a user. When DeepCode analyzes this code, it can provide specific feedback on potential issues, such as validation errors or security concerns (Credit: Nathan, `https://www.geekpedia.com/deepcode-ai-code-review-bug-detection/`).

```ruby
# Sample Ruby on Rails code snippet
class UsersController < ApplicationController
  def create
    @user = User.new(user_params)

    if @user.save
      # Successful user creation logic here
      flash[:success] = 'User created successfully.'
      redirect_to @user
    else
      # Handle validation errors
      flash.now[:error] = 'Error creating user.'
      render 'new'
    end
  end

  private

  def user_params
    params.require(:user).permit(:name, :email, :password)
  end
end
```

Figure 6-2. *DeepCode analysis (Credit:* https://www.geekpedia. com/deepcode-ai-code-review-bug-detection/)

Pros:

- **Early Detection:** AI tools like Factory.AI can predict performance bottlenecks or security flaws before they cause issues.

- **Efficiency:** Developers save time by focusing only on flagged issues, avoiding unnecessary manual code reviews.

- **Learning from Data:** AI tools improve over time as they analyze more codebases and detect patterns, becoming more accurate and helpful.

- **Scalability:** AI tools are particularly useful for large codebases, identifying bugs that human reviewers might overlook.

Cons:

- **False Positives:** These tools may occasionally flag non-issues, wasting time as developers investigate false alarms.

- **Overreliance on Patterns:** If the bug is novel or specific to the project, AI may not catch it since it's unfamiliar with the unique pattern.

- **Integration Costs:** Some tools may require a learning curve and time investment to integrate seamlessly into existing workflows.

Intelligent Documentation and Code Search

AI can enhance the developer experience by generating documentation and improving code search capabilities, making large codebases easier to navigate and understand. With AI, developers can automate documentation creation and retrieve relevant code snippets across vast repositories.

Tools:

- **Sourcegraph:** An advanced search tool that allows users to search across multiple codebases and repositories, powered by AI to provide intelligent results.

- **Codeium:** A free AI-powered code completion and documentation tool that provides real-time assistance to developers by predicting code and enhancing documentation.

- **Poolside:** A new AI tool for improving developer workflows by integrating intelligent code search and documentation features, particularly useful for large and distributed teams.

Consider a use case where a new developer on a large team is trying to understand an older function in the company's legacy codebase. They use Sourcegraph to search for all instances of the function and its dependencies. Codeium assists by generating inline documentation that describes the function's behavior and its role in the codebase. Meanwhile, Poolside offers quick access to relevant code snippets and past comments, streamlining the onboarding process.

Nutanix used Sourcegraph to fix Log4j issues quickly and confidently with Sourcegraph. Nutanix was able to see where JMSAppender existed, fix it, and send out a release, all in less than five minutes. It took four days for Nutanix to deliver patches to its customers that fully remediated the Log4j vulnerability. They were also able confidently identify every instance of Log4j across their sprawling codebase. The detailed article is available as a case study at `https://sourcegraph.com/case-studies/nutanix-fixed-log4j-with-sourcegraph`. Figure 6-3 shows Code Search in action within Sourcegraph.

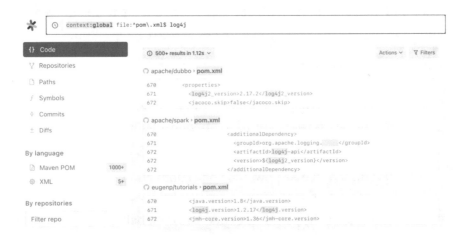

Figure 6-3. *Code Search in Sourcegraph (Credit:* `https://sourcegraph.com/code-search?`)

Pros:

- **Onboarding Efficiency:** New developers can quickly grasp complex codebases with AI-generated documentation and intelligent search tools.

- **Consistency:** Tools like Codeium provide uniform, machine-generated documentation, ensuring that all code is annotated, even older or neglected parts.

- **Cross-Repository Search:** Advanced search tools like Sourcegraph allow developers to search across multiple repositories in seconds, making it easier to trace logic and understand dependencies.

- **Developer Productivity:** Poolside's integrated features improve team collaboration, documentation creation, and search capabilities, reducing manual effort.

Cons:

- **Lack of Context:** AI-generated documentation may lack the nuance of human-written docs, leading to overly simplistic or irrelevant explanations.

- **Clutter:** Automated documentation tools may over-document, adding unnecessary comments that can clutter the code.

- **Limited Creativity:** AI tools follow patterns and might not capture creative or unique aspects of certain solutions.

Intelligent Debugging

AI-powered debugging tools aim to help developers identify and fix issues more quickly by analyzing code, logs, and runtime behavior. These tools can suggest probable causes for errors and offer real-time insights into the system's behavior during runtime.

Tools:

- **Rookout:** A dynamic debugging tool that allows developers to collect data from live environments without redeploying the app, thereby enhancing visibility into production issues.

- **Cursor:** A newer AI debugging tool that assists developers by analyzing error logs and suggesting potential fixes in real-time, often reducing the time to resolve critical issues.

- **Cognition:** This AI-driven debugging platform enhances the developer's ability to debug by learning from historical bug data and offering fix suggestions based on past experience.

Consider a scenario where Cursor offers several intelligent debugging features to help developers identify and fix issues in their code. The AI will analyze the code and provide suggestions based on the context of the project. There are multiple ways to work with the AI agent in Cursor to receive recommendations. The following recommendations come from the AI assistant on `https://docs.cursor.com/`:

1. **AI Fix in Chat**: You can quickly fix linter errors by hovering over the error in the editor and clicking the blue AI Fix button. The keyboard shortcut for this is Ctrl/⌘+Shift+E.

2. **Codebase-aware debugging**: Using the @Codebase feature, Cursor Chat can scan your entire codebase to find relevant code chunks, rerank them based on your query, and provide context-aware debugging suggestions.

154

3. **Model selection**: You can choose different AI models for debugging assistance, including GPT-4, Claude, and Cursor's custom models. Toggle between models using Ctrl/⌘ /.

4. **Follow-up instructions**: After receiving an initial response, you can refine your debugging query by adding more instructions in the prompt bar and pressing Enter for a regenerated response.

5. **Context-aware suggestions**: Cursor Chat automatically includes context from your codebase, searches the web, and indexes documentation to provide more accurate debugging assistance.

Pros:

- **Reduced Downtime:** Tools like Rookout provide real-time insights from live systems, enabling faster debugging without disrupting operations.

- **Automated Suggestions:** AI tools like Cursor and Cognition can offer potential fixes, drastically reducing the time it takes to isolate and resolve the root cause of a bug.

- **Learning from History:** By analyzing past issues, tools like Cognition can suggest solutions that have worked before, thereby speeding up the debugging process.

Cons:

- **Performance Overhead:** Live debugging tools like Rookout might add some performance overhead, especially in highly sensitive production environments.

- **Inaccurate Fixes:** AI-driven debugging tools may occasionally suggest incorrect solutions, leading developers down the wrong path.

- **Dependence on AI Suggestions:** Developers might become overreliant on AI tools, potentially losing deep debugging skills over time.

AI is increasingly influencing the software development process. New tools like GitHub Copilot, Tabnine, Factory.AI, Poolside, Codeium, Cursor, and Cognition are pushing the boundaries of AI's role, enhancing efficiency and reducing manual effort. However, while the benefits are significant—such as improved code quality, faster issue resolution, and enhanced productivity—there are also challenges to overcome, such as false positives, context understanding, and security concerns in production environments.

AI can complement human effort but requires careful implementation to maximize its value without overwhelming developers or introducing unnecessary complexity into workflows

A Different Perspective

While writing about interesting elements, use cases, and benefits of infusing AI into development activities, I came across an interesting article titled, "Do Users Write More Insecure Code with AI Assistants?," by Neil Perry, Megha Srivastava, Deepak Kumar, and Dan Boneh. (See `https://arxiv.org/abs/2211.03622v3`.)

In the full version of the paper, the paper highlights a crucial issue with the adoption of AI code assistants—while they offer productivity benefits, they also pose risks related to code security. The findings suggest that the current generation of AI tools may inadvertently contribute to the creation of insecure code, emphasizing the need for improvements in both the tools themselves and in developer training.

The paper investigates the security implications of using AI-powered code assistants like GitHub Copilot. It specifically aims to understand whether these tools influence developers to write more insecure code.

The experts call out: *"Overall, we find that participants who had access to an AI assistant based on OpenAI's codex-davinci-002 model wrote significantly less secure code than those without access. Additionally, participants with access to an AI assistant were more likely to believe they wrote secure code than those without access to the AI assistant. Furthermore, we find that participants who trusted the AI less and engaged more with the language and format of their prompts (e.g. re-phrasing, adjusting temperature) provided code with fewer security vulnerabilities"*

This review underscores the importance of balancing productivity gains with security considerations in software development.

Key concepts that were covered in the paper included multiple observations and datasets covering AI code assistants and insecure code (code that is vulnerable to security risks, which could be exploited by attackers). The paper focuses on whether AI tools contribute to the generation of insecure code.

Their methodology was as follows:

1. **Experimental Design**: The authors conducted a series of experiments involving participants who were asked to write code both with and without the assistance of AI tools. The AI tool used was GitHub Copilot.

2. **Security Analysis**: The generated code was reviewed for common security vulnerabilities, including issues like SQL injection, cross-site scripting (XSS), and insecure data handling.

3. **Control Group**: To assess the impact of AI assistants, the study compared the results from developers using AI tools with those who wrote code manually without any AI assistance.

The study found that code written with the help of AI assistants contained more security vulnerabilities compared to code written without such assistance. The findings include these:

1. **Impact on Security Practices**: Developers relying on AI tools were observed to have a reduced awareness of secure coding practices. This suggests that the convenience of AI assistance might lead developers to overlook important security considerations.

2. **Tool Limitations**: AI assistants often suggested code snippets that were technically correct but lacked security best practices, highlighting the limitations of current AI tools in addressing security concerns.

Implications that they called out in the paper include these:

1. **Need for Improved AI Tools**: The results suggest a need for enhancing AI code assistants to better handle security aspects. Incorporating security awareness into these tools could help mitigate the risks.

2. **Developer Education**: The paper emphasizes the importance of educating developers about secure coding practices. Relying solely on AI tools without understanding the security implications can lead to vulnerabilities.

3. **Tool Integration**: Future development of AI assistants should consider integrating security checks and recommendations to ensure that code suggestions align with security best practices.

Overall, AI is increasingly influencing the software development process, and this section has covered various use cases, tools, and methodologies required to write better, high-quality code while still fast-tracking the development process. The next section looks at how AI can be infused into the software build process.

The Software Build Process

After the coding is complete, the next step is the build process, where the source code is transformed into an executable or deployable package. This often involves compiling, which converts human-readable code into machine-readable instructions that can be executed on a computer.

Managing dependencies is a crucial part of the build process. Most applications rely on external libraries or packages to extend functionality, and tools like Maven, Gradle, and npm handle these dependencies, ensuring that the correct versions of each library are included in the build.

In modern software development, continuous integration (CI) plays a pivotal role. CI tools like Jenkins, CircleCI, Harness, and GitLab CI automate the build process by continuously integrating changes into the codebase and triggering automated builds with every code commit. This ensures that the codebase is always in a deployable state, even as new features or bug fixes are added.

There are several use cases (see Figure 6-4) on how AI is being used during the build or the CI process, including automated CI/CD pipeline creation, intelligent build optimization, predicting build failure, and intelligent resource allocation.

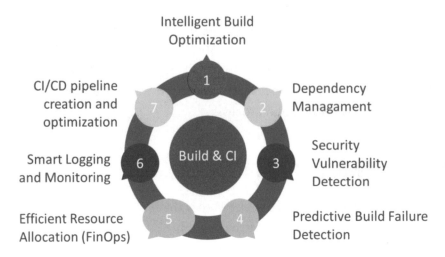

Figure 6-4. *Key use cases of AI infusion into the build and CI process*

The following sections dive deep into few of the key use cases.

AI-Driven Build Optimization

The build process in application development involves compiling source code, running tests, packaging applications, and deploying them to different environments. Continuous integration and continuous deployment (CI/CD) are practices that automate these processes, allowing for more frequent and reliable software releases. AI is increasingly being integrated into CI/CD tools to enhance their capabilities, making the build process more efficient and less prone to errors.

This section explores some of the current CI tools available in the industry and explains how AI can be used across various elements.

Harness

- **Overview**: Harness is a modern CI/CD platform that uses AI to automate and optimize the software delivery process. It provides features like continuous delivery, continuous verification, and cloud cost management.

- **AI Integration**: Harness's AI-driven features include automatic rollback in case of deployment failures, predictive analytics to optimize pipelines, and continuous verification to monitor deployment health.

- **Use Cases**: Harness is particularly effective in environments where reliability and efficiency are critical. It's used by enterprises to manage complex, multi-service deployments with minimal manual intervention.

Google Cloud Build

- **Overview**: Google Cloud Build is a CI/CD service that automates the process of building, testing, and deploying applications on the Google Cloud Platform (GCP).

- **AI Integration**: Google Cloud Build uses AI to optimize build processes by predicting bottlenecks, parallelizing tasks, and minimizing build times. It also integrates with Google's broader AI and machine learning services for more advanced use cases.

- **Use Cases**: Ideal for organizations using GCP, Google Cloud Build is used to manage and optimize build pipelines, particularly in cloud-native applications.

CircleCI

- **Overview**: CircleCI is a CI/CD platform that automates the software delivery process with a focus on speed and flexibility. It supports a wide range of environments, from containers to virtual machines.

- **AI Integration**: CircleCI's AI-driven insights help teams optimize their build pipelines by analyzing performance data and suggesting improvements. It also provides predictive analytics to identify potential failures before they occur.

- **Use Cases**: CircleCI is often used by startups and mid-sized companies that need a fast, reliable CI/CD solution. Its AI features help teams optimize build times and ensure high reliability.

GitHub Actions

- **Overview**: GitHub Actions is a CI/CD tool integrated into GitHub that allows developers to automate the build, test, and deployment processes directly within their repositories.

- **AI Integration**: GitHub Actions integrates with GitHub Copilot and other AI-driven tools to automate code reviews, generate test cases, and optimize workflows.

- **Use Cases**: GitHub Actions is popular among open source projects and small to medium-sized teams that need a seamless integration with their version control system. AI features help streamline the CI/CD process and improve code quality.

Jenkins

- **Overview**: Jenkins is an open source automation server widely used for building, testing, and deploying software. It supports a wide range of plugins and integrations.

- **AI Integration**: While Jenkins itself is not AI-driven, there are plugins and third-party tools that integrate AI capabilities into Jenkins pipelines. For example, the Jenkins plugin for Blue Ocean can use AI to visualize pipeline performance and suggest optimizations.

- **Use Cases**: Jenkins is often used in large enterprises with complex build pipelines. AI integrations can help optimize these pipelines by predicting failures and suggesting improvements.

The next section looks at some of the pros and cons of using AI during software build optimization.

Pros:

- **Efficiency Gains**: Optimized builds reduce development cycle times, meaning quicker feedback and more rapid iteration.

- **Cost Reduction**: By optimizing resource consumption, AI can reduce infrastructure costs, especially in cloud-based environments.

- **Real-Time Feedback**: AI tools can monitor ongoing builds and make real-time recommendations.

Cons:

- **Complex Setup**: It can take significant time to integrate and configure AI tools into existing build pipelines.

- **Initial Overhead**: The benefits of AI-driven optimizations might not be immediately visible, as they require time to learn and adjust.

Predictive Build Failure Analysis

Predictive build failure analysis is another area where AI is making significant inroads. By analyzing historical build data, AI models can predict potential failures before they occur, allowing developers to take proactive measures.

Tools like Harness and Gitlab CI provide insights into build failure issues. These tools analyze patterns in code changes, environment variables, and build configurations to identify potential issues and suggest corrective actions.

Figure 6-5 shows how Harness AIDA (AI Developer Assistant) can quickly predict a build failure, analyze the code, and provide a recommendation to fix the issue. AIDA Assist is continuously monitoring the CI pipelines and helps with resolution. This use case helps cut down several human interactions and multiple ticket creation, and it lessens the burden of the developer or DevOps engineer.

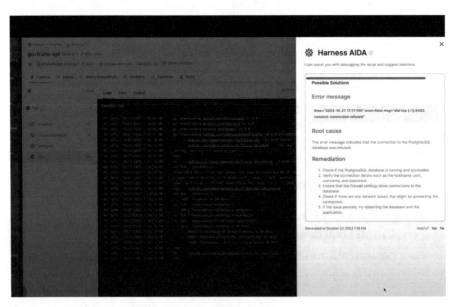

Figure 6-5. *Harness AIDA predicting a build failure (Credit:* `https://developer.harness.io/docs/platform/harness-aida/` `aida-ci/)`

Apart from the Harness AIDA module, you can customize or integrate Jenkins or Travis with new plugins to achieve the same outcome.

- **Jenkins with Machine Learning Plugins**: Jenkins offers plugins that integrate machine learning models to predict build failures based on historical data. These plugins analyze patterns in code changes, environment variables, and build configurations to identify potential issues.

- **Travis CI with AI Modules**: Travis CI can be enhanced with AI modules that predict build failures and suggest corrective actions.

Some of the real-world examples include a large organization with multiple teams working on a shared codebase. In this case, Harness uses AI to predict build failures by analyzing recent code commits. If a failure is likely, Harness alerts the development team, who can then address the issue before initiating the build.

Intelligent Dependency Management

Managing dependencies in application development is a complex task, particularly when dealing with large codebases and numerous third-party libraries. AI can simplify this process by automating dependency updates, ensuring compatibility, and identifying potential security vulnerabilities.

Tools like Dependabot, Snyk, and Renovate can be integrated with CI tools like GitHub and Harness. Dependabot automatically checks for updates to dependencies in a project's codebase. Snyk is known for providing security insights and updates for open source libraries and frameworks. It uses AI to assess the impact of updates and generates pull requests for safe updates, whereas Renovate is an open source tool that automates dependency updates. It uses AI to determine the best time to apply updates, balancing the need for security with stability.

In Figure 6-6, you can see how Dependabot is connected to GitHub to analyze dependencies and create automated alerts when it identifies vulnerabilities. The alerts can be auto-triaged using Dependabot's rules.

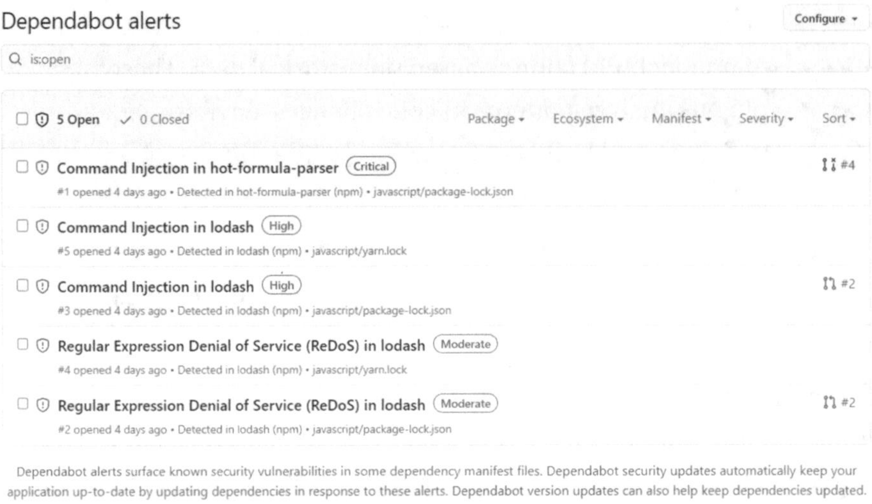

Figure 6-6. *Dependabot analysis and alerts (Credit:* https://docs. github.com/en/code-security/getting-started/dependabot-quickstart-guide#viewing-dependabot-alerts-for-your-repository)

Pros:

- **Timesaving**: Developers no longer need to track down and manually update dependencies.

- **Security**: AI ensures that dependencies are continuously monitored and updated, thereby reducing the risk of security breaches.

- **Automatic Updates**: Some tools will automatically generate pull requests with updated dependencies, allowing for seamless integration.

Cons:

- **Breaking Changes**: Automatic dependency updates might introduce breaking changes, which could lead to integration or runtime errors.

- **Dependency Overload**: Too many automated update requests can overwhelm teams, leading to potential issues being overlooked.

One of the challenges that we see is managing a balance between keeping dependencies up-to-date and not disrupting development with too many changes.

AI-Driven Security and Compatibility

Security vulnerabilities pose significant risks in the software development lifecycle, especially as threats become more sophisticated. Traditional methods of vulnerability detection often involve manual reviews or basic scanning tools that require human oversight. AI-driven tools revolutionize this process by continuously analyzing code and dependencies for potential vulnerabilities, providing real-time alerts, and offering actionable recommendations to address security issues. With the inclusion of tools like Harness AIDA, AI doesn't just detect vulnerabilities; it also provides actionable insights, reducing the time developers spend on manual security checks

AI can detect issues such as:

- Outdated dependencies with known vulnerabilities.

- Injection attacks (e.g., SQL injection).

- Weak cryptographic implementations.

- Insecure configurations, such as hardcoded credentials or improperly configured access control.

By embedding AI within the pipeline, vulnerabilities are caught early—during the build or commit phase—before they reach production, thereby minimizing the risk of breaches.

Tools:

- **Harness AIDA (AI-driven Incident Detection and Alerting)**: Harness AIDA extends AI capabilities into the security realm by providing real-time detection of security vulnerabilities during the CI/CD process. It integrates with existing pipelines to automatically detect vulnerabilities, generate actionable alerts, and suggest fixes.

- **Snyk**: Provides comprehensive vulnerability scanning for open source dependencies and offers patching recommendations.

- **GitHub Advanced Security**: Includes automated vulnerability detection and secret scanning, integrated directly into the GitHub development workflow.

Pros:

- **Proactive Protection**: AI enables continuous scanning, providing developers with real-time security insights during development and significantly reducing the risk of vulnerabilities reaching production.

- **Automated Fixes**: Many AI tools not only detect vulnerabilities but also suggest or even automatically apply fixes, saving developers time.

- **Historical Learning**: AI learns from past incidents and adjusts its detection mechanisms, ensuring the system grows more robust over time.

- **Faster Incident Response**: With Harness AIDA's alerting mechanisms, developers receive instant notifications when vulnerabilities are detected, allowing immediate remediation. This reduces potential security threats and costs related to incident response.

Cons:

- **False Positives**: AI-powered vulnerability detection can sometimes generate false positives, flagging benign issues that may distract developers.

- **Overreliance on AI**: While AI is powerful, it may miss context-specific vulnerabilities that require human judgment or business knowledge, especially with custom-built frameworks or unique configurations.

- **Setup Complexity**: Implementing AI-based security tools like Harness AIDA requires configuration and integration into existing workflows, which may involve significant setup time and effort.

While tools like Harness AIDA are effective at generating security alerts, too many alerts can overwhelm teams, causing alert fatigue and leading to important issues being missed. AI can flag vulnerabilities, but developers still need security training to properly address complex or critical vulnerabilities. AI should supplement, not replace, secure coding practices.

Also, AI tools may not always understand the business context of an application, which can result in over-flagging issues that are acceptable in certain situations (e.g., security exceptions made for internal tools).

AI-driven tools for security vulnerability detection—such as Harness, Snyk, GitHub Advanced Security, WhiteSource, Checkmarx, Aqua Security, and Fortify—provide robust capabilities for identifying and addressing security issues in real-time. By incorporating these tools into the development pipeline, teams can significantly enhance their security posture and reduce the risk of vulnerabilities impacting their applications.

CI and CD Pipeline Creation and Optimization

CI/CD pipelines are essential for automating the integration, testing, and deployment of software, helping development teams deliver high-quality applications more efficiently. Creating and optimizing these pipelines involves setting up automated processes that handle code integration, testing, and deployment, as well as continuously improving these processes to enhance performance, reliability, and speed. By leveraging modern tools and practices, teams can streamline their workflows, reduce manual errors, and accelerate the delivery of new features and updates.

Creating and Optimizing CI/CD Pipelines: The process involves configuring a sequence of automated steps that handle code integration, testing, and deployment. Optimizing these pipelines focuses on improving their efficiency and effectiveness by reducing build times, automating repetitive tasks, and incorporating advanced features like predictive analytics and real-time monitoring. Some of the use cases include migrating pipelines from one tool to another. Developers can use tools like GitHub Copilot to generate code, which can help automate bulk CI/CD pipeline creation or migration.

Figure 6-7 shows Harness in action, creating CI/CD pipelines based on user inputs by analyzing the technology patterns.

Figure 6-7. *Harness CI pipeline creation (Credit:* `https://www.harness.io/products/continuous-integration`*)*

Table 6-2 compares the various AI-driven CI/CD tools on the market.

Table 6-2. *Comparison of AI-Driven CI/CD Tools*

Feature	Harness	GitLab CI	GitHub Actions	Jenkins	CircleCI
Build Automation	Advanced automation with customizable build workflows	Integrated build pipelines with customizable stages	Supports automated build workflows with YAML configuration	Highly customizable builds with extensive plugin support	Fast and efficient build automation with predefined configurations
Build Speed	Optimized for efficiency with AI-driven insights into build performance	Efficient with good performance for integrated pipelines	Good build speed, with performance scaling based on usage	Depends on the setup; can be optimized with plugins	Known for fast build times, especially with cloud-native infrastructure
Scalability	Highly scalable, suitable for large enterprises	Scales well with GitLab's infrastructure	Scales with GitHub's cloud infrastructure	Scales with proper setup; can handle large projects	Scales effectively in cloud environments; suitable for high-performance needs

AI-Driven Build Optimization	AI-driven insights for optimizing build processes and predicting build times	Basic performance insights; less focus on AI-driven optimization	Limited AI integration for build optimization	Relies on plugins; limited native AI-driven build optimization	Provides performance insights and suggestions for optimization; AI features growing
Deployment Automation	Advanced deployment strategies including canary releases, blue-green deployments	Supports complex deployment strategies with automated pipelines	Provides workflows for automated deployment; integrates with various tools	Highly customizable with plugins for deployment strategies	Efficient deployment automation with various strategies supported

(continued)

173

Table 6-2. (*continued*)

Feature	Harness	GitLab CI	GitHub Actions	Jenkins	CircleCI
Predictive Analytics	AI-driven predictions for deployment success, failure risk, and rollback triggers	Basic insights into build and deployment performance	Limited predictive analytics; focuses on workflow automation	Limited out-of-the-box predictive analytics; relies on plugins	Provides performance insights and suggestions; AI-driven features growing
Continuous Verification	Real-time monitoring and automated rollback based on AI predictions	Integrated monitoring and performance metrics; supports custom verification stages	Provides tools for integrating testing and verification stages	Supports various plugins for testing and verification stages	Integrated testing and monitoring tools; customizable verification stages

Integration	Integrates with various VCS, monitoring tools, and alerting systems	Native integration with GitLab repositories and third-party tools	Seamless integration with GitHub repositories and GitHub Marketplace actions	Extensive plugin ecosystem for integration with numerous tools and platforms	Integrates with popular VCS platforms like GitHub, Bitbucket, and GitLab
Ease of Use	Intuitive UI with advanced features tailored for enterprises	User-friendly with a comprehensive set of features in one platform	Easy to use with a straightforward interface within GitHub	Requires setup and configuration; learning curve for beginners	User-friendly with pre-built configurations and workflows
Cost	Premium pricing with advanced features; higher cost	Free tier available, with paid plans offering additional features and support	Free tier available with a pay-as-you-go pricing model for additional use	Open source and free; costs associated with infrastructure and plugin maintenance	Free tier available, with paid plans offering additional features and support

(continued)

175

Table 6-2. (*continued*)

Feature	Harness	GitLab CI	GitHub Actions	Jenkins	CircleCI
Pros	Advanced deployment strategies, AI-driven build optimization, predictive analytics	Integrated DevOps suite, flexible pipeline configuration, strong community support	Direct integration with GitHub, easy setup, extensive marketplace for actions	Highly customizable, extensive plugin support, active community	Fast build times, easy integration, cloud-native with strong scalability
Cons	Higher cost, complexity for smaller teams	Complexity for non-GitLab users; performance issues reported in large instances	Limited to GitHub repositories; less feature-rich compared to some other CI/CD tools	Complex setup and maintenance, requires manual configuration for advanced features	Limited advanced features in the free tier, reliance on cloud infrastructure

Some use cases in continuous integration/continuous deployment (CI/CD) include these:

> **Use Case 1**: A software development team working on a microservices architecture uses CircleCI to manage their CI/CD pipeline. AI analyzes the build history and predicts which microservices are likely to fail during the build. By prioritizing these services in the build queue, the team reduces downtime and accelerates deployment.

> **Use Case 2**: An enterprise development team uses Google Cloud Build to manage their build process. AI optimizes the allocation of compute resources during the build, ensuring that the most critical tasks are completed first. This leads to faster and more efficient builds.

Pros and Cons of AI in CI/CD

Pros:

- **Increased Efficiency**: AI optimizes build and deployment processes, reducing the time and effort required to release new features.

- **Error Reduction**: AI-driven tools can predict and prevent issues, reducing the likelihood of deployment failures and rollbacks.

- **Continuous Improvement**: AI tools continuously learn from past deployments, improving the accuracy and efficiency of future builds.

Cons:

- **Complexity**: Implementing AI-driven CI/CD pipelines can be complex and can require significant setup and maintenance.

- **Cost**: AI-powered CI/CD tools may come with higher costs, particularly for advanced features like predictive analytics and automated rollbacks.

Key Challenge for AI in CI/CD Is the Dependence on Data

The effectiveness of AI in CI/CD depends on the availability of high-quality data for training models and making accurate predictions. Optimizing CI/CD pipelines enhances the software development process by automating integration, testing, and deployment, thus improving efficiency and reliability. Tools like GitLab CI/CD, CircleCI, Travis CI, and Harness offer various features to support and optimize these pipelines. While the benefits include increased speed and reliability, key challenges to address include managing complexities and costs and ensuring security. Chapter 8 covers the other key use cases (such as resource allocation and management) and Chapter 9 covers smart logging and monitoring.

AI is transforming application development, offering new tools and techniques that enhance every stage of the development lifecycle. From automated code generation and build optimization to predictive analytics and application modernization, AI is enabling developers to build more robust, scalable, and intelligent applications faster than ever before.

However, integrating AI into application development is not without its challenges. Developers must navigate technical complexities, address ethical concerns, and remain vigilant to the potential risks associated with AI-driven decisions. By embracing AI thoughtfully and strategically, organizations can harness its full potential, driving innovation and ensuring that their applications are built for the future.

Summary

The infusion of AI into application development represents a significant shift in how software is built and maintained. By embracing AI, developers can unlock new levels of efficiency, quality, and innovation, ensuring that their applications are not only built to meet today's demands but are also ready to adapt to the challenges of tomorrow.

This chapter provided a comprehensive exploration of AI's impact on application development and the software build/CI process by offering real-world examples, tools, and considerations. It also covered the concept of application modernization, making it a thorough guide for anyone interested in the intersection of AI and software engineering.

CHAPTER 7

Infusing AI into Software Testing

When the evolution of DevOps and continuous delivery began, one of the biggest challenges involved testing. Could software be tested at the required speed? Could test cases be executed without error? There were also questions around how test data would be generated. Could automation reduce the burden by allowing testers to script repetitive tasks?

The infusion of AI into software testing is not just an incremental improvement but a big leap forward. Traditional testing methods have long been dependent on manual effort and scripted automation. They are increasingly being augmented or replaced by AI-driven techniques. AI tools can analyze vast amounts of data, analyze or learn from patterns, and adapt to changes in real-time. Its ability to predict defects and generate intelligent test cases makes AI uniquely suited to address the challenges of the next generation of software development.

This chapter explains how AI is transforming software testing. It explores the evolution of testing practices, the specific AI technologies being applied, and the benefits and challenges of AI-based testing. It also includes real-world examples of organizations that have successfully integrated AI into their testing processes.

© Abhinav Krishna and Vamshidhar Meda 2024
A. Krishna and V. Meda, *AI Integration in Software Development and Operations*,
https://doi.org/10.1007/979-8-8688-1044-2_7

The Evolution of Software Testing

In the early days of software and application development, testing was a manual, labor-intensive process. Testers would execute test cases by hand, compare the results to expected outcomes, and manually log any defects they found. This approach was sufficient for simple or small applications but was not scalable and quickly became unsustainable as the software grew in complexity and scale.

As part of manual testing process, testers would follow predefined test cases, which were often documented in Word or Excel documents. Each test case would describe a series of steps or tasks to execute and the expected results. If the actual result differed from the expected result, the tester or a quality analyst would report a defect using the defect tracking tool.

The primary limitation of manual testing is its scalability. As the number of test cases grows, so does the time required to execute them. Manual testing is also prone to human error, as testers may miss steps or misinterpret results.

The Automation Era

To address the limitations of manual testing, automation tools were developed. These tools allowed testers to write scripts that could execute test cases automatically. Automation significantly reduced the time required to run tests and increased the reliability of test execution.

Early automation tools used scripting languages like Selenium, which allowed testers to write scripts that could interact with web browsers and simulate user actions. These scripts could be executed repeatedly, ensuring that the application behaved as expected after each code change.

While automation reduced the manual effort required for testing, it introduced new challenges. Writing and maintaining test scripts is a time-consuming process, and scripts can be fragile—breaking when the application's user interface or functionality changes.

The Rise of AI in Testing

The introduction of AI into software testing represents a significant leap forward. Unlike traditional automation, which requires explicit instructions, AI can learn from data and adapt to changes in real-time. This capability allows AI-driven tools to handle more complex testing scenarios and reduce the need for manual intervention.

Machine Learning (ML) algorithms can analyze historical test data to identify patterns and make predictions. For example, an ML model might predict the areas of an application that are most likely to contain defects, allowing testers to focus their efforts where they are needed most.

Natural Language Processing (NLP) allows AI tools to interpret and understand human language. This capability can be used to automatically generate test cases from user stories or requirements documents, reducing the time required to create test scripts.

How AI Enhances Software Testing

AI brings a variety of technologies into the software testing process, each with unique capabilities that enhance different aspects of testing.

ML Algorithms

ML algorithms can analyze historical test data to identify patterns, predict potential defects, and optimize test coverage. ML models can also continuously learn and improve as they process more data, making them increasingly effective over time.

For example, suppose a retail application has a history of defects in its payment processing module. An ML model trained on past defect reports might predict that new code changes in this module have a high likelihood of causing issues. This prediction would prompt targeted testing, focusing efforts on areas most likely to contain defects.

Natural Language Processing (NLP)

NLP enables AI systems to understand and process human language, which can be incredibly useful in generating test cases from textual requirements or user stories.

For example, imagine a scenario where a project manager writes a user story describing a new feature: "As a user, I want to receive an email confirmation after completing a purchase." An NLP-powered AI tool can interpret this user story and automatically generate relevant test cases to ensure that the email confirmation functionality works as expected.

Neural Networks

Neural networks, particularly deep learning models, are adept at recognizing complex patterns in data. They can be used in visual testing to detect UI anomalies that are difficult for traditional automation to catch.

A neural network might analyze screenshots of a mobile application's user interface across different devices and operating systems, identifying subtle visual inconsistencies that could impact the user experience.

AI's Impact on Software Testing

AI's impact on software testing can be observed in several key areas:

1. **Test Case Generation**: AI tools can automatically generate test cases based on code changes, user stories, or past defect data. This process ensures comprehensive test coverage with minimal manual effort.

   Consider a scenario where a development team is updating an e-commerce platform with new features. An AI tool analyzes the recent changes in the codebase and generates a suite of test cases targeting the new functionalities, ensuring that all critical areas are tested.

2. **Test Optimization**: AI can optimize test cases by identifying redundant or obsolete tests, ensuring that the testing process is efficient and focused on high-risk areas.

   For example, large test suites can become bloated with redundant tests that slow down the testing process. An AI-enabled tool can identify tests that no longer provide value and provide recommendations on removal or optimize the test cases. This will help in streamlining the testing process by analyzing the test cases or test suite.

3. **Automated Test Execution**: AI-driven tools can execute tests automatically, adjusting to changes in the codebase and providing real-time feedback.

   For example, in a CI/CD pipeline, an AI tool continuously monitors code commits and automatically executes relevant regression tests whenever new code is integrated. This ensures that new changes do not introduce defects, maintaining the stability of the application.

4. **Defect Prediction**: AI models can predict potential defects based on historical data and recent code changes, allowing teams to proactively address issues before they become problematic.

   For example, an AI system trained on a company's past defect data might flag a recent change in a module as high-risk, prompting additional security testing to catch potential vulnerabilities early.

5. **Test Data Management**: AI can generate and manage realistic test data, ensuring that testing is executed by quality engineers under conditions that closely mirror real-world usage.

I have seen scenarios in which an AI tool generated a diverse set of test data to simulate different user behaviors on an online banking platform, ensuring that all potential scenarios, including edge cases, were covered in the testing process.

AI offers significant advantages over traditional testing methods:

- **Automation of Repetitive Tasks**: While traditional automation can handle repetitive tasks, it still requires significant manual effort to create and maintain test scripts. AI, on the other hand, can generate and update tests as the application evolves.

- **Intelligent Adaption**: Traditional testing scripts can break when the application's UI or functionality changes, requiring manual updates. AI tools, however, can adapt to these changes in real-time, ensuring that tests remain valid and effective.

- **Deep Analysis**: AI's ability to process and analyze large datasets allows it to uncover patterns and insights that would be impossible to detect manually. This leads to more accurate defect prediction and risk assessment.

Key Benefits of AI in Software Testing

Table 7-1 provides the key benefits of leveraging AI in software testing, along with example scenarios.

Table 7-1. *Key Benefits of AI in Software Testing*

Key Benefit	Description	Scenario
Enhanced accuracy and precision	AI significantly enhances the accuracy and precision of software testing by reducing human error and providing intelligent analysis.	An AI tool that automates regression testing ensures that every test is executed by quality engineers precisely as intended, without the risk of missed steps or incorrect inputs.
Analyze large amounts of data	AI's ability to analyze large datasets and detect subtle patterns means that it can identify defects that might be overlooked by human testers.	A financial services company uses an AI-powered testing tool to analyze transaction data and identifies a rare but critical defect in the payment processing system. The defect had previously gone undetected in manual testing.
Improved efficiency and speed	AI can execute tests much faster than human testers or traditional automated scripts. This speed is particularly valuable in CI/CD pipelines, where quick feedback is essential.	In a CI/CD environment, an AI tool automatically executes a comprehensive suite of tests after each code commit, providing developers with immediate feedback on the impact of their changes.
Efficient use of resources	AI optimizes the use of testing resources by focusing efforts on high-risk areas and automating routine tasks. This allows testing teams to concentrate on more complex and value-added activities.	A development team uses an AI tool to automate regression testing, freeing up testers to focus on exploratory testing and user experience validation.

(continued)

Table 7-1. (*continued*)

Key Benefit	Description	Scenario
Scalability and adaptability	AI-driven testing is inherently scalable and adaptable, making it well-suited to the demands of modern software development.	As software applications grow and become complex, the ability to scale testing efforts becomes increasingly important. AI tools can handle large and complex test suites, ensuring that all critical areas are tested.
Cost-effectiveness, long-term cost savings	AI reduces the need for large testing teams and extensive manual effort, leading to significant cost savings over time.	A technology startup invests in an AI-driven testing platform. Although the initial cost is high, the company sees a 40% reduction in testing costs within the first year due to decreased manual effort and faster release cycles.

Challenges in Implementing AI in Software Testing

Some of the challenges in implementing AI into the software testing process include data quality and data availability. Gathering and maintaining the data needed for AI training can be challenging, particularly in test and production environments where data privacy and security are critical concerns.

- Compatibility issues often arise when integrating existing systems and workflows, as many of the tools and platforms are not compatible.

- The technical complexity of integrating AI into existing workflows can be a significant barrier, requiring specialized knowledge and expertise.

- AI models can inherit biases from the data they are trained on, leading to biased testing outcomes. For example, if a model is trained on data that underrepresents certain user demographics, it may not perform well for those users.

- Talent upskilling and learning curve issues often exist. Implementing and managing AI-based testing systems effectively requires specialized skills and knowledge, which may be in short supply.

- The upfront costs of AI tools, training, and integration can be substantial, particularly for small and medium-sized organizations.

- Organizations must carefully consider the initial costs versus the long-term benefits of AI in testing.

How the V-Model Has Evolved with AI Testing

The V-Model for software testing is a widely used software development framework that maps the stages of development with corresponding testing activities. The V-Model ensures validation and verification at each step. After the infusion of AI into software testing, several key changes and enhancements are made to the traditional V-Model, making it more adaptive, efficient, and capable of handling complex, modern systems.

Figure 7-1 illustrates the V-Model of software testing.

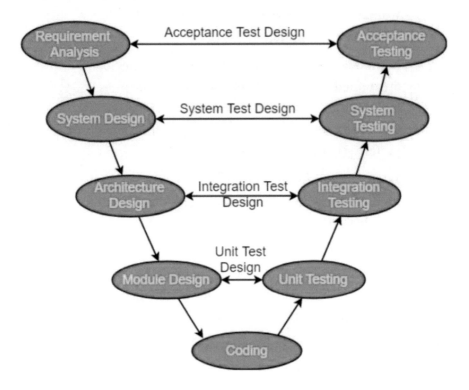

Figure 7-1. *The V-Model for SDLC testing (Credit:* `https://www.`
`geeksforgeeks.org/software-engineering-sdlc-v-model/)`

Table 7-2 shows how the V-Model has evolved in each software
testing stage.

Table 7-2. *V-Model Evolution Due to AI*

Software Testing Stage	Traditional V-Model	AI-Infused V-Model
Early Test Planning and Requirement Analysis	The requirements analysis phase corresponds with the user acceptance testing (UAT) on the testing side of the "V." The system's functional requirements are documented, and UAT is planned.	AI enhances requirements analysis by processing large volumes of historical project data and feedback. NLP-based AI tools can help identify inconsistencies, ambiguities, or gaps in the requirements and automatically map them to test cases early in the process. AI-powered requirements analysis also suggests potential areas of high risk, providing testers with the ability to proactively address them in UAT planning.
System Design	System design phases (high-level design and detailed design) map to integration testing and system testing. Test plans are manually created to validate components and the system.	AI can automatically generate test cases from design artifacts, such as UML diagrams or system flow charts. This reduces manual effort in designing test cases, especially for complex systems. AI can analyze design documents and generate optimized test scenarios by learning from previous designs and testing outcomes.

(continued)

Table 7-2. (*continued*)

Software Testing Stage	Traditional V-Model	AI-Infused V-Model
Unit Testing	Involves manual or script-based testing of individual units or components to ensure they function correctly.	AI automates unit test case generation and execution. It can also intelligently select the most important unit tests to run based on code changes, optimizing test coverage. Machine learning models identify redundant test cases and suggest areas where additional tests are necessary, reducing the manual burden and increasing efficiency
Integration Testing	Integration testing checks the interactions between different system components and subsystems, typically based on manually created test cases.	AI optimizes integration testing by predicting which integration points are most prone to errors based on historical defect data. It can prioritize and execute tests that focus on high-risk areas, identifying defects before they propagate through the system. AI also supports intelligent regression testing, determining the minimal set of test cases needed to validate the integrations after a code change.

(*continued*)

Table 7-2. (*continued*)

Software Testing Stage	Traditional V-Model	AI-Infused V-Model
System Testing	System testing evaluates the system, covering functional and non-functional requirements. Traditionally, tests are manually created, executed, and reported.	AI-enhanced tools automatically generate functional test cases and execute them across different environments, covering a broader spectrum of scenarios than would be possible manually. AI-driven visual regression testing, performance testing, and security testing tools enhance non-functional testing by automatically detecting UI changes, performance bottlenecks, or security vulnerabilities.
Acceptance Testing	User acceptance testing (UAT) involves verifying that the system meets the end user's requirements and is ready for deployment. Test cases are often based on predefined acceptance criteria.	AI augments UAT by analyzing user behavior and feedback to optimize test cases, ensuring they align with real-world usage. AI can simulate various user interactions and edge cases, allowing testers to focus on critical areas. AI-based tools also help predict user acceptance issues before deployment, using historical data and models trained on similar applications.

The ways of working have also changed with the infusion of AI into the software testing phase.

AI-Driven Testing Tools

AI-driven testing tools offer a wide range of capabilities, from automated test case generation to defect prediction and visual testing. This section looks at some of the more popular tools.

Tool: Appvance

Appvance's AI-driven testing platform offers features such as automated test case generation, regression testing, and performance testing. The platform uses ML algorithms to optimize test coverage and reduce testing time.

This tool is best suited for organizations looking for a comprehensive testing solution that combines AI with traditional test automation techniques. It includes the AIQ Platform, which offers a wide range of features, including automated test case generation, regression testing, and performance testing.

Figure 7-2 shows see how Appvance enables supervised AI-driven exploratory script generation. It increases or completes test coverage where bugs are found, heals the bugs, and helps solve complex testing needs.

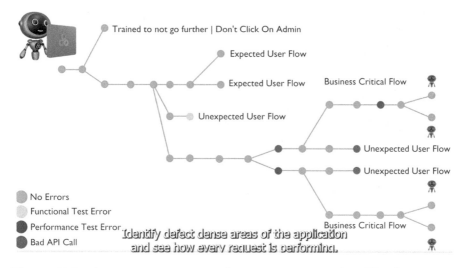

Figure 7-2. *Appvance automated test case generation (Credit:* `https://appvance.ai/aiq-platform)`

Tool: Testim

Testim is an AI-driven testing tool that focuses on mobile and web applications. It uses ML to automatically generate test cases and execute them across different devices and browsers.

Testim Copilot provides the following functionalities:

- Automatically produces custom test steps from a text description using generative AI.

- Provides clear explanations of JavaScript code, enhancing understanding and facilitating documentation and reuse.

- Accelerates debugging by automatically analyzing code and suggesting corrections.

Testim can generate a test to check whether a web page contains a header image followed by a login prompt automatically as part of the execution. This is shown in Figure 7-3.

Figure 7-3. *Generate automated test code using Testim (Credit:*
https://www.testim.io/test-automation-tool/)

Tool: Applitools

Applitools is a leading AI-powered visual testing and monitoring tool that focuses on ensuring the accuracy and consistency of user interfaces (UIs) across different browsers, devices, and screen sizes. It uses Visual AI to automatically compare visual elements, identify inconsistencies, and validate that the UI looks and behaves as expected. This is crucial in modern web and mobile applications where responsive design and cross-browser compatibility are important.

Key features of Applitools are:

1. **Visual AI**: Applitools' Visual AI engine uses machine learning to detect UI anomalies such as layout shifts, broken elements, misalignments, missing components, and style mismatches. It can detect differences that human testers might miss.

2. **Cross-Browser and Cross-Device Testing**: The tool allows you to perform visual tests across different browsers (Chrome, Safari, Firefox, etc.) and devices (desktops, tablets, and smartphones). This ensures consistent UI experiences.

3. **Root Cause Analysis**: The tool provides AI-powered root cause analysis by pinpointing the source of visual bugs. This helps developers quickly resolve issues.

4. **Self-Healing Tests**: Applitools automatically adapts to minor changes in the UI, reducing false positives caused by minor tweaks, such as font changes or button color adjustments.

5. **Ultrafast Grid**: Applitools' Ultrafast Grid accelerates visual tests by running tests in parallel across multiple environments and platforms simultaneously. It ensures that visual validation is done quickly and efficiently without redundant tests.

6. **Collaboration and Reporting**: Applitools provides a collaborative interface for developers, testers, and designers, where test results can be reviewed, approved, and shared. Its detailed reporting makes it easy to understand visual changes and track issues.

Figure 7-4 outlines the process of implementing visual UI testing. It typically involves four basic steps:

1. Write a test that exercises your application's UI by sending simulated mouse and keyboard events to enter various states and capture a screenshot in each of these states.

    a. Send simulated mouse and keyboard events to enter various states.

    b. Capture a screenshot in each of these states.

2. Compare the captured screenshots to previously captured baseline images.

3. Review the resulting differences and:

    a. Identify cases where differences were caused by a new feature that does not appear in the baseline image and accept the new screenshot. From that point forward, the new screenshot is used as the new baseline image for that checkpoint.

    b. Identify cases where differences indicate a bug that needs to be fixed, report the issue, and reject the image, meaning that the baseline image is not updated and remains as is.

4. Save the baseline updates, so that they can be used in the next test run.

    The first time a test is run, there are no baseline images, so the screenshots that are captured are adopted as the baseline images. On subsequent runs, it will evaluate and compare any changes.

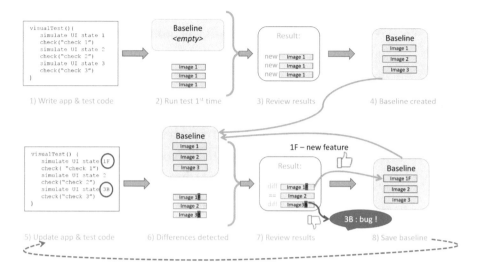

Figure 7-4. *Visual UI testing with Applitools (Credit:* `https://applitools.com/docs/topics/overview/overview-visual-testing.html`*)*

Tosca is a leading AI-infused continuous testing platform, ideal for large-scale and complex testing needs

1. AI-Powered Capabilities:

   • Tosca Copilot: A newly introduced generative AI assistant that optimizes testing processes by helping with test portfolio management, explaining complex test cases, and offering actionable insights on execution failures. It uses advanced Large Language Models (LLMs) for these tasks, allowing non-technical users to manage test automation efficiently.

- Vision AI: Employs patented neural network technology to ensure resilient UI automation and includes self-healing features to adapt tests dynamically

2. Test Automation Features:

    - Fully codeless, model-based testing for UI, API, and data layers across 160+ technologies, including enterprise, mobile, and custom applications

    - Features like risk-based testing, test data management, and service virtualization enable faster and more robust testing. These capabilities minimize dependencies and bottlenecks during the testing lifecycle

3. Execution & Reporting:

    - Supports distributed testing by running multiple tests in parallel across various infrastructures for scalability

    - Includes detailed testing reports and analytics for informed decision-making and faster issue resolution

4. Integration & Flexibility:

    - Seamlessly integrates with CI/CD pipelines and various enterprise applications.

    - Offers cross-platform testing for web, mobile, and desktop environments.

5. Cost & Productivity Gains:

    - Automating repetitive tasks and enabling faster onboarding with tools like the AI-powered Tosca Copilot reduces testing costs and cycle times

Other Testing Tools

Other tools in the AI-driven testing area include the following:

- **Functionize:** Functionize combines AI with traditional test automation techniques to deliver a comprehensive testing platform. It offers features such as automated test case generation, test execution, and defect prediction.

- **Microsoft's AI Testing Strategies:** Microsoft uses AI-driven tools to optimize its testing processes, including defect prediction, test case generation, and automated test execution. The company has also developed AI models that predict the impact of code changes on system performance, allowing for more targeted testing.

- **Facebook's Infer Tool:** This is an AI-powered static analysis tool that identifies bugs and security vulnerabilities in code before it is deployed. Facebook implemented Infer to improve the quality and security of its codebase. The tool uses AI to analyze code changes and detect potential issues, allowing developers to fix them before they reach production.

- **Google's AI-Driven Testing Framework**: This uses ML to analyze code changes and predict their impact on the system. This allows Google's testing teams to prioritize high-risk areas, ensuring that critical issues are identified and addressed quickly.

Capabilities and Features

Each AI-driven testing tool offers a unique set of capabilities and features. This section looks at some of the key functionalities involved in testing, as represented in Figure 7-5, and explains how AI tools can help.

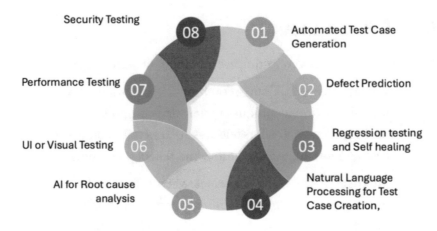

Figure 7-5. *Key functionalities required for AI-based testing*

1. **Automated Test Case Generation**: Tools like
   Appvance and Functionize use AI to automatically
   generate test cases based on code changes or user
   stories. This reduces the time required to create and
   maintain test cases, ensuring comprehensive test
   coverage.

2. **Defect Prediction**: Tools such as Test.ai and
   Functionize use ML algorithms to predict potential
   defects based on historical data and recent code
   changes. This allows testing teams to focus their
   efforts on high-risk areas, reducing the likelihood of
   critical defects reaching production.

3. **Regression Testing:** Regression testing ensures that
   changes to the codebase do not introduce new defects.
   AI-powered tools can intelligently select which test
   cases to run and automate the execution of these tests.

4. **Self-Healing Test Automation**: In traditional automated testing, minor UI changes can break tests, requiring frequent maintenance. AI-driven tools offer self-healing capabilities where the AI adapts the test scripts to changes in the application.

5. **Natural Language Processing for Test Case Creation:** NLP-driven AI tools can understand human language and automatically convert plain language requirements or user stories into test cases.

6. **AI for Root Cause Analysis**: When a test fails, identifying the root cause of the issue can be time-consuming. AI-driven testing tools help by performing root cause analysis, identifying which part of the system is responsible for the defect.

7. **UI or Visual Testing**: Applitools uses AI-powered visual testing to detect UI anomalies across different devices and screen sizes. This ensures that the user experience remains consistent, even as the application evolves.

8. **Performance Testing**: Appvance offers AI-driven performance testing, which simulates real-world usage scenarios to identify potential bottlenecks and performance issues.

9. **Security Testing**: AI-driven tools can automate security testing by scanning the application for vulnerabilities, analyzing security logs, and predicting potential threats.

Comparison of Tools

Table 7-3 compares the leading AI-driven testing tools and reveals the strengths and weaknesses of each tool.

Table 7-3. *AI-Driven Testing Tool Comparison*

Tool Name	Key Features	Test Case Generation	Self-Healing	Defect Prediction	Visual Testing	Performance Testing	Security Testing	Root Cause Analysis	Unique Use Cases
Testim	AI-powered functional test automation	Automatic test generation based on UI flows	Yes	No	No	No	No	Yes	Predictive test selection based on user behavior
Functionize	Self-healing tests, cloud-based execution	Auto-generation from user flows	Yes	No	Yes	No	No	Yes	Continuous functional testing with natural language support
Applitools	AI-based visual testing and monitoring	No	Yes	No	Yes	No	No	No	Visual testing and UI regression testing
Appvance AI	AI-driven test automation with regression	Automatic test generation	Yes	Yes	No	No	No	No	Test automation with AI for regression and functional testing
Applitools Eyes	Visual UI testing for functional, cross-browser, and mobile	No	Yes	No	Yes	No	No	No	Comprehensive visual testing across multiple devices and platforms
NeoLoad (Neotys)	AI-enhanced performance testing for enterprise applications	No	No	No	No	Yes	No	No	Simulates real-world performance conditions to detect bottlenecks
Tricentis Tosca	Model-based test automation, AI-powered Vision AI, Tosca Copilot	Automatic model-based test case generation	Yes	Yes	No	No	No	Yes	AI-powered continuous testing with Vision AI for UI resilience, scalable distributed execution, and Tosca Copilot for intelligent automation.
Fortify (Micro Focus)	AI-driven security testing for identifying vulnerabilities	No	No	No	No	No	Yes	Yes	Detects security vulnerabilities during static and dynamic testing
Test.ai Predictive	Predictive defect and performance testing based on historical data	Yes	No	Yes	No	Yes	No	Yes	Predicts the most likely defect-prone areas before code is tested

Best Practices for Implementing AI in Software Testing

1. **Start Small and Scale Gradually**: Implementing AI in software testing is a complex process that requires careful planning and execution. One of the best practices is to start small and scale gradually.

2. **Use Pilot Projects**: Begin with a pilot project that focuses on a specific area of testing, such as regression testing or defect prediction. This allows the organization to test the waters and evaluate the effectiveness of AI-driven tools before committing to a full-scale implementation.

For example, a software development company starts with a pilot project that uses AI to automate regression testing in a single application. Based on the success of the pilot, the company gradually expands AI-driven testing to other areas of its development process.

3. **Incrementally Scale**: Once the pilot project is successful, gradually scale AI-driven testing to other areas of the development process. This approach allows the organization to build expertise and confidence in AI-driven testing before fully committing to it. Consider a scenario where an e-commerce company, after a successful pilot project, expands its use of AI-driven testing to include defect prediction and visual testing, eventually integrating AI into its entire testing process.

4. **Ensure Data Quality and Data Collection**: Collect and curate high-quality data for training AI models. Ensure that the data is diverse and representative of the different scenarios the application may encounter.

   For example, a financial institution invests in data collection and curation to ensure that its AI-driven defect prediction model is trained on high-quality data. The model's accuracy improves significantly, leading to more reliable defect predictions.

5. **Implement Data Management**: Implement robust

data management practices to ensure that the data used for training AI models is accurate, up-to-date, and secure. For example, a healthcare software company implements strict data management practices, including regular data audits and encryption, to ensure the integrity and security of the data used to train its AI models.

6. **Address Bias and Ethical Concerns**: Bias in AI models can lead to inaccurate predictions and unethical outcomes. Implement strategies to identify and mitigate bias in AI models, such as using diverse training data and regularly auditing models for bias. Consider the ethical implications of AI-driven testing, particularly in areas like data privacy and user consent.

7. **Adopt Continuous Learning and Improvement Strategies**: AI-driven testing is not a one-time implementation but a continuous process of learning and improvement.

   - **Model Training:** Regularly train and update AI models to ensure that they remain effective as the application and its environment evolve.

   - **Feedback Loops:** Implement feedback loops to continuously monitor the performance of AI-driven testing tools and adjust as needed.

8. **Collaborate Between AI and Human Testers**: AI-driven testing tools are not a replacement for human testers but a complement to them.

   - **Human-AI Collaboration:** Foster a collaborative relationship between AI-driven testing tools and human testers, with each complementing the strengths of the other.

   - **Training and Education:** Provide training and education to testers on how to effectively use AI-driven testing tools and interpret their results.

Challenges with AI-Driven Testing Implementation

1. **Learning Curve for Teams**: Adopting AI-driven testing tools requires teams to familiarize themselves with new technologies, concepts, and workflows. This can be daunting, especially for teams used to traditional manual or automated testing processes.

   For example, a team skilled in Selenium-based testing may find it challenging to adapt to an AI-powered tool like Appvance or Applitools, as the approaches to setting up tests, handling failures, and interpreting results differ significantly.

2. **False Positives and Overreliance on AI**: The models can generate false positives (incorrectly flagged defects) or false negatives (missed defects). These inaccuracies may stem from training data quality, model tuning, or insufficient learning cycles.

3. **Data Dependency and Model Training**: AI testing tools depend on data for training models. The quality and quantity of historical test cases, user interactions, and defect data directly impact how well the AI can predict defects, optimize test cases, and perform root cause analysis. With tools like Appvance AI or Testim, the AI learns from previous test executions. If the historical data is inconsistent or incomplete, the AI may not perform optimally, leading to inaccurate predictions or inadequate test coverage.

4. **Complex Scenarios and Non-Deterministic Behavior**: Complex systems, such as those involving heavy data processing, asynchronous tasks, or machine learning-driven applications, may be difficult for AI-driven testing tools to handle due to non-deterministic behavior.

   AI models struggle with applications where results vary based on user input or dynamic data (e.g., an AI recommendation engine). This non-deterministic behavior can cause unpredictable results during testing.

5. **High Initial Investment and Setup Time:** AI-driven testing tools often come with higher upfront costs compared to traditional testing tools. The setup, training of the AI models, and integration into existing CI/CD pipelines may require significant time and resources.

Tools like Tricentis Tosca and Functionize may require detailed configuration to align with project-specific workflows. Additionally, integrating AI-driven testing tools into complex enterprise environments can be expensive.

6. **Customization Limitations**: Tools may lack flexibility for handling custom or niche requirements. Certain AI algorithms may not work effectively for unique use cases or application-specific behavior, in industries with regulatory compliance (e.g., healthcare, finance), the specific requirements for testing certain functionalities may not be easily adaptable to AI-driven tools.

7. **Handling Legacy Systems**: Many organizations still run legacy systems with outdated architecture, which may not be compatible with modern AI-driven testing tools. Testing such systems often involves complex integrations or even manual workarounds.

   For example, a legacy banking system that has been running for over a decade may not support the automation capabilities of newer AI testing tools, leading to additional manual effort in creating test cases or maintaining tests.

8. **Integration with Existing Tools and Workflows**: Testing tools need to be integrated seamlessly with existing CI/CD pipelines, bug tracking systems, and version control platforms. In some cases, achieving this integration requires additional customization and maintenance.

9. **Ethical and Legal Concerns**: The use of AI in testing can raise ethical questions, particularly when testing applications related to privacy, security, or user data. Organizations must ensure that their AI models are transparent, ethical, and legally compliant. For example, AI-driven testing for financial or healthcare applications can raise privacy concerns, especially if the AI needs access to sensitive data during testing. Data protection regulations (e.g., GDPR) may require additional considerations.

10. **Bias in AI Models**: AI models are trained on specific datasets, and there is always the risk that these datasets may contain biases. If not properly addressed, AI-driven testing may focus on certain types of defects or scenarios, while overlooking others. An AI testing tool trained primarily on web applications may not perform well when used on mobile apps due to differences in user interfaces, workflows, or interaction patterns.

Future Trends in AI and Software Testing

1. **AI-Driven Test Orchestration:** The future of software testing is likely to see more advanced AI-driven test orchestration, where AI tools autonomously manage the entire testing process.

2. **End-to-End Automation:** AI-driven test orchestration will enable end-to-end automation of the testing process, from test case generation to execution and defect management.

3. **Adaptive Testing:** AI-driven test orchestration will enable adaptive testing, where AI tools dynamically adjust the testing process based on real-time data and feedback.

4. **AI-Augmented Exploratory Testing:** Relies heavily on human intuition and creativity and will benefit from AI augmentation.

5. **AI Assistance**: AI tools will assist human testers in exploratory testing by providing insights, recommendations, and real-time analysis.

6. **Enhanced Coverage**: AI-augmented exploratory testing will enable more comprehensive coverage by combining the strengths of human intuition with the analytical capabilities of AI. A gaming company uses AI-augmented exploratory testing to uncover complex bugs in its latest release. The AI tool assists testers by identifying high-risk areas and suggesting test scenarios, leading to more thorough testing and a higher-quality product.

7. **AI in Testing of AI Systems**: As AI systems become more prevalent, the need for testing AI systems themselves will grow. Testing AI systems presents unique challenges, such as the need to validate complex and dynamic models. New tools and techniques will emerge to address the challenges of testing AI systems, including model validation, bias detection, and explainability.

AI in software testing is transforming the industry, offering significant benefits in terms of efficiency, accuracy, and scalability. However, organizations must carefully navigate the challenges of AI implementation, including data quality, integration, and bias. By following best practices and staying ahead of emerging trends, organizations can harness the full potential of AI to improve the quality and reliability of their software products.

Summary

This chapter looked at how artificial intelligence brings significant value to the world of software testing.

There are several key benefits to leveraging AI in software testing, including testing precision, large data analysis, and efficiency, to name a few. While AI can be a beneficial integration, it is not straightforward. It adds a level of complexity and there is a learning curve in getting AI-based testing right.

The chapter covered looked at a few tools, including Appvance, Testim, and Applitools, that are in vogue in the software industry. It also compared some of the tools that are used commonly today.

CHAPTER 8

AI in Continuous Delivery

"Continuous delivery is a software development discipline where you build software in such a way that the software can be released to production at any time."

—Martin Flower

The key insight here from Martin Flower's quote is that continuous delivery (CD) isn't about automating the pipeline but about structuring the entire software development process to ensure that the system is always in a "ready-to-release" state.

This means every code change, whether small or large, is integrated, tested, and validated in such a way that it could be deployed at any moment. It reflects a mindset of continuous readiness, where teams focus on frequent, small, incremental changes rather than large, infrequent releases. Flower underscores the goal of CD as reducing the risks and challenges typically associated with deployment, by making the process routine and automated.

The real benefit of this approach is in its ability to respond quickly to business needs or bug fixes, enabling faster time to market, more frequent updates, and the flexibility to address issues without delay. CD encourages

© Abhinav Krishna and Vamshidhar Meda 2024
A. Krishna and V. Meda, *AI Integration in Software Development and Operations*, https://doi.org/10.1007/979-8-8688-1044-2_8

high-quality practices, automated testing, and efficient collaboration across teams, ensuring that software is always in a deployable state, which directly supports agility and resilience in modern software development.

Continuous delivery (CD) has come a long way from traditional deployment practices. Initially, deployments were manual and infrequent and teams would gather for "big bang" releases, often scheduled on weekends or late nights to avoid impacting business operations. This manual process was time-consuming and error-prone, with a high risk of failure, leading to downtime, frustration, and unhappy users.

Then came the era of automation, where tools like Jenkins, Bamboo, and CircleCI started automating build pipelines. While these tools solved the problem of manual deployments, they still required a lot of human intervention—deciding when to deploy, monitoring releases, and managing failures in production.

We're now entering the next phase: the AI-driven era of CD. AI has the potential to fundamentally change how we deliver software by automating not only the technical processes but also decision-making, risk assessment, and even post-deployment monitoring.

The Role of AI in Continuous Delivery

Imagine a scenario where, instead of relying on developers or DevOps/SRE engineers to manually monitor performance dashboards, AI analyzes data in real-time, predicts failures, and acts automatically. AI not only handles the mechanics of deployment but also understands the complexities behind code changes, deployment patterns, dependencies, user traffic, and infrastructure behavior. It uses predictive models to determine the best time to deploy, dynamically adjusts infrastructure, and even rolls back faulty deployments without requiring human intervention.

This transformation is a huge step forward in achieving zero-downtime deployments and higher reliability across distributed systems.

Key Areas Where AI Can Make a Difference

AI is a game-changer in all phases of DevOps, especially in continuous delivery. It mainly impacts deployment, release, and infrastructure management, as indicated in Figure 8-1.

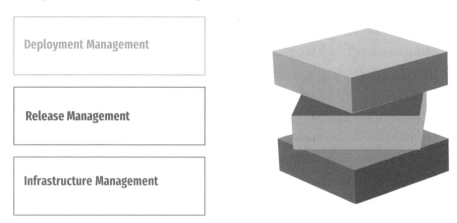

Figure 8-1. *Three key areas where AI can make a difference in continuous delivery*

- **Deployment Management:** AI can predict the success or failure of deployments by analyzing past deployment data, performance metrics, and infrastructure behavior.

- **Release Management:** By leveraging machine learning models, AI can intelligently orchestrate releases across global environments, ensuring the right features are rolled out to the right users at the right time.

- **Infrastructure Management:** AI can dynamically provision and scale resources based on real-time traffic and performance data, ensuring that infrastructure is always optimized without manual intervention.

AI in Deployment Automation

In today's fast-paced software development landscape, businesses must continuously deliver new features and updates while maintaining the stability and performance of their applications. Deployment automation has become essential in achieving these goals because it removes manual bottlenecks and ensures faster, more reliable releases.

However, traditional deployment automation has limitations when it comes to flexibility, adaptability, and predictive capabilities. This is where AI steps in. AI can analyze vast amounts of data, predict outcomes, and even adapt to changing conditions in real-time. By applying AI to deployment automation, organizations can improve their CI/CD pipelines, minimize human intervention, and reduce errors.

AI transforms deployment from a manual or rule-based process to one driven by machine learning models that learn from past deployments, real-time performance data, and environmental conditions. This section explores the key use cases, challenges, tools, and the significant impact AI brings to deployment automation.

AI in deployment automation refers to the application of artificial intelligence, machine learning, and data science techniques to automate and optimize the process of deploying applications and services. AI augments traditional deployment pipelines by predicting issues, automating decision-making, and optimizing performance across various environments.

Unlike traditional automation, which follows predefined steps, AI-driven automation leverages historical data and real-time metrics to continuously learn and improve the deployment process. AI algorithms can detect patterns in system behavior, analyze logs and metrics, and adapt deployment strategies based on live data.

For instance, in a deployment pipeline, instead of following a rigid step-by-step process, AI can dynamically adjust the sequence of deployment tasks based on the current system load, network traffic, and the health of application services.

The journey from manual deployment to AI-powered automation has been transformative for software development. In the early days, deployment was a manual process involving developers and system administrators physically moving code to production environments. This approach was prone to errors, time-consuming, and inconsistent.

As CI/CD pipelines emerged, deployment automation became a standard practice, allowing teams to automate repetitive tasks like building, testing, and deploying code. Tools like Jenkins, GitLab CI, and CircleCI helped streamline this process by following predefined workflows. However, these pipelines, while efficient, often lacked flexibility and adaptability.

The introduction of AI into deployment automation marked the next evolution. AI systems now enable pipelines to "learn" from past deployments, dynamically adjusting steps based on real-time data and previous experiences. This makes deployments faster, smarter, and more resilient.

Benefits of Using AI in Deployment Automation

- **Predictive Insights:** AI can predict potential issues in deployments, allowing developers to take proactive measures.

- **Dynamic Decision-Making:** Instead of fixed deployment strategies, AI allows for decisions to be made based on real-time data.

- **Reduced Manual Intervention:** AI can automate complex tasks like rollbacks, pipeline optimization, and scaling decisions, freeing up developers and DevOps engineers.

Key Use Cases of AI in Deployment Automation

The key use cases for AI in deployment automation are illustrated in Figure 8-2.

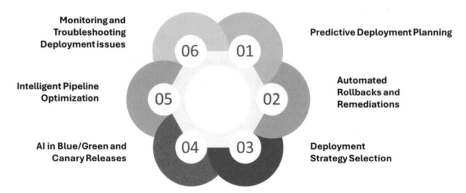

Figure 8-2. *Key use cases for AI infusion in deployment management*

Predictive Deployment Planning

Predictive deployment planning is one of the most promising use cases of AI in deployment automation. It involves using machine learning models to predict the best time and method for deploying software updates to minimize risk and downtime. By analyzing historical performance data, traffic patterns, server load, and past deployment outcomes, AI can determine the optimal time to deploy.

For example, imagine a retail company that experiences high traffic during peak hours. AI models can predict traffic spikes based on historical data, allowing the system to schedule deployments during low-traffic hours to reduce the risk of server overload. Additionally, if AI detects that a specific server is experiencing higher than usual load, it can reroute the deployment to other, less busy servers.

Benefits:

- **Minimized Disruption:** By predicting when traffic is low, AI ensures that deployments happen when they are least likely to affect users.

- **Improved Reliability:** AI can flag deployments that have a high probability of failure based on code analysis or system health.

- **Optimized Resource Utilization:** Predictive models can help balance workloads across servers, ensuring optimal performance during deployments.

Automated Rollbacks and Remediations

Rollbacks are critical when something goes wrong during deployment. Traditionally, developers or operations teams must manually initiate rollback processes when they detect an issue. AI automates this process by detecting deployment failures in real-time and automatically initiating rollback actions without human intervention.

For example, an e-commerce platform deploys a new update, but AI detects an anomaly in the response times of the key API services. Based on predefined metrics and historical data, AI identifies this as a failure pattern and automatically rolls back to the previous version before customers experience any major disruption.

Benefits:

- **Reduced Downtime:** By automating rollbacks, AI minimizes the time between detecting a problem and reverting to a stable version.

- **Faster Recovery:** AI can diagnose the root cause of failures and trigger specific remediation steps, such as restarting services or scaling infrastructure.

- **Self-Healing Systems:** AI-driven systems can automatically take corrective actions without waiting for human intervention.

Deployment Strategy Selection

In most CD environments, deployment strategies (Canary, Blue/Green, etc.) are pre-configured based on best practices. But no two deployments are the same, and fixed strategies don't always work for every situation. AI can change that by analyzing the context of the deployment and selecting the best strategy dynamically.

Say that a healthcare provider wants to roll out a critical update to the patient records system. AI analyzes the deployment environment and user traffic patterns, identifying that a Canary release would minimize risks. It then proceeds to deploy the update to a small group of users while closely monitoring performance metrics, ensuring that the broader user base is unaffected until the update is confirmed stable.

AI in Blue/Green and Canary Releases

In traditional Canary or Blue/Green releases, teams often rely on manual monitoring to ensure there are no issues. This can be tedious and error prone. AI enhances these strategies by providing real-time analysis and decision-making capabilities.

Consider a scenario where a large retailer uses Blue/Green deployments for its e-commerce platform. During the holiday season, AI analyzes traffic, server load, and error rates to decide when to switch traffic from the Blue environment (old version) to the Green (new version). If AI detects abnormal behavior in the Green environment, it delays the switch and alerts the operations team, preventing costly outages during peak shopping times.

The release management section of this chapter dives deep into this topic.

Intelligent Pipeline Optimization

AI optimizes deployment pipelines by continuously learning from past performance, error rates, and bottlenecks. It can dynamically adjust the pipeline configuration based on real-time data, identifying inefficiencies and automatically optimizing pipeline steps to improve performance and reduce execution time.

A CI/CD pipeline might involve multiple stages, such as building, testing, deployment, and post-deployment verification. AI can monitor these stages, identify which steps are consistently slow or prone to errors, and recommend or implement optimizations, such as parallelizing certain tests or reordering steps for better performance.

Benefits:

- **Faster Pipelines:** By optimizing pipeline steps and reducing bottlenecks, AI can significantly shorten deployment times.

- **Improved Efficiency:** AI eliminates unnecessary steps and improves resource utilization, resulting in more efficient deployments.

- **Continuous Improvement:** The system learns from each deployment, continuously refining the pipeline for future runs.

Monitoring and Troubleshooting Deployment Issues

AI continuously monitors the deployment pipelines by analyzing deployment logs and patterns and can automatically provide recommendations or take actions to remediate deployment issues depending on the rules or configurations set up by the DevOps engineers.

Benefits:

- **Faster Resolution:** By remediating the deployment issues, it helps remove the human intervention or handshakes across teams. This also reduces operational costs.

- **Continuous Improvement:** The system learns from each deployment activity and helps remediate deployment issues.

Challenges in AI-Powered Deployment Automation

AI-powered deployment automation is not without its set of challenges. The following sections touch upon those challenges.

Data Quality and Volume

AI systems rely heavily on large volumes of high-quality data to make accurate predictions and decisions. In the context of deployment automation, data includes metrics from past deployments, performance logs, error reports, and real-time monitoring data. Poor-quality data can lead to incorrect predictions, faulty optimizations, and erroneous actions by the AI system.

If logs are incomplete or formatted incorrectly, AI may not be able to accurately detect patterns of failure, leading to missed alerts or false conclusions about the success of a deployment. It is important to ensure that all systems provide consistent, reliable data across environments and AI systems must be able to filter out irrelevant data or noise to focus on meaningful insights.

Model Interpretability and Reliability

One of the biggest challenges in deploying AI is model interpretability. AI models, especially those based on deep learning, can be difficult to interpret, making it challenging to Understand why specific decisions were made. This can lead to hesitation in trusting the AI's actions, especially in critical scenarios like rolling back a deployment or modifying pipeline steps.

We have seen scenarios where a machine learning model flags a deployment as risky, but the reason for this prediction is unclear to the DevOps team. Without understanding the model's decision-making process, it becomes difficult for the team to validate or trust the AI's actions.

Also, many AI models are opaque, making it hard to understand their decision-making process. Relying too heavily on AI without understanding its limitations can lead to unforeseen issues during deployments.

Integration with Existing CI/CD Pipelines

Integrating AI into existing CI/CD pipelines can be complex, particularly for organizations that have heavily customized pipelines. AI requires access to large volumes of data, which may not always be readily available in traditional CI/CD setups. Moreover, retrofitting AI-driven automation into legacy pipelines can be a resource-intensive process.

There is significant re-engineering work required for older pipelines, as they may not be designed to work with AI-driven systems. Integrating AI into pipelines often requires using additional tools and frameworks, increasing overall system complexity.

Security Concerns

Introducing AI into deployment pipelines also raises security concerns. AI systems can be vulnerable to adversarial attacks, where malicious actors manipulate data inputs to deceive AI models. Additionally, AI systems that have access to sensitive deployment data must be protected from unauthorized access or tampering.

For example, an attacker might inject malicious data into the logs or performance metrics used by AI models to cause the system to make incorrect decisions, such as triggering an unnecessary rollback or scaling down services at critical times.

Cultural and Organizational Adoption

For AI deployment automation to succeed, it requires more than just technical integration—it also requires cultural and organizational buy-in. Many teams, especially those with long-established processes, may resist adopting AI-driven approaches. There may be concerns about job security, loss of control, or skepticism about the effectiveness of AI systems.

Some DevOps teams that have traditionally relied on manual rollbacks and troubleshooting might resist adopting AI-driven automation, fearing that they will lose visibility and control over deployments. It is important for organizations to invest in training to help teams understand how to work with and manage AI-driven systems.

Tools and Platforms Leveraging AI in Deployment Automation

There are several AI-powered tools and platforms designed to automate and optimize the deployment process. These tools integrate with CI/CD pipelines to bring intelligent automation capabilities such as predictive insights, anomaly detection, and self-healing infrastructure.

Harness.io

Harness.io is a continuous delivery as a service (CDaaS) platform that leverages AI and machine learning to automate deployment pipelines and improve pipeline efficiency. One of its standout features is its AI-powered Continuous Verification, which automatically analyzes deployment health by comparing metrics before and after a deployment. Harness also provides intelligent rollback mechanisms based on real-time performance data.

AIDA in Harness (see Figure 8-3) has infused AI in the CI/CD pipelines, including an agent that helps create pipelines, troubleshoots deployment issues, enables best practices, remediates security vulnerabilities, and other use cases.

Figure 8-3. *AIDA in Harness (Credit:* `https://harness.io`*)*

Features:

- **Automatic Canary Analysis:** AI-driven analysis of Canary deployments to determine if a new release is healthy or needs to be rolled back.

- **Intelligent Rollbacks:** If AI detects performance issues or errors during deployment, it can automatically trigger rollbacks to the previous stable version.

- **Self-Healing Pipelines:** The platform continuously learns from deployment data and optimizes pipelines to reduce errors and improve performance.

Spinnaker with Machine Learning Integrations

Spinnaker is an open source, multi-cloud continuous delivery platform designed to manage deployments across various environments. While not AI-driven out of the box, Spinnaker can be integrated with machine learning systems to bring AI-powered capabilities into the deployment pipeline.

By integrating a machine learning model into Spinnaker, teams can build a system that predicts the success or failure of deployments based on historical data. This prediction can help teams decide when to proceed with a deployment or whether to delay it based on real-time system health.

Features:

- **Multi-Cloud Deployments:** AI can help optimize deployments across multiple cloud environments by predicting resource availability, cost, and performance.

- **Risk Prediction:** Machine learning models can be used to predict the likelihood of deployment success or failure.

- **Traffic Management:** AI can dynamically manage traffic routing during Blue/Green or Canary deployments to minimize risk.

GitHub Copilot for Deployment Automation Scripts

GitHub Copilot is an AI-powered coding assistant tool that helps developers write code more efficiently. While it is primarily known for assisting in coding, it can also be used to streamline the creation of deployment automation scripts, infrastructure-as-code, and configuration files.

For example, a developer working on a Terraform configuration for deploying infrastructure on AWS can use GitHub Copilot to generate the necessary script components based on natural language prompts or code examples.

Features:

- **Automated Script Generation:** Copilot helps developers write deployment scripts, reducing the time and effort required to set up automation.

- **Contextual Suggestions:** The AI-powered tool can provide suggestions for deployment configurations based on the developer's code context.

- **Improved Productivity:** Developers can quickly generate boilerplate code for deployment pipelines, reducing the cognitive load and allowing them to focus on higher-level tasks.

AI-Powered Observability Platforms (Datadog, New Relic)

Observability platforms like Datadog and New Relic use AI and machine learning to enhance monitoring, alerting, and performance analysis for deployed applications. These platforms provide advanced anomaly detection, predictive alerts, and insights into system behavior based on historical and real-time data.

Datadog's AI-driven anomaly detection feature uses machine learning to automatically detect abnormal behavior in metrics, logs, and traces. This allows DevOps teams to identify issues before they impact users and take corrective action.

Features:

- **Anomaly Detection:** AI models automatically detect unusual behavior in system performance, helping teams identify potential issues before they become critical.

- **Predictive Alerts:** AI-driven alerts notify teams of potential problems based on patterns in historical data.

- **Real-Time Insights:** Machine learning models continuously analyze data to provide insights into system performance and health.

The Impact of AI in Deployment Automation

The impact of AI in deployment automation is profound, reshaping the way software is deployed, maintained, and scaled. By automating decision-making processes, AI drives efficiency, reliability, and cost savings across the deployment lifecycle.

Speed and Efficiency Gains

AI-driven deployment automation enables faster and more efficient deployments by optimizing pipeline configurations, predicting potential issues, and dynamically adjusting deployment steps based on real-time data.

For example, a deployment pipeline that typically takes two hours to complete can be optimized by AI to run in parallel, reducing the time to 30 minutes. AI might also identify steps that can be skipped or adjusted to further reduce pipeline execution time.

Benefits:

- **Faster Time to Market:** AI helps teams release new features and updates faster, allowing organizations to stay competitive.

- **Reduced Deployment Times:** By optimizing pipeline steps and eliminating bottlenecks, AI shortens the overall time needed for deployments.

- **Continuous Improvements:** AI learns from each deployment and continuously refines the pipeline for future releases.

Reduction of Human Errors

Human errors, such as misconfigurations or missed steps in the deployment process, can lead to failures and downtime. AI reduces the likelihood of these errors by automating critical tasks, such as rollbacks, pipeline optimizations, and anomaly detection.

One scenario where AI can be used is when a developer accidentally configures a wrong parameter in the deployment script, which can lead to a service outage. AI can detect the configuration mismatch and automatically correct it before deployment.

Benefits:

- **Increased Reliability:** By eliminating manual intervention, AI ensures that deployments follow best practices and avoid common mistakes.

- **Consistency:** AI-driven automation ensures that deployments are consistent across different environments and teams.

- **Lower Risk:** AI-driven systems can automatically detect and correct potential errors, reducing the risk of deployment failures.

Cost Optimization

AI helps optimize the cost of deployments by predicting resource usage, reducing unnecessary infrastructure scaling, and identifying inefficiencies in the pipeline. This leads to significant cost savings, especially in cloud-based environments where resource usage directly impacts costs.

An example of cost optimization is when an AI model predicts that a certain cloud region is experiencing lower than expected traffic and automatically scales down instances to save on cloud costs. Alternatively, AI could recommend switching to a different instance type to optimize performance and cost.

Benefits:

- **Optimized Resource Usage:** AI ensures that resources are used efficiently during deployments, reducing unnecessary infrastructure costs.

- **Cost-Effective Scaling:** AI-driven systems can automatically scale infrastructure based on real-time demand, avoiding over-provisioning.

- **Lower Operational Costs:** By automating tasks like rollbacks, monitoring, and scaling, AI reduces the need for manual intervention and operational overhead.

Improved DevOps and Developer Experience

AI enhances the DevOps experience by automating repetitive tasks, providing intelligent recommendations, and reducing cognitive load on developers. This allows teams to focus on higher-level tasks like improving code quality and building new features.

For example, a developer using an AI-powered deployment tool receives recommendations on how to optimize pipeline steps based on past performance, allowing them to make more informed decisions and streamline the deployment process.

Benefits:

- **Increased Productivity:** AI-driven tools help developers and DevOps teams work more efficiently by automating low-level tasks and providing actionable insights.

- **Reduced Cognitive Load:** By automating complex processes, AI reduces the mental burden on teams, allowing them to focus on innovation and problem-solving.

- **Improved Collaboration:** AI-driven systems can provide recommendations and insights that help developers and operations teams work together more effectively.

Scalability and Flexibility

AI enables systems to scale dynamically based on demand, improving flexibility and ensuring that deployments can handle varying traffic loads. This is especially critical in cloud-native environments where applications need to scale quickly to meet user demand.

For example, an e-commerce platform experiences a sudden spike in traffic due to a flash sale. AI automatically scales the infrastructure to meet demand, ensuring that the platform remains responsive and available to customers.

Benefits:

- **Dynamic Scaling:** AI-driven systems can automatically scale infrastructure based on real-time traffic, ensuring that applications can handle demand without manual intervention.

- **Improved Flexibility:** AI allows for more flexible deployment strategies, such as Canary releases or Blue/Green deployments, which can be dynamically adjusted based on real-time performance data.

- **Increased Resilience:** AI ensures that applications remain resilient by automatically detecting and responding to infrastructure failures, scaling issues, and performance bottlenecks.

Future Trends and the Road Ahead

The integration of AI into deployment automation is still in its early stages, but the potential for future growth is immense. As AI models become more sophisticated, we can expect even greater levels of automation, including fully autonomous deployment pipelines that require minimal human intervention.

Trends to Watch

- **Autonomous Deployment Pipelines:** AI systems may eventually handle all aspects of deployment, from code commits to production releases, with minimal human involvement.

- **AI-Driven Security Automation:** AI will play a key role in automating security checks, vulnerability assessments, and compliance audits in deployment pipelines.

- **Increased Adoption of AI-Powered Observability:** AI-driven observability platforms will continue to evolve, providing even deeper insights into system performance and health.

- **Collaboration Between AI and Human Teams:** AI will increasingly work alongside human teams, providing intelligent recommendations and automating low-level tasks while allowing humans to focus on higher-level decision-making.

AI-Powered Release Management

Release management refers to the processes, workflows, and methodologies used to deliver software or features into production environments. In the past, releases were rigid and scheduled infrequently, typically in large, monolithic deployments. However, the rise of DevOps, CI, and CD has transformed release management into a more agile, incremental process.

This transformation laid the foundation for progressive release management—where features and updates are delivered incrementally to small subsets of users, before expanding to the broader user base. This minimizes risk and allows for real-time feedback.

However, as the complexity of releases grows, with microservices, multi-cloud environments, and user-centric feature rollouts, traditional manual release management struggles to keep pace. This is where AI steps in to add intelligence, automation, and predictive insights into the release cycle, enabling more dynamic, adaptive, and progressive releases.

AI and the Shift Toward Progressive Release Management

Progressive release management emphasizes gradually deploying features to ensure stability, using techniques such as Canary releases, feature flags, and Blue/Green deployments. We have seen a paradigm shift in moving from traditional release management to progressive release management with automation and data-driven predictions to make the right choices on when and how to deploy features.

Key Aspects of Progressive Release Management Enhanced by AI

The following are some of the key aspects of progressive release management:

- **Canary Releases**: Deploying or releasing new updates to a small subset of users before gradually rolling them out to the entire user base.

- **Feature Flagging**: Controlling feature releases to specific user segments or regions dynamically.

- **Incremental Rollouts**: Slowly deploying features in stages to mitigate risk.

- **Automated Rollbacks**: Reverting updates when errors or anomalies are detected during releases.

AI enhances these strategies by analyzing historical data, user behavior, and real-time system metrics to make intelligent decisions, predict issues, and respond swiftly to failures. Progressive release management powered by AI provides not only speed and automation but also confidence and reliability in releases.

Key AI Use Cases in Release Management

There are several use cases for release management where AI can be infused, and six key ones are outlined in Figure 8-4.

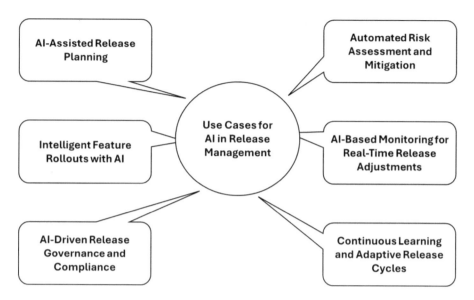

Figure 8-4. *Key AI use cases in release management*

AI-Assisted Release Planning

AI-powered release planning analyzes historical release data, system performance, and resource usage to suggest optimal windows for future releases. By identifying the best times to execute releases (e.g., low traffic periods, stable system health), AI enhances decision-making around release scheduling.

Consider a scenario where a global e-commerce platform needs to plan its quarterly release. The AI system analyzes traffic patterns and previous release outcomes, identifying that a particular window on a Sunday morning is optimal, reducing the risk of customer disruptions while ensuring sufficient engineering resources are available.

Mechanism and Process:

1. **Data Aggregation**: Collect historical data on past releases, including success rates, timing, system performance, and user impact.

235

2. **Feature Engineering**: Identify key factors that influence release success, such as time of day, day of the week, system load, and recent changes.

3. **Model Development**: Develop machine learning models (e.g., regression models, time-series analysis) to predict the success probability of releases at different times.

4. **Scheduling Recommendations**: Based on predictions, AI suggests optimal release windows and schedules that align with historical success patterns and current system conditions.

AI can struggle with limited or inconsistent data, potentially leading to inaccurate release recommendations. For effective AI-driven planning, data collection and accuracy are crucial.

- **Data Quality**: The accuracy of predictions depends on the quality and completeness of historical data.

- **Changing Conditions**: Factors affecting release success can change over time, requiring models to be regularly updated.

Impact:

- **Reduced Release Risks:** By scheduling updates during optimal periods, risk is lower.

- **Improved Operational Efficiency:** AI helps avoid releases during high-risk periods (e.g., peak traffic), which improves efficiency.

Intelligent Feature Rollouts with AI

AI plays a critical role in managing incremental feature rollouts through feature flags and Canary releases. Using real-time data, AI can decide when and to whom new features should be released, gradually increasing the release footprint as performance and user engagement metrics are monitored.

For example, an organization like Netflix rolls out a new recommendation algorithm to 5 percent of its users in a Canary release. AI monitors user behavior and system load, and after detecting positive results (e.g., improved engagement, and stable performance), it increases the rollout to 30 percent, then 50 percent, and eventually to the full user base.

Mechanism and Process:

1. **Real-Time Monitoring**: AI systems continuously monitor system performance, user feedback, and error rates during the release.

2. **Anomaly Detection**: Machine learning models detect anomalies or deviations from expected behavior. For example, sudden spikes in error rates or performance degradation are flagged as potential issues.

3. **Automated Rollback**: When anomalies exceed predefined thresholds, AI triggers an automatic rollback to the previous stable version. The rollback process is executed with minimal manual intervention.

4. **Remediation Recommendations**: Post-rollback, AI analyzes the cause of the issue and provides recommendations for remediation to prevent future occurrences.

Challenges include when AI must balance rapid feature deployment with careful monitoring, avoiding premature releases to the entire user base without adequate testing on smaller groups.

- **Threshold Management**: Setting appropriate thresholds for triggering rollbacks can be complex and may require fine-tuning.

- **False Positives**: AI may sometimes flag benign issues as critical, leading to unnecessary rollbacks.

Impact:

- **Reduced Risk of Feature Failures:** By using a staged, data-driven approach to rollouts, risk is reduced.

- **Improved User Experience:** New features are released only when they are validated by real-world performance data.

- **Quick Recovery**: Automated rollbacks ensure rapid recovery from problematic releases, minimizing downtime.

- **Reduced Manual Intervention**: Lowers the need for manual oversight during critical failures, speeding up the response.

AI-Driven Release Governance and Compliance

AI assists with release governance by ensuring that all necessary checks (e.g., security, compliance, and performance) are satisfied before allowing a release to proceed. This automates governance by scanning code for vulnerabilities, regulatory issues, and other risks, flagging non-compliance in real-time.

Consider a scenario where a financial services firm uses AI to ensure that all releases comply with strict regulatory requirements (e.g., GDPR, PCI-DSS). The AI continuously scans for compliance issues, automatically blocking any release that introduces non-compliant code or violates governance policies.

Compliance-related AI models can produce false positives, which may delay legitimate releases. Fine-tuning is necessary to balance compliance enforcement without overly restrictive rules.

Impact:

- **Improved Regulatory Compliance:** AI automates governance checks.

- **Faster Release Cycles:** AI reduces the manual burden of compliance verification.

Automated Risk Assessment and Mitigation

AI can predict release risks by analyzing code changes, dependency trees, test results, and historical incident data. It identifies potential high-risk areas, allowing teams to focus testing and mitigation efforts where they are needed most.

For example, an AI system detects a potential conflict between new code and a legacy system's database structure. It automatically flags the release as high-risk and suggests additional testing or postponement until the issue is resolved.

Mechanism and Process:

1. **Risk Identification**: AI systems scan code changes, dependency trees, and historical incident data to identify potential risks.

2. **Risk Assessment**: Machine learning models evaluate the severity and likelihood of identified risks, categorizing them into high, medium, or low risk.

3. **Mitigation Recommendations**: Based on risk assessment, AI provides recommendations for mitigating risks, such as additional testing or phased rollouts.

4. **Continuous Monitoring**: AI continuously monitors the release environment for new risks and adjusts mitigation strategies as needed.

Inaccurate or incomplete risk models can either miss critical issues or overestimate risks, causing unnecessary delays. Continuous refinement of AI models is necessary to improve accuracy:

- **Complex Dependencies**: Analyzing complex interdependencies and integrations can be challenging.

- **Dynamic Environments**: Risks can evolve rapidly, requiring continuous monitoring and adaptation.

Impact:

- **Reduced Release Failures:** By identifying high-risk areas early in the process, failures are reduced.

- **More Efficient Resource Allocation:** Teams can prioritize testing efforts on risky components.

- **Enhanced Risk Management:** AI helps identify and mitigate risks early, reducing the likelihood of release failures.

- **Efficient Resource Allocation:** Focuses testing and mitigation efforts on high-risk areas, optimizing resource usage.

AI-Based Monitoring for Real-Time Release Adjustments

Once a release is in progress, AI continuously monitors system performance, user behavior, and error rates. Based on predefined thresholds or anomaly detection models, AI can dynamically adjust the release (e.g., pause, rollback, or proceed with the release) in real-time.

For example, during a mobile app update rollout, AI can detect a spike in crash reports for a specific device model. It can then pause the release for that device while continuing to roll out the update to other users. The issue can be fixed before re-enabling the release to the affected users.

One of the key challenges for AI models during real-time monitoring is that they require robust data pipelines and real-time analytics capabilities, which can be difficult to implement in environments with fragmented or siloed data sources.

Impact:

- **Improved Release Stability:** Adjusting rollouts based on real-time performance data makes the releases more stable.

- **Reduced User Impact:** Potential issues are identified and resolved during the release.

Continuous Learning and Adaptive Release Cycles

Continuous learning involves AI systems that evolve and improve over time by learning from each release. Adaptive release cycles leverage AI's ability to continuously learn and adjust strategies based on real-time data and feedback.

Mechanism and Process:

1. **Data Collection**: AI collects data from each release, including performance metrics, user feedback, and incident reports.

2. **Model Update**: Machine learning models are continuously updated with new data, allowing them to adapt and improve their predictions and recommendations.

3. **Adaptive Strategies**: Based on learned patterns, AI adjusts release strategies, such as updating rollout schedules or modifying risk management practices.

4. **Feedback Loop**: The system incorporates feedback from post-release analyses to refine its models and recommendations.

For example, an online marketplace uses AI to analyze performance data from each release. The system learns that releases with extensive UI changes tend to have higher error rates. Based on this, the AI tool recommends a more cautious rollout approach for future UI updates, incorporating additional testing phases.

It is very complex to manage and process large volumes of data from multiple releases and AI models may experience drift, where their performance degrades over time if it's not properly maintained.

Impact:

- **Improved Release Strategies**: Adaptive strategies based on continuous learning led to more effective release management.

- **Enhanced Decision-Making**: Provides teams with up-to-date insights and recommendations for optimizing release cycles.

AI mechanisms in release management significantly enhance the ability to manage complex release processes with precision and efficiency. From predictive modeling and risk management to intelligent automation and continuous learning, AI brings valuable capabilities that help in optimizing release cycles, minimizing risks, and improving overall stability. By integrating these AI-driven approaches, organizations can achieve more reliable and Agile release management, leading to better software quality and enhanced user experiences.

Tools Currently Focused on Release Management

Table 8-1 provides an overview of the popular tools used in release management.

Table 8-1. Release Management Tools and their Features

Feature	LaunchDarkly	Harness	Spinnaker	Azure DevOps	GitLab	Plutora
Feature flagging	Yes	Yes	Yes	Yes	Yes	Yes
Predictive analytics	Limited	Limited	Basic	Advanced	Advanced	Advanced
Risk assessment	Basic	Advanced	Basic	Advanced	Basic	Advanced
Automated rollbacks	Basic	Advanced	Basic	Basic	Basic	Advanced
Resource allocation	No	Yes	No	Yes	Yes	Yes
Multi-cloud support	No	Yes	Yes	No	No	No
CI/CD integration	Yes	Yes	Yes	Yes	Yes	Yes
Real-time monitoring	Yes	Yes	Yes	Yes	Yes	Yes
AI-driven recommendations	Basic	Advanced	Basic	Advanced	Advanced	Advanced
Automated testing	No	Yes	No	Yes	Yes	No
Anomaly detection	No	Yes	Basic	Yes	Yes	Advanced
Continuous learning	No	No	No	Yes	Yes	Yes

AI-Driven Infrastructure Management

In modern infrastructure, test environments allow teams to validate features, functionality, security, and performance in a controlled setting before deploying to production environments. Production environments, on the other hand, represent the live system, hosting real user interactions with high availability, security, and scalability requirements. The complexity of managing these environments has grown exponentially with the adoption of cloud, microservices, and container-based architectures.

Key Components of Test and Production Environments

The following are the key components from an environment perspective:

- **Infrastructure:** Compute, storage, and network resources provisioned via AWS, Azure, or Google Cloud, Private Cloud, or Data Center

- **Networking:** Virtual private clouds (VPCs), subnets, and peering to replicate production-level networking

- **Security Layers:** Firewalls, identity, and access management (IAM), and encryption across all environments

- **Monitoring and Logging:** Centralized monitoring systems and log aggregators like Datadog and ELK Stack

Traditional Environment Management Challenges

Before AI, managing environments was a highly manual, error-prone process. The following sections cover some of the common challenges.

Complexity in Environment Setup

Traditional environment setups are complex and vary depending on the system's scale and architecture. Cloud-native applications are especially complicated due to their reliance on microservices, containers, and orchestrators like Kubernetes.

Configuration Drift

Inconsistent configuration between environments (test vs. production) is a significant cause of deployment failures. Even small discrepancies—like differences in database versions or network configurations—can cause applications to behave unexpectedly once they move to production.

Infrastructure automation tools like HashiCorp Consul and Puppet ensure that configurations remain consistent across environments, reducing such risks.

Tools for Solving Configuration Challenges

- **Puppet:** Automates infrastructure configurations and manages drift by ensuring environments remain consistent.

- **Chef Automate:** Provides automated configuration management and detailed monitoring.

Challenges

- **Integration:** Integrating configuration management tools with existing infrastructure can take time, requiring a full audit of current configurations.

- **Ongoing Monitoring:** Even with AI tools, monitoring for configuration drift must be continuous to ensure reliability across environments.

AI Technologies Enhancing Test and Production Environments

There are multiple use cases and tools currently where AI is in play across infrastructure management. This section lists 20+ use cases with the associated tools or platforms currently in use across the industry. These use cases cover key infrastructure components such as environment provisioning, network, security, access, database, and others.

Figure 8-5 summarizes all these use cases.

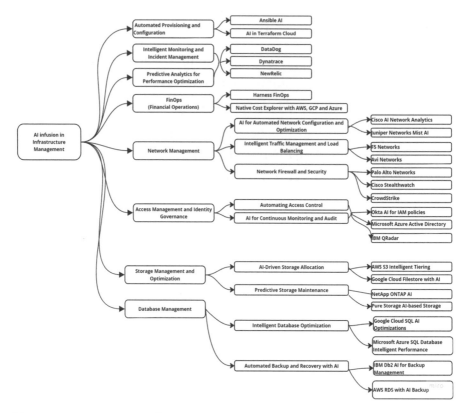

Figure 8-5. *Use cases for AI in infrastructure management*

The following sections dive deep into each infrastructure area and look at use cases, tools, challenges that I have come across as part of AI infusion in infrastructure management.

AI-Driven Automated Provisioning and Configuration

Automated provisioning removes the need for manual setup and human error, which can delay projects and introduce bugs into production. AI-driven tools provision environments on-demand, automatically adjusting configurations, scaling resources, and applying security policies.

Use Case

A large enterprise undergoing cloud migration used Terraform Cloud + AWS to automate their entire infrastructure setup. With AI-enabled tools like Ansible AI, they could spin up cloud infrastructure for testing in minutes instead of hours, with configurations that exactly mirrored production.

Tools and Technologies

- **Terraform Cloud:** Provides Infrastructure as Code (IaC) solutions that automatically provision environments.

- **Ansible AI:** Enhances configuration management and infrastructure setup with AI-driven insights and automations. See Figure 8-6.

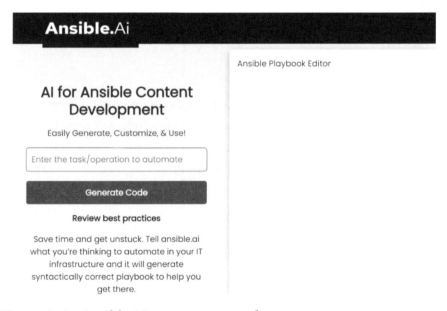

Figure 8-6. *Ansible AI can generate code*

Challenges

- **Complexity of Hybrid Environments:** Many companies have hybrid cloud environments with both on-premise and cloud systems. Automating setup across hybrid environments adds complexity, especially when integrating legacy systems.

- **Cost Management:** Automating environment creation can lead to over-provisioning if AI tools are not calibrated correctly, thus increasing cloud costs unnecessarily.

Intelligent Monitoring and Incident Management

Real-time monitoring tools powered by AI not only detect anomalies but also recommend or enact solutions before they become production issues. AI-driven monitoring tools learn normal behavior patterns from logs and metrics to predict potential problems.

Use Case

A financial institution adopted Splunk's AI for IT operations to monitor real-time metrics and logs. When an unusual pattern in API response times was detected, the system automatically suggested scaling the backend server capacity, preventing downtime during a critical financial reporting period.

Tools and Technologies

- **Splunk AI:** Delivers AI-driven insights from logs and metrics, identifying anomalies and predicting incidents.

- **Datadog:** Uses AI to provide full-stack observability, automatically detecting issues in cloud infrastructure.

Challenges

- **False Positives:** AI-driven monitoring systems need to be fine-tuned to avoid alert fatigue, when too many false positives overwhelm the operations team.

- **Data Complexity:** Large-scale applications generate massive amounts of data, making it difficult to train AI systems effectively without powerful computing resources.

Predictive Analytics for Performance Optimization

AI's predictive analytics capabilities enable infrastructure managers to foresee system bottlenecks or failures and optimize resources in advance. This is especially useful in production environments where downtime or slow performance can directly impact users.

Use Case

An e-commerce platform noticed consistent traffic surges during promotions. Using New Relic AI, it predicted and scaled the infrastructure based on expected user load. This proactive scaling prevented server slowdowns, ensuring a seamless shopping experience.

Tools and Technologies

- **New Relic AI:** Provides predictive analytics and resource optimization based on historical performance and traffic patterns.

- **Dynatrace:** Offers AI-powered insights for preemptively scaling cloud infrastructure to meet traffic demands.

Challenges

- **Data Volume:** Predictive analytics require massive amounts of data. Systems without adequate logging and monitoring can struggle to provide enough input to train AI algorithms.

- **Cost Optimization:** Scaling proactively based on predictive analytics can inadvertently increase costs if not carefully monitored.

AI in FinOps (Financial Operations)

Using AI in FinOps (Financial Operations) is crucial for managing and optimizing cloud expenditures, especially in large-scale and dynamic environments. Harnessing AI for FinOps allows organizations to gain real-time insights, automate cost management, and improve budget forecasting. The following sections take a detailed look into how AI is transforming FinOps, with a focus on tools and real-world applications, including the role of Harness FinOps.

AI-Driven Cost Optimization

Cloud environments often suffer from inefficiencies due to over-provisioning or underutilization of resources. AI-driven cost optimization tools analyze usage patterns, predict resource needs, and automatically adjust infrastructure to minimize costs while maintaining performance.

Use Case

A technology firm used Harness FinOps, an AI-powered cost management tool, to automatically optimize cloud resource usage. By identifying underutilized instances and suggesting optimal resource allocation, the firm was able to reduce its cloud spending by 28 percent.

Tools and Technologies

- **Harness FinOps:** Provides real-time cost visibility, optimization recommendations, and automated resource adjustments across multi-cloud environments. The tool uses AI to analyze spending patterns and suggest cost-saving actions.

- **CloudHealth by VMware:** AI-driven insights into cloud usage, providing actionable recommendations for cost savings.

- **AWS Cost Explorer (AI-powered):** Offers predictive analytics to help customers optimize cloud costs based on usage patterns.

Challenges

- **Balancing Cost and Performance:** While AI-driven optimizations can reduce costs, they must be carefully managed to ensure they do not negatively impact performance or user experience.

- **AI Model Training:** Ensuring the AI model is trained on accurate and comprehensive data is crucial for providing reliable cost optimization recommendations.

AI in Network Management

AI for Automated Network Configuration and Optimization

AI helps network administrators automatically configure and optimize network settings. By analyzing network traffic patterns, AI systems adjust configurations to ensure optimal performance, reducing latency and improving throughput.

Use Case

A global financial institution implemented Cisco AI-enhanced network management, which automatically adjusted routing policies based on real-time traffic patterns. This resulted in a 20 percent increase in network performance during trading hours.

Tools and Technologies

- **Cisco AI Network Analytics:** Uses AI to optimize routing, detect network issues, and adjust network configurations automatically.

- **Juniper Networks Mist AI:** Provides AI-driven network management, automatically optimizing configurations to enhance performance.

Challenges

- **Complex Network Topologies:** Managing and optimizing large, hybrid networks can be challenging for AI systems, especially when dealing with legacy infrastructure.

- **Security Considerations:** Automated network changes must be carefully managed to avoid opening new vulnerabilities or disrupting existing security policies.

Intelligent Traffic Management and Load Balancing

AI-driven tools help manage network traffic by automatically optimizing routes and balancing loads across servers. This ensures smooth performance, especially during peak traffic periods.

Use Case

A global SaaS provider faced intermittent performance issues due to traffic spikes across regions. By integrating F5 Networks AI-based load balancing, the platform automatically routed traffic to the most responsive servers, significantly improving user experience.

Tools and Technologies

- **F5 Networks:** Provides AI-powered load balancing to optimize traffic management.

- **Avi Networks (VMware NSX Advanced Load Balancer):** Offers AI-based traffic routing and load balancing for dynamic traffic flows.

Challenges

- **Latency in Dynamic Networks:** AI-powered traffic routing can struggle with real-time latency issues, especially in geographically dispersed networks. This requires continuous monitoring and optimization to avoid performance degradation.

- **Network Security:** Network-level AI tools must integrate security policies to ensure malicious traffic does not get routed to sensitive parts of the infrastructure.

AI for Network Security

Network security is another area where AI shines, particularly in threat detection and response. AI-driven tools can analyze traffic patterns and detect anomalies that may indicate malicious activity, providing real-time threat responses.

Use Case

A retail company faced constant cyberthreats targeting its network infrastructure. Using Palo Alto Networks' AI security tools, the company detected malicious traffic signatures before they could breach firewalls, reducing security incidents by 50 percent.

Tools and Technologies:

- **Palo Alto Networks:** Offers AI-powered threat detection and response for enterprise networks.

- **Cisco Stealthwatch:** Uses AI to detect abnormal network traffic and security breaches in real-time.

Challenges

- **False Positives:** AI-based security systems need to avoid generating too many false positives, which can overwhelm security teams and reduce effectiveness.

- **Real-Time Threat Response:** AI systems need to operate in real-time, which requires high-performance computing resources, especially for large-scale, distributed networks.

AI in Firewall and Security Management

AI-Driven Threat Detection and Automated Security Responses

Firewalls are the first line of defense in any network, and AI has enhanced their capabilities by automating threat detection and response. AI-driven firewalls can analyze traffic for malicious patterns, automatically blocking or rerouting traffic when threats are detected.

Use Case

A healthcare provider using CrowdStrike's AI-driven firewall saw a 60 percent reduction in potential data breaches by blocking malicious traffic at the firewall level before it could reach sensitive internal systems.

Tools and Technologies

- **CrowdStrike:** Offers AI-driven firewall capabilities for threat detection and blocking.

- **Fortinet FortiGate with AI:** Provides AI-powered threat intelligence and firewall management.

Challenges

- **False Positives and Negatives:** Just like with network security, AI-based firewalls must strike a balance between detecting real threats and avoiding false positives.

- **Security Policy Complexity:** AI tools must integrate seamlessly with an organization's security policies and ensure they are enforced across distributed environments.

AI in Access Management and Identity Governance

Automating Access Control

Access management is critical in test and production environments, particularly when handling sensitive data. AI enhances identity and access management (IAM) by automating access controls, thereby ensuring the right people have the right access at the right time.

Use Case

A financial institution implemented Okta's AI-driven IAM to automatically manage user permissions. When users changed roles or left the company, AI-based workflows adjusted their access automatically, reducing the risk of insider threats.

Tools and Technologies

- **Okta Identity Governance:** Automates access management based on user roles and behaviors.

- **IBM Cloud Identity with AI:** Uses AI to dynamically adjust access permissions based on user behavior and compliance requirements.

Challenges

- **Balancing Security and Usability:** Striking the right balance between restrictive access control and user convenience is difficult. Too much automation can inconvenience users if access is denied incorrectly.

- **Managing Legacy Systems:** Integrating AI-driven IAM solutions with older, legacy systems can be complex, as many legacy platforms do not support AI-based interfaces out-of-the-box.

AI for Continuous Monitoring and Audit

AI can continuously monitor access to resources, automatically flagging suspicious activity or violations of security policies. This reduces the need for manual audits and helps teams identify potential risks faster.

Use Case

A healthcare provider utilized IBM QRadar to monitor access to sensitive patient data. AI flagged suspicious access attempts outside business hours, which allowed the security team to prevent a potential breach.

Tools and Technologies

- **Microsoft Azure Active Directory Identity Protection:** Leverages AI to detect suspicious login attempts and other access anomalies.

- **IBM QRadar:** Uses AI to detect and flag access control violations in real-time.

Challenges

- **False Positives:** AI systems often generate false positives, which can overwhelm security teams if they are not tuned properly.

- **Scalability:** Monitoring large, distributed environments can generate a lot of data, and AI systems must be able to scale to handle real-time analysis of this information.

AI in Storage Management and Optimization

AI-Driven Storage Allocation

AI optimizes storage allocation by analyzing usage patterns and automatically redistributing storage resources to areas with the most demand. This ensures that production environments remain performant even as storage needs fluctuate.

Use Case

A logistics company used AWS S3 Intelligent Tiering to automatically move infrequently accessed data to cheaper storage classes. This reduced storage costs by 25 percent without sacrificing performance.

Tools and Technologies

- **AWS S3 Intelligent Tiering:** Automatically moves data between storage classes based on access patterns.

- **Google Cloud Filestore with AI:** Uses AI to optimize file storage performance and costs.

Challenges

- **Data Security:** As AI systems move data between storage tiers, security and compliance must be maintained, particularly when handling sensitive or regulated data.

- **Balancing Cost and Performance:** AI-driven storage systems must strike a balance between reducing storage costs and ensuring that data is available when needed.

Predictive Storage Maintenance

AI can predict when storage hardware (in on-prem environments) or cloud storage services will fail or degrade, allowing for proactive maintenance and resource reallocation.

Use Case

An enterprise using NetApp ONTAP AI predicted impending storage failures based on performance telemetry, which allowed them to move critical data to healthy storage nodes before failure occurred.

Tools and Technologies

- **NetApp ONTAP AI:** Provides predictive maintenance capabilities for enterprise storage systems.

- **Pure Storage AI-based Storage Management:** Optimizes storage performance and lifecycle through AI analytics.

Challenges

- **Data Integrity:** During predictive maintenance, data must be carefully managed to ensure integrity and prevent loss during migrations.

- **Interruption-Free Maintenance:** Performing maintenance without interrupting services or impacting performance requires advanced AI models and orchestrated workflows.

AI for Database Management

Intelligent Database Optimization

AI improves database performance by continuously analyzing query performance, indexing strategies, and data distribution. AI-powered tools can automatically apply optimizations like indexing and partitioning to improve performance.

Use Case

A fintech company utilized Google Cloud SQL with AI enhancements to analyze database query performance and automatically optimize indexing for common queries. This reduced query times by 40 percent in production.

Tools and Technologies

- **Google Cloud SQL AI Optimizations:** Provides AI-driven query analysis and indexing.

- **Microsoft Azure SQL Database Intelligent Performance:** Uses AI to automatically optimize database performance.

Challenges

- **Complex Query Patterns:** Complex, ad hoc query patterns can be challenging for AI systems to analyze and optimize in real-time, especially for large, distributed databases.

- **Tuning AI Models:** AI-driven database optimization tools need to be carefully tuned to avoid making too many unnecessary changes that could disrupt normal operations.

Automated Backup and Recovery with AI

AI-powered systems can automate database backups and ensure faster, more reliable recovery in case of a failure. By analyzing data access patterns, AI can determine the optimal backup schedule and retention policies.

Use Case

An insurance company used IBM Db2 AI to automate backup and recovery, reducing manual interventions and ensuring faster recovery times after a database crash.

Tools and Technologies

- **IBM Db2 AI for Backup Management:** Automates backup scheduling and recovery processes based on data usage and risk factors.

- **AWS RDS with AI Backup:** Automates backup, retention, and recovery for relational databases.

Challenges

- **Data Volume:** Managing backups for large-scale databases, especially in distributed environments, requires advanced AI models capable of handling massive datasets.

- **Data Restoration Speed:** AI systems need to ensure that recovery times meet service level agreements (SLAs), which can be challenging for large or complex databases.

Future Trends in AI-Driven Infrastructure Management

1. **Increased Integration of AI Across Hybrid and Multi-Cloud Environments:** As hybrid and multi-cloud strategies become more prevalent, AI tools will evolve to provide seamless management across different cloud platforms, optimizing resource allocation, cost management, and security across diverse environments.

2. **Advanced AI for Predictive Analytics and Proactive Management:** Future AI systems will focus more on predictive analytics, enabling proactive management of infrastructure. This includes predicting hardware failures, optimizing maintenance schedules, and preemptively scaling resources based on advanced usage forecasts.

3. **AI-Driven Automation in DevOps:** AI will play a crucial role in enhancing DevOps practices by automating code deployment, continuous integration, and monitoring processes, leading to faster and more reliable software development cycles.

4. **Enhanced Security Through AI-Powered Threat Detection:** AI-driven security tools will become more sophisticated, leveraging machine learning to detect and mitigate increasingly complex threats in real-time. This will include automated responses to potential breaches and the dynamic adjustment of security policies.

5. **AI-Powered Sustainability and Cost Efficiency:** As organizations focus more on sustainability, AI tools will optimize infrastructure management to reduce energy consumption and minimize carbon footprints, aligning with global sustainability goals.

6. **Ethical AI and Compliance in Infrastructure Management:** The future will see a stronger emphasis on ethical AI, ensuring that AI-driven infrastructure management tools comply with privacy laws, data protection regulations, and ethical standards.

AI's role in infrastructure management is set to grow, driving efficiency, cost savings, and innovation across all aspects of IT operations. Organizations that leverage AI in infrastructure management will be better positioned to handle the complexities of modern IT environments and remain competitive in a rapidly evolving digital landscape. The next chapter looks at how AI can be infused in the operations, reliability, capacity, and availability elements (aka SRE) found in the application landscape.

Summary

This chapter focused on continuous delivery—deployment, release, and infrastructure management. This is one of the critical phases of SDLC, as it crosses a bridge from development to production, and anomalies and mishaps at this stage can result in service outage.

This chapter covered many use cases and tools, but they are essentially the tip of the iceberg. Every use case is a project of its own and the objective of sharing the use cases is to show what is possible.

CHAPTER 9

Operations, Observability, and Site Reliability Engineering

Innovating and developing new features and applications determines how organizations fare in the marketplace. The ones that continue to grow continue to innovate. That is just one half of the story. For organizations to truly sustain growth, to continue earning their customers' trust, to keep the lights on, there is much more that needs to be done. That *more* is the operations process, which is often put on the backburner. In reality, operations is the most critical cog in the wheel. It helps organizations grow and not worry about maintaining what they've already built.

Operations runs hand in hand with observability—aka, monitoring. Operations becomes effective through monitoring the critical paths of an organization's delivery to their customers, their critical development engines, and all other bits and pieces that keep it all together. The operation-focused site reliability engineering (SRE) framework works on the principle of automation, self-healing, and prevention.

© Abhinav Krishna and Vamshidhar Meda 2024
A. Krishna and V. Meda, *AI Integration in Software Development and Operations*,
https://doi.org/10.1007/979-8-8688-1044-2_9

These areas of operation, when used with AI, are instant winners. They help organizations focus on innovation while AI can maintain the status quo. This chapter is all about infusing AI into the world of operations—specifically into the SRE framework.

The Operations Quagmire

Operations is a broad topic. Every area of study has its own set of operations to manage. For example, a business needs to be managed through business operations, a store needs its own set of operations, and IT operations have their own set of processes and guidelines. For example, a store's operation involves supply chain processes, ensuring that the aisles are filled with designated products, the products are accurately represented on the billing software, and the billing matches the sales, which should match the products missing from the shelves. Likewise, business operations for a bank revolves around banking disciplines. The scope of each operational discipline varies. However, the common thread is that operations keeps the business running and ensures that there is foundational support for growth. Customers' point of contact is generally the operational teams. The performance of the operations will reflect on the organization. Therefore, it is even more critical that operational processes be tightened and given due focus. This chapter refers to IT operations simply as operations.

Operations is challenging. You never know from which side things are going to start going south. You never know if a new government policy will shake the operational process. You never know if a knock-on effect will paralyze operations and require a major reboot. Operations has a lot of dependencies, and any of these dependencies can affect it at the most unexpected times. This also provides an opportunity to build an operations system that's flexible, that can pivot on a moment's notice, and that can serve the business needs. Operations is therefore fun, in the spotlight, and challenging—all at the same time.

When an organization finds itself in financial trouble, the first casualty is the operations department. The rationale is that operations maintains the status quo and, if done effectively, it can be done with fewer resources and lower costs. Innovation and development require dedicated people, so those areas aren't cut until things take a more dire turn.

Finding the right talent for operations is a difficult task. These people troubleshoot, maintain, and fix problems, and it is not the most sought-after role in the job market. Working with people who are not the best can lead to its own set of challenges—operations can be compromised and downtime can increase, which can lead to a host of other collateral implications.

With remote working and increased threats from cyber-attackers, work environments have been hardened. Accessing environments has become a circuitous process with multi-factor authentication and plenty of checks and balances to ensure that those logged in are human and employees. All this adds to the complexity and gets in the way of efficient operations.

Operations is considered a reactive process where teams react to incidents, fix problems, and try to put out fires. Although this is mostly the case, there is more to it than meets the eye. Operations can be proactive and practice good problem management—identifying and implementing preventive fixes and building automation and self-healing measures. When there are innovative ideas, operations can be as interesting as the developmental process itself.

Site Reliability Engineering

DevOps is development plus operations, and yet the focus is mostly on the development side of activities. If you observe the processes closely, the operation in DevOps looks through the lens of development. Developers either double up to do operations or dedicated operational folks handle incidents and maintenance fixes.

Now flip the switch and shift the focus toward operations. Look at development through the lens of operations. The focus is then on operational tasks at the center while developing new features. Enter Site Reliability Engineering (SRE). SRE is a methodology that focuses on attaining production stabilization to begin with, before embarking on developing and rolling out new features.

SRE is the brainchild of Google. It dates back to 2003 when their senior vice president, Ben Treynor, who was leading technical operations, was tasked with creating integrated teams. The main objectives of SRE at the time of conception were to use engineering with a software development background to do operations work and to automate everything through these smart engineers. According to Ben, SRE is what happens when you ask a software engineer to design an operations team.

SRE focuses on creating scalable and highly reliable software systems. It blends principles from software engineering and applies them to infrastructure and operations problems. Like DevOps, the primary goal of SRE is to bridge the gap between development and operations, ensuring that software systems are not only functional but also reliable, available, and efficient in a production environment.

SRE is a fast-growing practice across organizations. According to Gartner, around 10 percent of organizations have implemented some form or shape of SRE. This number is expected to grow rapidly, to 75 percent, by 2027. Organizations are seeing the value of optimizing their design, cost, and operations while satisfying their customers.

Considering SRE versus DevOps, the question isn't about which one to choose, but rather how to integrate the two to get the best of both worlds. While DevOps is strong on the development processes, focusing on rapid development and faster releases, SRE focuses on operations, stabilization, and scalability of the production systems. Underlying them is the common objective of automating whatever is possible and ensuring that the customers' objectives become the North Star for the rest of the activities to follow. The culture behind DevOps and SRE couldn't be more similar—both methodologies insist on building a blameless culture that revolves around looking at problems objectively, learning from failures, and encouraging collaboration, transparency, and continuous improvement.

How SRE Works?

DevOps embeds Agile processes and the roles that it carries become an inherent part of DevOps—such as product owner, scrum master, and Agile team members. Apart from this, DevOps engineers and architects are responsible for putting together the solution and implementing the DevOps architecture—continuous integration, continuous delivery, and continuous deployment. Likewise, on the SRE end, a site reliability engineer is a developer who does operations. The expectation is that they will keep the product stable, reliable, and scalable. In comparison, the DevOps engineer and site reliability engineer's roles are similar, but the latter comes with a background in software development, which is an added advantage to stabilize the product. Both roles are expected to be adept at tool configuration, integration, and automation.

Focusing on work areas, SRE relies on operations being managed on the back of principles, as shown in Figure 9-1.

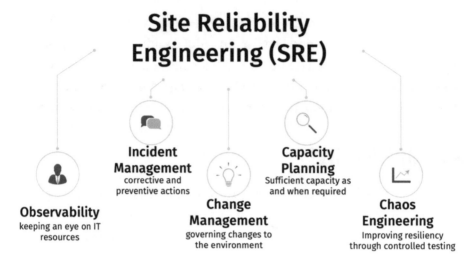

Figure 9-1. *SRE principles*

The Role of AI in SRE

IT is rapidly moving toward employing AI, and that includes SRE. In fact, the SRE role has become prominent given the technological advancements in the AI field. SRE practices of software engineering and operations have become enriched by AI.

What makes AI a formidable ally is the vast amounts of data generated daily. The underlying message from the data is deciphered by the AI tool, and technologies such as predictive analytics are capable of automating tasks that result from pattern recognition. AI can identify potential incidents and even resolve them, leading to decreased downtime and an increased customer satisfaction. Through auto-scaling and efficient resource distribution, optimal performance can be achieved.

AI can be of immense value in incident and problem management areas. Through machine learning, AI can understand what "normal" looks like, and any anomaly that causes downtime/incidents can be automatically resolved by AI. This self-healing capability can potentially be a gamechanger. It prevents delays due to the time humans would need to react, analyze, and execute. All of this can be carried out in one quick swoop.

By thoroughly analyzing incidents, logs, and other pertinent data, AI can help identify the root cause of incidents and recommend permanent solutions to prevent future incidents. The analytical powers of AI can accurately pinpoint root causes. This prevents the potential lost time for users, which can be expensive depending on the type of business.

On the cloud, the auto-scaling and descaling features are triggered based on factors such as utilization, sessions, and so on. Although this scaling happens proactively, it is reactive in nature, where certain thresholds must be met for certain actions to take place. With AI, the resource allocation is done based on analysis of historical data, usage trends, and environmental conditions. This ensures the right provisioning of resources, leading to reduction in operational costs and ensuring that the performance parameters stay green.

Observability

Observability is a relatively new concept. It's a step or two more advanced than event management and monitoring. Observability is the capability that allows developers to understand the state or health of a system. This is done by obtaining data from logs, metrics, and traces and making sense of that information.

With the cloud, there is no set boundary to measure since the embedded resources (microservices, serverless functions, databases, etc.) are distributed across geographies and are dynamic. This has led to a complex structure where system errors can lead developers down a rabbit hole, and finding the smoking gun could be more challenging than finding water on the moon.

The logs, metrics, and traces are considered the three pillars of observability, and when they are used in conjunction other and with a contextual view, it is possible to obtain a comprehensive view of what is happening inside the system.

Monitoring vs. Observability

Monitoring is basic. Monitoring is old school. Monitoring should have been retired. It is still around because organizations have not upgraded to the latest kid on the block—observability.

Monitoring tools measure systems with the intent of flagging anomalies. The goal is to alert developers when a system behaves abnormally. The entire monitoring process can be defined in four steps:

1. Identify what needs to be monitored.

2. Set the thresholds.

3. Start measuring.

4. Send an alert when the thresholds are breached.

There is no intelligence or reasoning behind the threshold breach and there is absolutely no way to prevent it. It is like the judges on the *Masterchef* show, who tell you only if your food is good or not, and not how to make it better.

Observability addresses these shortcomings. It can do everything—starting by mimicking Simon Sinek (asking *why*). The same set of logs that tells developers that a threshold has been breached also gives them a peek into what caused it. Observability digs deep to not only find out why but also to ensure that it doesn't recur.

The limitation with monitoring is because there is a set scope. The system, its metrics, and its follow-up actions define its scope. Whereas observability is like a startup organization, where everybody does everything. There is no predefined scope, so basically observability can check various systems and processes—to find the smoking gun and to stop these issues from happening again.

A typical use-case with observability tools, such as distributed tracing systems, is one that allows developers to follow the path of a request through a complex microservices architecture. They can see where delays are occurring, how services are interacting, and where the potential bottlenecks might be.

Observability and AIOps

AIOps stands for *Artificial Intelligence in IT Operations*. It is a term coined by Gartner, and in its nascent stages, it was heralded as the next big thing. But over time, especially after observability came into the mainstream, AIOps has faded away.

The goal of AIOps is to simplify operations through the employment of AI, and to rapidly resolve incidents through predictive data analytics. The primary approach was to collect and integrate vast amounts of data from various sources, including logs, metrics, events, and traces. Humongous volumes of data are bound to be tricky for humans to decipher, but for a well-trained AI, they are child's play. The other anticipated capabilities were to identify the root cause of incidents as a preventive measure against downtime ,thus enabling automation and boosting management information systems (MIS).

The industry started to incorporate AIOps, with Moogsoft and Big Panda leading the way. Their intent was to feed all the logs, metrics, and other available monitoring information into these products and have them sift through the rubble to find the gold dust—the events that require attention and the potential set of follow-up actions. This plan failed, as these tools did not live up to their expectations. The ingested data was not sufficient to determine such problems. Slowly, the world of AIOps started to lose its charm.

Then came other tools—such as AppDynamics, Splunk, Dynatrace, and Datadog—whose platforms were branded under the observability banner. Their data collection could tell the story, which allowed them to get insight into problems and the potential risks. These observability tools outperformed the AIOps tools, so these days, the industry chatter centers on observability more than on AIOps.

While AIOps may not find feet today, I wouldn't count it out. In IT, especially with AI, what goes out often comes back in another shape or form. Frankly, IT operations at some stage in the future will primarily be run by AI. Whether we call it observability or a new name, essentially it will be AI in IT operations.

The Role of AI in Observability

AI greatly enhances observability capabilities by improving the ability to monitor, analyze, and understand the behavior of complex systems in real-time. Before AI, this involved manual data aggregation, and analysis of logs, metrics, and traces to gain insights into system performance and health. This was time consuming, and perhaps not accurate, owing to human shortcomings. This task is getting more complex, and AI has been leading the way by automating data analysis, detecting anomalies, predicting potential issues, and providing actionable insights that help maintain system reliability and performance.

The following sections look at some areas of observability where AI tools have made a significant impact.

Unified View

AI tools generate data in their respective formats. There are AI tools, such as Datadog, that can integrate into existing observability platforms to provide a unified view of system operations. The AI unification tool carries out real-time extract transform load (ETL) activities to bring all the relevant data in one place, with AI-driven insights that help elucidate the broader context of system behavior.

The Datadog tool is capable of integrating with the majority of the tools in the market. In a single pane view, customers, operation teams, and other stakeholders can get a unified view of the health of systems—allowing them to visualize and troubleshoot efficiently. This is represented in Figure 9-2.

Figure 9-2. *Datadog integrations (Credit:* `https://datadog.com`)

Dynatrace's AI engine, Davis, is another popular tool that can automatically correlate data across the entire tech stack—applications, infrastructure, and user experience—providing a unified view of operations. It brings together metrics, logs, and traces into a single unified interface, allowing teams to monitor and analyze their entire ecosystem without switching between multiple tools. Figure 9-3 shows a dashboard that incorporates various workloads.

Figure 9-3. Dynatrace Davis AI dashboard (Credit: https://www. dynatrace.com/platform/application-observability/)

Anomaly Detection

Detecting anomalies is an art. To begin, the normal expectations need to be well understood. AI tools have become experts in anomaly detection, with the majority of the tools capable of detecting anomalies quite effectively.

AppDynamics, the popular observability tool that specializes in application performance monitoring, employs AI to predict potential performance issues by analyzing data patterns. It helps identify potential problems before they affect end users.

The Anomaly Detection methodology in the AppDynamics document (https://docs.appdynamics.com/) states that it employs multiple techniques to ensure that the data gathered is clean and accurate.

- The AI tool disregards any temporary spikes and periods of no data

- It normalizes the metric data. For example, when
  determining the EPM metric data, spikes may not
  indicate a real problem unless there is a corresponding
  increase in Calls per Minute (CPM). EPM data may not
  be useful in itself, so anomaly detection uses error rate
  (EPM/CPM). Figure 9-4 indicates an anomaly detection
  pattern.

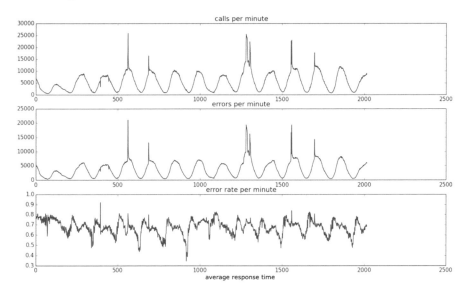

Figure 9-4. *Anomaly detection in AppDynamics (Credit:* `https://`
`docs.appdynamics.com/`*)*

Datadog is a multi-pronged, extremely capable observability platform.
It uses machine learning to automatically detect anomalies in metrics and
logs. It uses past data to predict what is expected in the future. This also
means that new implementations may not work accurately, as the data is
in its nascent stages in that case.

Elastic Observability and New Relic are two other notable AI tools
capable of accurately generating anomaly alerts.

Predictive Analytics

Using data as a reference model, developers can predict future trends and scenarios—which is the basis for decision making at the highest echelons of organizations. Multiple algorithms are employed, including regression analysis and neural networks.

Davis AI from Dynatrace not only detects anomalies in real-time but also uses machine learning to predict potential issues. It analyzes historical data and trends to forecast future performance problems, helping teams address issues proactively. The tool provides actionable insights into resource utilization, application performance, and potential outages, allowing for preemptive action.

Moogsoft's AIOps tool leverages predictive analytics to anticipate incidents before they occur, reducing downtime and improving operational efficiency. The tool uses Big Data analytics to supervise machine learning in real-time. This learning is integrated with the central knowledge database, and when a similar incident takes place, it is handled immediately.

Service Mapping

Service mapping was traditionally referred to as a configuration management database (CMDB). It is a visual representation of components and services and their dependencies. It covers the infrastructure, application, and service/product layers.

Think about a service map as a blueprint to your home. Based on the blueprint, you know the electrical and plumbing circuitry, the partitions, and so on. When something goes wrong, say there's a leak in the kitchen, you know how the pipes are connected and the direction of water flow. You can take corrective actions with the aid of the blueprint, and this is precisely what operation teams do during incidents or when changes needed to happen. The service map guides the engineer on diagnosing and troubleshooting, helps identify the impact during changes, and acts as a catalyst for improving performance.

In the past, when developers built a service map, the process was manual. They consulted with architects for architecture diagrams and drew the service map with it as a reference. The common challenges they encountered were that the architecture diagrams were not updated following a change, so the service map turned out to be incorrect. This further required developers to talk to the folks on the ground to understand the reality. In all, it was a cumbersome process, but once it was built, it was powerful and helped the incident, problem, change, and release processes.

With automation and AI, the world of service mapping has changed. Developers now have tools that can flow through the service components and identify the architecture automatically. Any change in the reference architecture is flagged by the tools, keeping the environment pristine from unauthorized changes.

Dynatrace Smartscape is one such tool that can automatically discover and map all the components in the environment, including applications, services, processes, hosts, and data centers. The service map is updated in real-time, reflecting the current state of your infrastructure and services. The tool provides a bird's eye view of the entire stack, ranging from user interactions at the application level to backend services, databases, and infrastructure components. This end-to-end visibility is crucial for understanding complex environments. Figure 9-5 shows the Dynatrace Smartscape tool's service visualization.

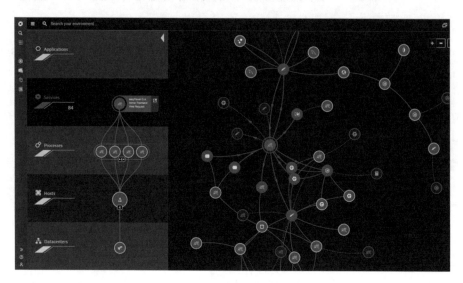

Figure 9-5. *Dynatrace Smartscape service map (Credit:* `https://` `www.dynatrace.com/platform/application-topology-discovery/` `smartscape/`*)*

Datadog is a powerful tool with service mapping. It automatically discovers services and their dependencies by analyzing traces, metrics, and logs. This reduces the manual effort needed to map complex environments. The service map is visually appealing and represents relationships between services, applications, and infrastructure. Similar to Smartscape, the service map in Datadog updates in real-time, reflecting any changes in the architecture or infrastructure. This is particularly useful in dynamic environments like microservices or cloud-native applications.

ServiceNow is an old warhorse that has been at the forefront of easing the pain of developing service maps. The CMDB module is capable of integrating either with its own Service Mapping module that automatically discovers and maps IT services by identifying the underlying infrastructure components (like servers, databases, and network devices), or it can be plugged into third-party tools such as Datadog and Dynatrace Smartscape. Figure 9-6 shows a service map on ServiceNow.

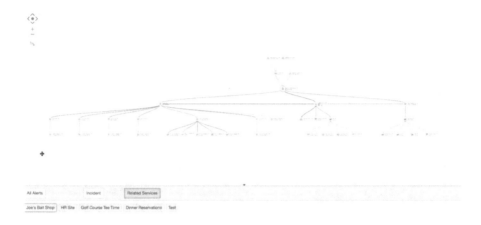

Figure 9-6. *ServiceNow's service map*

Incident Management

Incident management is a key process in operations which deals with the restoration of products and services. Products can be SaaS-based such as ServiceNow, Office 365, Salesforce, and MS Teams, or non-software products such as laptops, televisions, and sport utility vehicles. Examples of a service can be the Internet, electricity, and streaming platforms such as Netflix. Today, the gap between products and services is tightening as products are being offered as services.

Any deviation from the normal for a product or a service is an *incident*. Hereafter, I refer to products alone since they are more in line with the theme of this book. The incident management process' primary objective is to restore the product back to normalcy as quickly as possible—since time is money and every minute of downtime can lead to loss.

The nature of incident management is reactive. It is meant to come into play when a product breaks. It may be possible to detect the outage earlier and resolve the issue faster, and yet, this doesn't change its reactive nature. However, AI is changing the paradigm of operations by proactively identifying and resolving incidents before they happen, similar to the plot of *Minority Report*. where the police use a psychic technology to arrest and convict murderers before they commit the crime. Yes, purists would argue that it isn't incident management until there is a disruption, but with the transformation through AI, developers can see things through this different lens.

The Role of AI in Incident Management

When incident management was gaining popularity, it relied heavily on manual activities, where the incident detection was handled by users and the IT staff, and it was followed by diagnosis and resolution. This was fine when IT was limited to a handful of applications and a manageable number of servers and other infrastructure. However, as the scale and complexity of IT environments expanded, the manual activities proved to be inadequate, leading to longer response times, higher risks of human error, and increased operational costs. Then came the automation through the monitoring technologies. The resources of interest were monitored and when they failed the test of availability or capacity, this automatically flagged errors in the system. Then, integration built with IT service management ticketing tools such as ServiceNow and BMC Remedy automatically register incidents and assign them to the appropriate team. This is where automation stopped to this day, and the rest involved a manual approach as before.

AI is changing the paradigm of incident management and redefining the landscape, with new capabilities that considerably enrich the manner in which organizations handle unexpected disruptions. As digital infrastructures grow more complex and SaaS products boom, the need to integrate AI into an organization's fabric is pressing, especially given that teams that manage incidents are finding it ever more challenging.

Incident Prioritization

There was a time when developers created matrices for incident prioritization—the number of users, applications, geographies, and so on. The impact determined the priority of the incident. The service desk was trained to ask the right questions to prioritize the incident. While this was an important exercise to determine urgency, it took time. It led to an extension of the downtime. It was a beneficial monster. And today, some organizations still do this!

Other companies employ automation and AI to prioritize instantly. AI tools can determine the priority of the incident based on the impact and urgency. This is done using historical data and determining the resources and business that are impacted through various monitoring tools, configuration management (CMDB) relationships, and integrations.

ServiceNow is a popular IT service management ticketing platform. Its Predictive AIOps can assess incoming incidents by analyzing historical data and the incident's impact. It uses AI to predict the potential business impact of each incident and automatically prioritizes them based on urgency and severity. This ensures that critical issues are addressed first.

Self-Healing

The lifecycle of an incident is detection, diagnosis, and resolution. The diagnosis and resolution activities generally take time, and this usually represents downtime for the user. The downtime becomes longer when the engineer is held up with another incident or is unavailable when the incident is detected. When using people to solve such issues, timelines generally get longer.

AI can not only detect an incident but can diagnose and resolve it as well. AI can do this without delays and it's always available, which reduces the downtime considerably.

While there are many tools in the market that have self-healing capabilities, I want to mention a couple of tools specifically, starting with PagerDuty, which is a workhorse in this field. Developers can create runbooks for common incident scenarios, like executing scripts that address the issue without human intervention. The tool seamlessly integrates with the cloud, Ansible, Rundeck, and other automation platforms to execute custom actions when an incident occurs. These actions could include restarting services, scaling infrastructure, or performing other predefined remediation tasks.

For example, when the tool receives a trigger from a monitoring tool that a particular service is down, it can automatically trigger a runbook that not only restarts the service but also verifies its status, thus resolving the incident without human intervention. Or in response to a high CPU utilization alert from GCP Cloud Monitoring, PagerDuty can trigger an auto-scaling event through Cloud Functions to reduce the high CPU utilization. When the utilization subsides, it can trigger yet another event to scale down the serverless functions.

New Relic is another tool that is known for its self-healing prowess. The tool works in a similar fashion to PagerDuty, with runbooks. However, this tool can analyze incidents to find a pattern and eventually identify the root cause. Based on the root cause, New Relic can recommend permanent solutions. It leverages its machine learning algorithms to detect anomalies in real-time. These anomalies could be anything from intermittent spikes in utilization, to unexpected error rates, to resource consumption that deviates from normal patterns.

Root Cause Analysis

Incidents happen because something has gone wrong. The fundamental reason behind the incident is the root cause. Until the root cause of the incident is identified and a permanent solution is implemented, there is a possibility of the incident recurring.

In the traditional sense, root cause analysis (RCA) is the investigative activity carried out by engineers to identify the root cause and find a solution to address it permanently. This activity is really part of the problem management process, but developers tend to do things in parallel and dynamically, so they list it in the incident management process. Identifying the root cause is not easy or straightforward. It can happen over months and years, with little success. The elongated timeline and the impact beg for AI to take over.

With access to historical data, the architecture of the entire system and the capacity to analyze, AI is much better at dealing with the RCA process. AI tools use machine learning algorithms, correlation techniques, and data analytics to determine the root cause of incidents.

Every system collects data log. A tool such as IBM Watson AIOps reviews the operational data and leverages its AI and machine learning muscle to analyze and identify the root cause of incidents. It is capable of correlating incidents with specific changes, configurations, and other operational data. Another tool worthy of noting is AppDynamics, which is a monitoring tool. It uses AI to monitor the performance of applications and infrastructure. It correlates performance issues with specific root causes, such as code-level errors, resource bottlenecks, and external dependencies.

Change Management

Change management is the governance layer that ensures that only the changes approved by relevant stakeholders are placed into the production system. It is a gated approach to ensure that changes are introduced into the system in a systematic and controlled manner, and most importantly, done so with minimal risks.

Products that are in production continue to be in status quo until a change is introduced. If the change is successful, the products have better or new features. If the change goes south, then there is a possibility of instability, malperformance, and inefficiencies, which can lead to incidents. There was a time when the change management process was sacred to most organizations. Change advisory boards (CAB) governed all the changes, and the process was bureaucratic and time consuming. Although the process was beneficial to the end result, it made the entire process sequential, waterfall-ish, and slow.

While change management is still part of most organizations, some companies have diluted the process to provide an Agile boost, with the product owner handling deployment release. Progressive companies have created guiderails—such as a certain quality must be achieved to lead to production deployment—often through the continuous deployment process of CI/CD.

AI is a massive opportunity to marry the strong governance features and the required agility. Machines can do the analysis in the background to ensure that the decisions are made rapidly.

The Role of AI in Change Management

Since change management is a governance layer, it is expected to make decisions, a lot of them. These decisions are generally based on current and historical data points. What is the better than sifting through data and arriving at a decision than AI?

Risk Assessment

AI is best when it supports the change management process. Every change means risk, and that risk is based on the depth of the change, measured in terms of affected value streams, integrations, users, and financial implications, among others. AI can draw a picture of the risk profile of the change through predictive analytics, and based on the present and past data, it can pinpoint areas where additional focus is needed and highlight potential mitigation actions.

The Einstein Analytics tool can predict the success of change initiatives by analyzing historical data and identifying potential risks, enabling change managers to make informed decisions.

Digital.ai is another tool that can evaluate the potential impact of changes on different parts of the IT environment. It allows the stakeholders in charge of the change to take action or be prepared for the risk to materialize with mitigation.

Figure 9-7 shows the methodology employed by Digital.ai in predicting the risk factor of changes. The model predicts the risk factor of future changes based on the risks associated with similar changes in the past. For each change indicated (the CR*** numbers), there is a risk factor associated, based on who is carrying out the change, the history of similar changes in the past 90 days, and other factors. Based on these calculations, the AI tool predicts that the first change is likely to fail 5 percent of the time, while the second and third changes will fail at a rate of 45 percent and 67 percent, respectively.

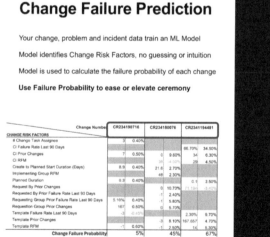
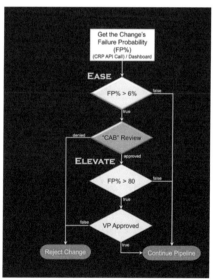

Figure 9-7. *Digital.ai prediction of risk factor (Credit: `https://digital.ai/resource-center/videos/introduction-to-change-risk-prediction/`)*

Change Simulation

How nice would it to be to know the future before releasing software into production—especially when there is a large userbase? Yes, there is Canary deployment, but there is a better solution through change impact solution by AI.

With Simio, developers can simulate and model capabilities to visualize and analyze the potential outcomes of changes. This gives them a view of what needs to be changed and refined before deployment.

AnyLogic is similar to Simio, where the changes can be simulated for complex environments, and different test data can be fed to check the impact.

Making Decisions

The elephant in the room is the decision to approve or reject moving a change to implementation. The CAB and change managers might wish for a magic wand to help them with this decision-making process.

Digital.ai is a tool that might not directly help with the decision, but can decide on the levels of approvals needed based on historical data. For example, if changes led by a particular project manager have always succeeded, the tool allows changes to be implemented without going to the CAB. Past results may not exactly reflect future results, but this is a good capability to have to focus on changes that do not have a good track record.

Sentiment Analysis

Sentiment analysis has multiple applications—all aimed at feeling the pulse of the user. With change management, change managers try to gauge whether employees are feeling positive, negative, or neutral about the change. Based on the sentiment, they can proactively address the concerns and misconceptions about the change. This real-time insight into employee sentiment helps maintain morale and ensure that any resistance is addressed promptly.

MonkeyLearn and Lexalytics are popular tools in the market that detect user/employee sentiment. They analyze social media, emails, surveys, and other digital channels to detect underlying sentiment. Figure 9-8 shows a screenshot of the MonkeyLearn dashboard.

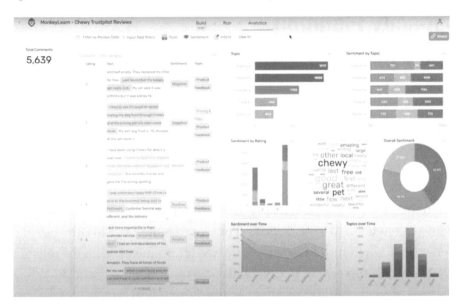

Figure 9-8. *The MonkeyLearn dashboard (Credit:* `https://www.youtube.com/watch?v=cAhw9ss1r5E`*)*

Stakeholder Engagement

There are certain changes that go on for a number of hours and days. Customers, users, and other stakeholders often feel the need to get a real-time update on the progress. Today, AI chatbots have become a common occurrence, and they can be employed to communicate and engage with various stakeholders during the change. They essentially provide real-time answers to questions, offer guidance on new processes, and gather feedback from employees. The constant communication is a powerful tool to increase the probability of change acceptance.

ChatGPT is a commonly used tool to implement AI based chatbots. ChatGPT can respond to stakeholders in a human-like manner. Talla is a similar tool that can be employed as well.

Capacity Planning

In the good old days of IT operations, where the majority of the processes were manual, developers used to drive a process called capacity management. It's a process that kept tabs on the capacity levels of components, services, and the business, and compared them against the optimal ranges/targets. Developers used to maintain Excel templates to document the capacity figures, and every week or month, depending on the criticality of the subject, the capacity levels were documented. When they were abnormal, the problem was reported to the problem management team to investigate and propose a solution. This process worked well when the IT infrastructure was on-premises. With the digital boom, everything seemed to expand like *Honey, I Blew Up the Kids*. Manually documenting capacities became impractical.

Enter SRE, automation, and now AI.

Sub-Processes of Capacity Planning

Because auditing the capacities of individual components or services is an outcome associated with observability, SRE now handles the planning and forecasting activities with the capacity planning process.

The two sub-processes that work as a single unit in realizing capacity-related nuances are as follows:

- **Capacity Planning:** This activity is tasked with implementing processes to ensure that the system can scale as needed, preventing outages and maintaining performance. It includes provisioning, monitoring, and adjusting resources. It comprises the immediate allocation of resources and long-term strategic planning. If there were to be capacity-related incident, this is the process that has failed.

- **Capacity Forecasting:** This activity predicts the future resource requirements (based on historical data, trends, and anticipated events)—be it software, hardware, licenses, and so on. This helps prevent situations in which resources become either insufficient or excessively over-provisioned. Forecasting is used to inform the decisions made during capacity planning.

The Role of AI in Capacity Planning

The capacity planning area is prime ground for AI to take shape, since planning and forecasting capacity requirements involves algorithms and historical trends.

Capacity Forecasting

Resource requirements are determined by intrinsic and extrinsic factors. The business requirements, along with the design specifications, provide half of the story in terms of capacity needs. There are also outside forces, such as income tax filing timelines, holidays, and others that provide insight into the possible traffic and hence the overall capacity. And yet, at times, the best capacity estimations go south owing to unseen circumstances. For example, a viral story could lead to exponential traffic or simultaneous large data file transfers could potentially derail capacity forecasts. When planning, therefore, developers consider the worst possible scenario, and yet stay on the side of optimum. A preferred outcome would be to enable agility such as auto-scaling to ensure that the technology supports capacity spikes and accounts for resource optimization.

Facebook's Prophet is an open source tool that is capable of forecasting based on historical data. Based on the data, the tool can automatically detect and model recurring patterns—such as identifying that the server load peaks every Friday evening due to a number of scheduled reports or that the traffic to a shopping portal increases every year during Diwali. It is possible that the time series data is not complete, with some missing pieces. Prophet can handle gaps in your data without requiring imputation. Also, built-in logic manages outliers, ensuring that they do not disproportionately affect the forecast. This is essential to cater to spikes and anomalies that can happen infrequently. Organizations use Prophet to forecast the required storage and to determine if and when additional capacity will be needed. The tool is often used to predict server load, to ensure that resources are efficiently allocated during peak periods, and to avoid over-provisioning during low-demand times.

Capacity Optimization

The main premise of moving to the cloud is to ensure that a whole array of infrastructure and other computing resources are not unused, wasting essential capital expenditure. Organizations do not have the luxury of bigger margins, so any expenditure that is saved will contribute toward growth. Therefore, optimizing capacity is an essential process that ensures that computing resources—such as CPU, memory, storage, licenses, and network bandwidth—are used as efficiently as possible. The goal is to maximize performance and minimize costs without compromising the reliability and availability of the system.

AppDynamics and Turbonomic are the current leaders in the capacity optimization space. AppDynamics, which is owned by Cisco, is an application performance management (APM) solution that provides deep insights into application performance, user experience, and infrastructure health. The tool can monitor complex system stacks in real-time, from end user interactions to backend databases and servers. Due to the breadth of its reach, it can access the requisite data and provide actionable insights and recommendations for optimizing application performance and resource usage. For example, it might suggest resizing a database instance or optimizing a resource-intensive piece of code. Turbonomic, which is owned by IBM, is an APM tool as well. In cloud environments, it can continuously optimize instance types, regions, and reservations, to decrease spending on cloud while ensuring that capacity meets demand.

Intelligent Scaling

Forecasting and optimization have application in reducing costs, but what they don't necessarily do is provide real-time solutions for anomalies that might seldom happen. The need of the hour is to assess the situation and take the necessary action to meet the new demand requirements. Intelligent scaling can truly change the way capacity planning is perceived. Yes, with the cloud, there are features that support auto-scaling based on certain criteria. But the answer to the scaling question may not necessarily lie in a few parameters to determine scaling. What is required is intelligence that can read the data and make a decision in a matter of seconds if not minutes.

AWS Auto Scaling with Predictive Scaling is a gamechanger. It enriches the traditional auto-scaling capabilities of AWS by incorporating machine learning to predict future traffic patterns and automatically scale resources in advance of expected demand. This helps ensure that applications have the necessary capacity to handle traffic spikes while minimizing costs during periods of lower demand.

Chaos Engineering

In the game of chess, a player's strength improves not only with knowledge but through the application of knowledge during games. The more games they participate in, the stronger they become as players. But what is generally not stated is that in between the games, every game is analyzed to the tee, weaknesses are identified, and targeted learning and practice is undertaken to overcome any shortcomings. This iterative process is the secret behind a player with professional success. Likewise, in the world of software, the chinks in the armor can only be exposed when certain conditions are encountered—some known, most unknown. Waiting for a condition to be satisfied in production is a disaster in the making.

To make software resilient to intrinsic and extrinsic conditions, it must be put through a full course of testing. Chapter 7 discussed different types of tests, and this section delves deeper into the resilience equation of software through chaos engineering.

Chaos engineering is primarily a SRE practice and is associated with resilience engineering, whereby developers intentionally introduce disruptions or failures into a system to test its resilience and identify its potential weaknesses. Netflix pioneered the practice with its tool called Chaos Monkey. Its premise is that if there is a possibility of something going wrong, let's determine the impact in the test environment, fix it if possible, or find alternatives before rolling out the environment into production. By breaking the software in a controlled manner, organizations can build better, more resilient systems that can withstand real-world problems. The goal is to ensure that systems can withstand unexpected events, such as hardware failures, network outages, and spikes in traffic, and continue to operate effectively.

Role of AI in Chaos Engineering

AI can drive chaos engineering by automating experiments, predicting system behavior, analyzing results, and improving overall resilience.

Identification and Automating Tests

AI is capable of understanding the architecture of a system, with the help of tools such as Dynatrace, and it can automatically design chaos experiments based on system data, previous failures, and known vulnerabilities. The tool can identify the scenarios with the maximum impact and run such scenarios for testing.

Machine learning models can be trained to recognize patterns in system behavior that precede failures. During chaos experiments, AI can monitor for these patterns and identify emerging issues before they become critical.

These tests are not planned completely in advance. The AI tool will dynamically adjust the parameters of chaos experiments in real-time based on system responses. For example, if AI detects that the system is taking the failure well, it might automatically decide to increase the intensity of the experiment to push the system further until such a point where the system is unable to bear the load.

Chaos Machine is another Netflix product. It is an extended version of Chaos Monkey and is targeted toward ensuring the resilience of their distributed systems. It leverages its machine learning ability to conduct deep analysis of system behavior and identify critical components that should be targeted in chaos experiments. This is a form of intelligent experiment generation, as the tool learns continuously over time regarding the parts of the system that are most vulnerable.

Chaos Machine can adapt its experiments based on the data it gathers, focusing more on areas that are identified as critical.

Steadybit is another chaos engineering platform that specializes in conducting resiliency tests on modern cloud-native and distributed systems. The tool uses lightweight agents that are deployed on the systems, allowing it to perform chaos experiments across a variety of environments, including Kubernetes, virtual machines, and cloud services. It provides tools for testing and validating the resilience of applications by simulating real-world failures. Figure 9-9 shows the Steadybit test management engine.

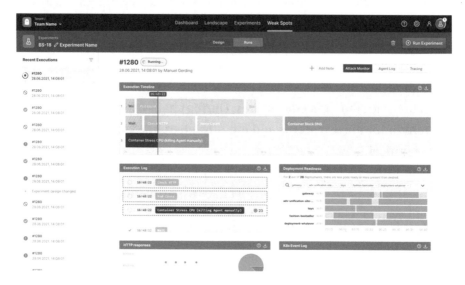

Figure 9-9. *Steadybit (Credit:* https://steadybit.com/features/designing-and-running-experiments*)*

Optimizing Experiment Scope

It is critical that not all the possible combinations of tests need to be imposed on the system. It is better to have a plan for the *madness.* Several tests could be conducted, but the tool must identify the critical path because the time is generally short between development and deployment.

AI tools can analyze historical system data and experiment outcomes to predict potential points of failure. This allows teams to focus their chaos experiments on the most vulnerable areas.

Unlike traditional chaos engineering tools that introduce randomness into the experiments, Chaos Machine is more focused. It strategically targets areas identified as critical to maximize the impact of chaos experiments and to gain more valuable insights.

Gremlin is another tool used for chaos engineering, and it provides a *blast radius* control, allowing teams to limit the scope of chaos experiments to minimize risk. This feature is generally used in production environments.

Summary

This chapter focused on operations—specifically site reliability engineering (SRE). In particular, it looked at how AI has boosted the operational activities across the operational lifecycle.

Observability is a field of study that builds on monitoring, and it aims to learn everything there is to about the scope in question. Incident management exists to restore products to their original state, thereby reducing the burden of downtime. Change management, which was once a bureaucratic department that held all the approvals to changes in the environment, has changed. Forecasting and managing are specialized processes that ensure that the right amount of capacity is available when it is required. Chaos engineering helps make applications resilient through controlled testing by introducing bugs into the system.

The areas of operations listed in the chapter are the critical ones, and AI has made a significant difference in each of these areas, making the process richer and the outcomes more meaningful.

Index

A

Access management, 258
Access management and identity
 governance
 automating access control
  challenges, 259
  tools and technologies, 258
  use case, 258
 continuous monitoring
  and audit
  challenges, 260
  tools and technologies, 259
  use case, 259
Affinity mapping, 72, 78, 79
Agile estimation
 affinity mapping, 78, 79
 benefits
  accuracy and efficiency, 71
  automation, 71
  collaboration, 71
  data-driven insights, 71
  flexibility, 72
  focus on value, 72, 73
  predictability, 71
  predictive analytics, 71
  resource allocation, 72

 bucket system, 79, 80
 dot voting, 77, 78
 planning poker, 73–75
 project management tools
  Asana, 89, 90
  Azure DevOps, 85, 86
  GitHub, 87–89
  JIRA, 83–85
  Trello, 86, 87
 three-point estimation
  technique, 80, 81
 T-shirt size estimation, 75–77
 use case points estimation
  technique, 82, 83
 in vogue, 73
Agile Poker for JIRA, 83
Agile Project Delivery Confidence
 study, 17
Agile project management, 17
AI-assisted release planning,
 235, 236
AI-driven build optimization
 application development, 160
 CI/CD tools
  advantages, 163
  CircleCI, 161, 162
  disadvantages, 163

© Abhinav Krishna and Vamshidhar Meda 2024
A. Krishna and V. Meda, *AI Integration in Software Development and Operations*,
https://doi.org/10.1007/979-8-8688-1044-2

AI-driven build
    optimization (*cont.*)
    GitHub Actions, 162
    Google Cloud Build, 161
    Harness, 160
    Jenkins, 162, 163
AI-driven storage allocation
    challenges, 261
    tools and technologies, 260
    use case, 260
AI-driven testing tools
    Applitools, 196–199
    Appvance, 194, 195
    best practices, software
      testing, 204–207
    capabilities and
      features, 201–203
    Facebook's Infer Tool, 201
    Functionize, 201
    Google's AI-Driven Testing
      Framework, 201
    key functionalities, 202
    Microsoft's AI Testing
      Strategies, 201
    Testim, 195, 196
    tool comparison, 204
AI-driven tools, 101
AI infused SDLC
    Agile estimation, 70–90
    building, 50, 51
    challenges, 46, 47
    data quality, 56
    deployment phase, 53, 54
    designing, 49, 50

    ethical and security
      concerns, 57, 58
    gathering requirements, 48, 49
    increased complexity, 55
    initial high cost and
      maintenance, 56
    integrating with existing
      systems, 57
    maintenance, 54, 55
    planning, 47, 48
    quality and development, 46
    testing, 51–53
AI/ML advantages, 8–11
AI/ML development steps
    deployment, 7
    design and train model, 7
    generate predictions, 7, 8
    maintaining models, 8
    monitor predictions, 8
    preparing data, 6
AI models training, 41
AI-powered code assistance, 51
AI techniques and algorithms
    deep learning algorithms, 36, 37
    evolutionary algorithms, 37
    fuzzy logic, 37
    into DevOps and MLOps, 34
    overview, 34
    reinforcement learning
      algorithms, 36
    supervised learning
      algorithms, 34, 35
    unsupervised learning
      algorithms, 35, 36

AI transforms the developer
        workflow
    application modernization, 140
    automated code generation, 138
    deployment automation, 139
    improve developer
        experience, 139
    intelligent code reviews, 139
    optimized testing, 139
    predictive analytics, 139
AI types
    limited memory/general AI, 5
    reactive machines/narrow, 4, 5
    self-awareness/Super AI, 5, 6
    Theory of mind, 5
Algorithm, 33
Amazon Alexa Voice Service
        (AVS), 121
Amazon CodeWhisperer, 142
Amazon's shopping
        recommendations, 30
Anodot, 124
Anomaly detection, 228, 278, 279
Ansible AI, 249
API design
    assistance, 126, 127
    authentication and
        authorization, 124
    data formats, 124
    documentation generation, 125
    endpoint definition, 124
    error handling, 125
    natural language interface for
        API queries, 127

request methods, 124
    validation, 126
AppDynamics, 287, 294
    anomaly detection
        methodology, 278, 279
    observability tool, 278
Applitools
    features, 197
    visual AI, 196
    visual UI testing, 198, 199
Appvance, 194, 195
Architect, 108
Artificial intelligence (AI)
    components, 27
    and DevOps, 23
    evolution, 3, 4
    performing tasks, 2
    project management, 48
    in SDLC, 43
    types, 4
Artificial Intelligence in IT
        Operations (AIOps),
        275, 276
Asana, 89, 90
Association Rule Learning, 36
Automated Analysis, 49
Automated code generation, 51
Automate disaster
        recovery, 131
Automated testing, 52
Automation, 14, 182, 214
Avi Networks (VMware NSX
        Advanced Load
        Balancer), 255

AWS Cost Explorer
(AI-powered), 253
Azure DevOps, 85, 86

B

Bias in AI models, 57
Bidirectional Encoder
Representations from
Transformers (BERT), 39
Big Data, 28
Bucket system, 79, 80
Bug detection, 147
Bug detection and prediction, AI
advantages, 150
Amazon CodeGuru, 149
DeepCode, 149
disadvantages, 151
Factory.AI, 149
Business operations, 268

C

CALMS, 13
Canary release, 237
Capacity forecasting, 293, 294
Capacity management, 292
Capacity optimization, 294, 295
Capacity planning
AI role
capacity forecasting, 293, 294
capacity optimization,
294, 295
intelligent scaling, 295

IT operations, 292
sub-processes, 292, 293
Car models, 7
Change advisory boards
(CAB), 288
Change management, 299
AI role
change simulation, 290
decision-making
process, 290
MonkeyLearn
dashboard, 291
risk assessment, 288, 289
sentiment analysis, 290, 291
stakeholder
engagement, 291
governance layer, 287
organizations, 288
products, 287
Change simulation, 290
Chaos engineering, 299
AI role
automating tests, 297, 298
experiment scope, 298, 299
identification, 297, 298
Netflix, 296
SRE practice, 296
Chaos Machine, 297, 299
Chaos Monkey, 296, 297
Chatbots, 99
ChatGPT, 292
CI/CD pipeline creation and
optimization
advantages, 177

AI-driven CI/CD tools
    comparison, 172
  disadvantages, 178
  Harness, 171
  key challenges, 178
  use cases, 170, 177
CircleCI, 161, 162
Cisco AI network analytics, 254
Cisco DNA Center, 132
Cisco Stealthwatch, 256
CloudHealth by VMware, 253
CodeGuru, 147
Codeium, 151, 152
Code reviews, 146–148
Codex, 143
Cognition, 154
Compliance-related AI
    models, 239
Component design
  API endpoints and
    methods, 116
  challenges, 119
  e-commerce application, 115
  efficient communication,
    117, 118
  human validation, 114
  individual components/
    modules, 114
  LLMs for interface design,
    118, 119
  microservice's responsibilities,
    115, 116
  optimal data exchange formats,
    116, 117

  service versioning and
    compatibility, 118
Configuration drift, 246
Configuration management
    database (CMDB), 280
Continuous delivery as a service
    (CDaaS), 225
Continuous delivery (CD),
    22, 23, 213
  AI-driven infrastructure
    management, 245
  AI-powered release
    management, 233
  automation era, 214
  deployment automation, AI,
    214, 216
  goal, 213
  key areas, AI, 215
Continuous delivery
    pipeline, 22, 23
Continuous integration (CI), 159
  definition, 18, 19
  quality checks, 19
  software delivery, 21
  unit tests, 20, 21
Continuous integration and
    continuous deployment
    (CI/CD), 53, 160
Continuous learning, 242
Convolutional neural network
    (CNN), 36, 78
Cost optimization, 230
COTS platform, 109
CrowdStrike, 257

Crucible, 44
Cursor, 154, 155
Customer relationship
    management (CRM)
    system, 93

D

Darktrace, 134
Data anomaly detection, 124
Database management, AI
    automate database backups and
       recovery
       challenges, 264
       tools and technologies, 263
       use case, 263
    intelligent database
       optimization, 262, 263
Data design
    automated data documentation,
       122, 123
    automated data modeling, 123
    components, 122
    data anomaly detection, 124
    database schemas, 122
    data structures, 122
    defining, 122
Datadog, 227, 251, 279, 282
Datadog tool, 276, 277
Data protection regulations, 210
DataRobot, 122
Data security, 57
Data structures, 123
Davis, 277, 278, 280

dbdesigner.AI, 123
Decision trees, 35
DeepCode, 147, 149, 150
Deep learning, 3, 36, 37
Deep Q-Networks (DQN), 36
Dependabot, 165, 166
Deployment automation, AI
    benefits, 217
    challenges
       cultural and organizational
          adoption, 224
       data quality and
          volume, 222
       integration with existing CI/
          CD pipelines, 223
       model interpretability and
          reliability, 223
       security concerns, 224
    CI/CD pipelines, 217
    future trends, 232, 233
    GitHub Copilot, 227
    Harness AIDA, 225, 226
    Harness.io, 225
    impact
       cost optimization, 230
       flexibility, 231, 232
       human errors
          reduction, 229
       improve DevOps and
          Developer experience,
          230, 231
       scalability, 231, 232
       speed and efficiency gains,
          228, 229

limitations, 216

manual process, 217

observability platforms, 227, 228

predefined steps, 216

spinnaker, machine learning integrations, 226

step-by-step process, 216

use cases, 218

automated rollbacks, 219, 220

Blue/Green and Canary releases, 220

deployment strategy selection, 220

intelligent pipeline optimization, 221

monitoring and troubleshooting deployment issues, 221, 222

predictive deployment planning, 218, 219

Deployment management, 215

DevOps, 1, 43, 47, 55, 269–271

examples, 11, 12

principles

automation, 14

culture, 13, 14

description, 12

learn, 15

measurement, 16

sharing, 16, 17

DevOps processes

continuous delivery, 21–24

continuous integration, 18–21

Dialogflow, 127

Digital.ai, 290

Dot voting (multi voting), 73, 77, 78

Dynamic Systems Development Method (DSDM), 17

Dynatrace, 252, 281, 282, 297

E

e-commerce application, 115

e-commerce platform, 123, 125, 231, 235, 251

Elastic observability, 279

Enterprise resource planning (ERP) system, 95

Error reduction, 118

Evolutionary algorithms, 37

F

F5 Networks, 255

Facebook's Prophet, 294

Factory.AI, 149

Feature Driven Development (FDD), 17

FinOps (Financial Operations), AI

AI-driven cost optimization challenges, 254

tools and technologies, 253

use case, 253

Harnessing AI, 252

Firewall and security management
    challenges, 258
      threat detection and
        response, 257
      tools and technologies, 257
      use case, 257
Functional requirement, 48, 96
Functional testing, 52
Fuzzy logic systems, 37

G

GDPR, 56
Generative Adversarial Networks
    (GANs), 37
Generative AI (Gen AI), 28, 41
    in software design, 107
Generative Pre-trained
    Transformer (GPT), 38
Genetic algorithms (GA), 37
GitHub, 87–89
GitHub Actions, 162, 172
GitHub Copilot, 142, 227
GitLab CI, 172
Google Cloud Build, 161
Google's AutoML, 112, 113
Google translate, 31
GPT-4, 61, 100–104, 142
Gremlin, 299

H

Harness, 160, 172
Harness AIDA, 164, 168, 169, 225, 226

Harness FinOps, 253
Harness.io, 225
HashiCorp Terraform, 129
Hierarchical clustering, 35
High-level design (HLD), 109
HIPAA, 56
HLD, 113
Holistic test, 52
Human errors, 229

I

IBM QRadar, 260
IBM Rational DOORS, 98
IBM Watson, 113
Incident management, 299
    AI role
      incident prioritization, 285
      RCA, 286, 287
      self-healing, 285, 286
    manual activities, 284
    operations, 283
    products, 283
    reactive nature, 283
    service, 283
Incident prioritization, 285
Infrastructure automation
    tools, 246
Infrastructure design
    automate disaster recovery, 131
    automated infrastructure
      provisioning, 129, 130
    disaster recovery and
      backup, 128

intelligent load balancing, 130, 131

intelligent network optimization, 131, 132

monitoring and management, 128

network architecture, 128

organization's IT environment, 127

predictive capacity planning, 129

security architecture, 128

server and storage design, 128

virtualization and cloud services, 128

Infrastructure management, 215

AI's role, 265

future trends, 264, 265

production environments, 245

test and production environments, 245

traditional environment management challenges

configuration drift, 246

environment setup, complexity, 246

tools, solving configuration challenges, 246, 247

use cases, AI, 248

Integrating AI and LLMs in planning phase, 60

Integration testing, 52

Intel AI Analytics, 113

Intelligent database optimization

challenges, 263

tools and technologies, 262

use case, 262

Intelligent debugging

advantages, 155

cognition, 154

cursor, 154, 155

disadvantages, 155

Rookout, 154

tools, 156

Intelligent dependency management

application development, 165

Dependabot, 165, 166

Renovate, 165

Snyk, 165

Intelligent feature rollouts, AI, 237, 238

Canary releases, 237

challenges, 238

feature flags, 237

impact, 238

mechanism and process, 237

Intelligent network optimization, 131, 132

Intelligent scaling, 295

Intelligent traceability, 102

IT requirements management

clear and concise documentation, 98

effective communication, 98

regular reviews and audits, 98

stakeholder engagement, 97

utilizing tools, 98

IT security, 45

J

Jenkins, 162, 163, 165, 172
JIRA, 83–85, 98
Juniper Networks Mist AI, 255

K

Kite, 142
K-means clustering, 35

L

Large Language Model (LLM),
    100–104, 115–119
  application sectors, 38
  definition, 38
  OpenAI's GPT, 38
  types, 38
Learning models, 28
Legacy banking system, 209
Limited memory/General AI, 5
Linear regression, 34
LLM types
  BERT, domain-specific tasks, 40
  BERT models, 39
  multilingual, 41
  T5, 40
  transformer-based models, 39
  XLNet, 39, 40
Logistic regression, 34
Long Short Term Memory
    Networks (LSTMs), 37
Low-level design (LLD), 109
Lucidchart, 114

M

Machine learning (ML), 26, 89,
    103, 297
  applications, 31, 32
  challenges, 32, 33
  definition, 27, 28
  future of, 33
  paradigm shift, 33
  types, 29
Machine Learning (ML)
    algorithms, 183
Mainline, 18
Manual testing
  primary limitation, 182
  testers, 182
Microservices architecture, 115
Microsoft Azure DevOps, 98
Minimum Viable Products (MVP), 50
ML types
  reinforcement learning, 30
  supervised learning, 29
  unsupervised learning, 29
Modular software, 109
Monitoring vs. observability,
    274, 275
Multilingual LLMs, 41

N

Natural language interface for API
    queries, 127
Natural language processing
    (NLP), 31, 38, 48, 49, 76, 99,
    121, 183, 184

NetApp ONTAP AI, 261
Network management, AI
    automated network
        configuration and
        optimization
        challenges, 255
        tools and technologies, 254
        use case, 254
    firewall and security
        management
        challenges, 258
        threat detection and
        response, 257
        tools and technologies, 257
        use case, 257
    intelligent traffic management
        and load balancing
        challenges, 256
        tools and technologies, 255
        use case, 255
    network security
        challenges, 257
        tools and technologies, 256
        use case, 256
Network security
    challenges, 257
    tools and technologies, 256
    use case, 256
Neural networks, 3, 184
New Relic, 227, 252, 279, 286
Non-functional requirement, 48, 96
Non-functional tests, 52
NoSQL databases, 123
Nutanix, 152

O

OAuth 2.0, 134
Observability, 227, 299
    AIOps, 275, 276
    AI tools
        anomaly detection,
         278, 279
        Datadog integrations, 277
        predictive analytics, 280
        unified view, 276–278
    capability, 273
    logs, metrics, and traces, 274
    service map, 280–282
    vs. monitoring, 274, 275
Okta Identity Governance, 258
OpenAI Codex, 112, 113, 115, 134
OpenAI's GPT, 38
Operations
    AI, 268
    business operations, 268
    dependencies, 268
    monitoring, 267
    performance, 268
    rationale, 269
    reactive process, 269

P

PagerDuty, 286
Palo Alto Networks, 256
Performance metrics, 104
Performance optimization, 147
Performance testing, 52

Planning management
   budgeting, 66
   communication plan, 67
   feasibility study
      economic feasibility, 63
      operational feasibility, 63
      technical feasibility, 62, 63
   project initiation
      define, 61
      identify stakeholders and
         expectations, 61, 62
      objectives and goals, 62
      triple constraints, 60
   project scheduling
      timeline development, 65
      triple constraints, 65
      use project management
         tools, 65
   QA planning, 69
   resource planning
      allocate roles and
         responsibilities, 64
      identify required
         resources, 64
   risk management
      identify potential
         risks, 68
      risk mitigation and
         contingency plans, 68
   SDLC projects, 60
Planning poker, 71, 73–75, 83
Policy Gradient Methods, 36
Poolside, 151, 152

Predictive alerts, 228
Predictive analytics, 54, 100, 280
Predictive build failure analysis
   Harness AIDA, 164
   Jenkins, 165
   tools, 164
   Travis CI, 165
Predictive deployment planning,
   218, 219
Predictive storage maintenance
   challenges, 262
   NetApp ONTAP AI, 261
   tools and technologies, 261
Principal Component Analysis
   (PCA), 35
Prioritizing requirements, 96
Production environments, 245
Progressive release management
   deploy features, 233
   features, 233
   key aspects, 234
Project management office
   (PMO), 103
Prototypes/mockups, 97

Q

Q-Learning, 36
Quality assurance (QA) planning
   quality control and assurance
      activities, 69
   quality metrics and
      standards, 69

R

RAML, 126

Random forest, 35

Reactive machines/narrow AI, 4, 5

Real-time insights, 228

Real-time monitoring tools, 250

Recurrent Neural Networks
(RNNs), 37

REINFORCE algorithm, 36

Reinforcement learning, 30, 36

Relational databases, 123

Release management, 215

   AI use cases, 235

      adaptive release cycles,
242, 243

      AI-assisted release planning,
235, 236

      AI-based monitoring,
real-time release
adjustments, 241

      automated risk assessment
and mitigation, 239, 240

      continuous learning,
242, 243

      intelligent feature rollouts,
237, 238

      release governance and
compliance, 238, 239

      tools and features, 244

   definition, 233

   progressive release
management, 233, 234

Renovate, 165

Requirements gathering

   analysis, 100, 101

   automated documentation, 101

   capturing and deploying, 91

   continuous improvement,
103, 104

   LLMs, 100

   NLP, 99

   non-functional
requirements, 92

   requirements
management, 92–97

   SDLC lifecycle, 91, 94

   stakeholders, 91

   techniques, 95

   and traceability, 102, 103

   validation, 102

Requirements management

   analysis, 96

   communication pathway, 94

   documentation, 96

   in IT projects, 97, 98

      business and IT goals, 92, 93

      cost and time efficiency, 93

      reducing project risks, 93

   skills, 94

   and traceability, 97

   validation, 96, 97

Resource management

   cost savings and effective, 45

Return on investment (ROI), 63

Risk assessment, 133, 288, 289
Risk management, 81
    proactive, 45
Risk mitigation, 93
Rollbacks, 219
Rookout, 154
Root cause analysis (RCA), 287

S

Security Audits, 147
Security design
    access control, 132
    anomaly detection, 134, 135
    data encryption, 132
    endpoint security, 133
    framework, 132
    identity management, 133
    incident response, 133
    network security, 132
    recommendations, 134
    security monitoring, 134, 135
    threat modeling and risk
        assessment, 133
Security vulnerabilities, 167, 170
Selenium, 182
Self-Awareness/Super AI, 5, 6
Sentiment analysis, 49, 81, 290, 291
Service mapping
    automation and AI, 281
    challenges, 281
    CMDB, 280
    Datadog, 282

Dynatrace Smartscape, 281, 282
    manual, 281
    ServiceNow, 282, 283
ServiceNow, 282, 283, 285
Sharing, 16, 17
Site Reliability Engineering (SRE)
    AI role, 272, 273
    Google, 270
    objectives, 270
    organizations, 270
    primary goal, 270
    principles, 271, 272
    vs. DevOps, 270, 271
SMART (specific, measurable,
        achievable, relevant, and
        timebound) goals, 62
Snyk, 147, 165, 168
Social media platform, 126
Software build process
    advantages, 166
    AI-driven build
        optimization, 160
    AI-driven security and
        compatibility
    advantages, 168
    detect issues, 167
    disadvantages, 169
    Harness AIDA, 168
    security vulnerabilities, 167
    Snyk, 168
    challenges, 167
    CI tools, 159
    disadvantages, 167

intelligent dependency
management, 165–167
predictive build failure analysis,
164, 165
use cases, 159, 160
Software design
abstraction, 109
API design, 124–127
architecture, 110
cohesion, 109
component design, 114–119
components, 108, 111
coupling, 109
data design, 122–124
DevOps pipelines and
embedded
automation, 108
efficient development, 108
encapsulation, 109
HLD, 109
infrastructure design, 127–132
LLD, 109
modular designs, 108
modular software, 109
principles and practices, 109
process of development, 109
quintessential phase, 107
in SDLC, 107
system design, 111–114
Software development lifecycle
(SDLC), 21, 23
advanced decision
making, 44, 45

and AI infusion, 46–55
cost savings and effective
resource management, 45
developer onboarding, 46
DevOps, 43
planning, 60
proactive risk management, 45
requirements, 60
unparalleled quality, 44
Zenith in efficiency and
productivity, 44
Software development process
AI-based bug detection and
prediction tools
advantages, 150
Amazon CodeGuru, 149
DeepCode, 149, 150
disadvantages, 151
Factory.AI, 149
AI code assistants
implications, 158
methodology, 157
security vulnerabilities, 158
AI in code reviews
advantages, 148
AI enhances code reviews,
potential issues
detection, 146
disadvantages, 148
examples, 147
software development
process, 146
tools and technologies, 147

Software development
        process (*cont.*)
    use cases, 147
    automated code generation and
        refactoring
        advantages, 145
        AI tool comparison, 144
        Codex, 143
        disadvantages, 146
        GPT-4, 142
        scenarios, 143
        tools, 142
    automated testing, 141
    code reviews, 141
    coding phase, 140
    integration testing, 141
    intelligent debugging
        advantages, 155
        cognition, 154
        cursor, 154, 155
        disadvantages, 155, 156
        Rookout, 154
        tools, 156
    intelligent documentation and
        code search
        advantages, 153
        Codeium, 151, 152
        disadvantages, 153
        Poolside, 151, 152
        Sourcegraph, 151, 152
    testing, 141
    unit testing, 141
    use cases, 141

version control, 140
Software testing
    advantages, AI, 186
    AI's impact, 183–186
    automation era, 182
    best practices, implementing
        AI, 204–207
    challenges, AI-driven testing
        implementation, 207–210
    challenges, implementing AI,
        188, 189
    future trends, AI, 210–212
    key benefits, AI, 186, 187
    ML algorithms, 183
    neural networks, 184
    NLP, 184
    testers, 182
    V-Model, 189–191
SonarQube, 44
Sourcegraph, 151, 152
Spinnaker, 226
Splunk AI, 251
SQLPrompt, 123
Steadybit, 298
Storage management and
        optimization
    AI-driven storage allocation,
        260, 261
    predictive storage maintenance,
        261, 262
Supervised learning, 29, 34, 35
Support Vector Machines (SVM), 35
Swagger, 126

SwaggerHub, 125
System design
    architectures and predict, 111
    defining, 111
    high-level design, 112, 113
    low-level design, 113, 114
    recommendations of AI, 111
    security design, 132–135
    UI design, 119–121

T

Tabnine, 142
Terraform Cloud, 249
Test and production environments
    AI-driven automated provision
        and configuration
        challenges, 250
        tools and technologies, 249
        use case, 249
    intelligent monitoring/incident
        management
        challenges, 251
        tools and technologies, 251
        use case, 250
    predictive analytics,
        performance optimization
        challenges, 252
        tools and technologies, 252
        use case, 251
Testim, 195, 196
Text-To-Text Transfer Transformer
    (T5), 40

Theory of mind, 5
Threat modeling, 133
Three-point estimation
        technique, 80, 81
Toyota Production Systems (TPS), 15
Traceability matrix, 97, 102, 103
Transformer-based models, 39
Travis CI, 165
Trello, 86, 87
T-shirt size estimation
        technique, 75–77
Turbonomic, 129, 294, 295

U

Unsupervised learning, 29, 35, 36
User acceptance testing (UAT), 52,
        191, 193
User interface (UI) design
    advantages, 120
    analyzing, 120
    attractive and interact, 119
    integrating AI, 120
    personalized user design,
        120, 121
    and user behavior, 120
    voice-activated interfaces, 121

V

V-Model
    evolution, software testing
        stage, 191

V-Model (*cont.*)
    SDLC testing, 190
    software testing, 189, 190
Voice-activated interfaces, 121

W

Waterfall project management
    methodologies, 17
WebSockets, 126

X, Y

XLNet, 39, 40

Z

ZenHub, 87
Zenith
    in efficiency and
        productivity, 44

Printed in the United States
by Baker & Taylor Publisher Services